The

Capture stunning night photos, including light painting, light streaks, cityscapes, Milky Way landscapes, and astrophotography

NIGHT
Photography Book

Erik Kuna

Award-winning landscape, astro, and aerospace photographer

THE NIGHT PHOTOGRAPHY BOOK BY ERIK KUNA

PHOTOGRAPHY
Erik Kuna

MANAGING EDITOR
Kim Doty

COPY EDITOR
Cindy Snyder

ART DIRECTOR
Jessica Maldonado

PUBLISHED BY
Rocky Nook
1010 B Street, Suite 350
San Rafael, CA 94901
info@rockynook.com
(415) 747-8756

Composed in Myriad Pro, Univers LT, Input Serif, and Nimbus Sans (Adobe Systems Incorporated) by Kelby Media Group Inc.

TRADEMARKS

All terms mentioned in this book that are known to be trademarks or service marks have been appropriately capitalized. Rocky Nook cannot attest to the accuracy of this information. Use of a term in the book should not be regarded as affecting the validity of any trademark or service mark.

Photoshop and Lightroom are registered trademarks of Adobe Systems, Inc. iPhone is a registered trademark of Apple Inc.

WARNING & DISCLAIMER

This book is designed to provide information about night photography. Every effort has been made to make this book as complete and as accurate as possible, but no warranty of fitness is implied.

The information is provided on an as-is basis. The author and Rocky Nook shall have neither the liability nor responsibility to any person or entity with respect to any loss or damages arising from the information contained in this book or from the use of the discs, websites, videos, or programs that may accompany it.

ISBN: 979-8-88814-188-5
10 9 8 7 6 5 4 3 2 1

Printed in Korea
This book is printed on acid-free paper.

Distributed in the UK and Europe by Publishers Group UK
Distributed in the U.S. and all other territories by Publishers Group West

Library of Congress Control Number: 2023945247

www.rockynook.com
www.kelbyone.com

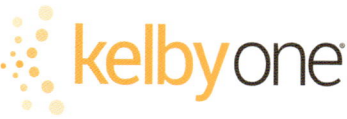

*To the One who breathed stars into being
and called light out of the darkness.
From something to everything, the One
who designed the work of art we call life.
Who set the heavens in motion, painted the sky
with wonder, and gave us eyes to see.
Every photograph, every frame, every fleeting
moment of light—this is my offering, a glimpse
of Your infinite glory and graceful majesty. If the
galaxies proclaim Your majesty, if creation reflects
Your beauty, if it all reveals Your nature, so will I.
This book is for You.*

ACKNOWLEDGMENTS

First, I want to thank God for creating the universe we get to observe and explore and, hopefully, one day, venture further into the stars of your creation. God's creation fuels my passion for photography and spaceflight. Second, I thank His Son, Jesus, for guiding me in all I do, in love.

To my wife: Nothing would be possible without your support. You are my soulmate, my rock, and without you, I would have never pushed myself to the limits I have. You make me a better person in every way. I love you.

To my daughter, the best gift ever: I love how you'll go out with me to chase the stars. I hope you never lose that curiosity and wonder for the universe. Love you always.

To my mother: Thank you for always supporting my nerdy ways and fostering my love for science and photography. **And, to my dad:** Though you're no longer here, your encouragement to push past my limits, keep questioning everything, and stay curious has stuck with me.

To my family: It's complicated, but I wouldn't change it for the world. I love you. And Riley, for always making us smile at every party or holiday.

To Scott Kelby: A huge thank you for all your support over the years. Your feedback and counsel have pushed me deeper into aerospace and astrophotography, making me a better photographer and a better person.

To the entire KelbyOne staff: From Books to Web, Marketing to Customer Service, and everywhere in between—your support makes this journey enjoyable, and I am grateful for all of you.

To the Video crew: Christina, Juan, Jason, Eric, Ron, and even Dobson—you guys make filming and teaching fun. Thanks for being a blast to work with on a weekly basis.

To the KelbyOne members and the incredible photography community that supports my work: I do this because I want others to have an easier time learning photography than I did.

Thank you to my publisher, Rocky Nook, and especially Scott Cowlin and Ted Waitt for believing in this book and the topic. I hope it's successful so you're not mad—LOL!

ACKNOWLEDGMENTS (continued)

Thank you to my mentors over the years: Joe McNally, Dave Black, Jay Maisel, Russell Preston Brown, Moose Peterson, and Serge Ramelli—your wisdom and guidance have been invaluable. I am forever grateful.

Next, to some photography friends who push me: First, John Kraus, for always being there to bounce around crazy photography ideas or just talk about the meaning of life and seeking balance.

To Ramtin Kazemi: For your inspirational eye and your "don't tread on me" attitude.

To Fernando Santos: For staying curious, even when we're out in the middle of nowhere outside Area 51.

To Joe Cacciopo: For always being up for crazy 7-hour drives to shoot the Milky Way or a rocket launch, or even a 3,000-mile drive to Utah. Just watch out for the deer.

To Jay Grammond: For encouraging me to step deeper into teaching workshops.

To my Sun 'n Fun photography crew: For all the years of hard work but fun times.

To my aerospace photojournalism colleagues: Keep up the hard work of telling one of the most important stories in modern history.

To all my clients and workshop attendees: Thank you for giving me the opportunity to teach and help—it is my passion.

To my editors, especially Robin and Supercluster, and clients like Stoke Space: Thanks for supporting my crazy ideas over the years and allowing me to create images that push the envelope. I wish more could trust the process, as crazy as the ideas sound. LOL!

I could keep going—Kalebra, Jean, Jory, Paul, Larry, Dan, James, Andy, Tom, Kristen, Mary Liz, Ryan, Tim, Dave, Gab, etc., but we all know the orchestra is going to play me off stage at some point. So, to everyone else in my life, thank you for your support and thanks for reading this book!

ABOUT THE AUTHOR

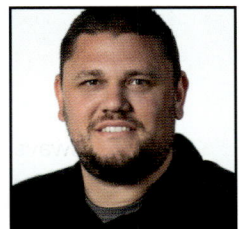

Erik Kuna

Erik Kuna is an award-winning aerospace and astrophotographer, educator, and speaker. As Vice President of Operations for KelbyOne, he plays a pivotal role in the online educational community for photographers and Photoshop and Lightroom users. His passion for spaceflight photography was ignited in 2015 after witnessing SpaceX's historic Falcon 9 booster landing, inspiring him to document the beauty and inspiration of space exploration.

Erik's work has been recognized internationally, winning multiple awards, including three first-place finishes in the Aviation Week Photo Contest in 2021 and 2023 for his breathtaking images of night spaceflight and aerospace technology. His photography has been featured in top industry publications and platforms, helping to tell the visual story of space exploration in a compelling and inspiring way.

Beyond his photography, Erik is a dedicated educator, teaching hundreds of thousands of photographers annually through KelbyOne's online platform and in-person workshops. He has spoken at premier conferences and events worldwide, including the Nightscapers Conference, Photoshop World, the Lightroom Conference, B&H's OPTIC, Imaging USA, NAB, and the Night Photo Summit. His expertise in Photoshop, Lightroom, and astrophotography has made him one of the most sought-after instructors in the industry.

Additionally, he can be found around NASA, the US Space Force, and other launch facilities photographing rocket launches for SpaceX, Stoke Space, Blue Origin, ULA, and other launch providers. Covering launches for multiple new agencies and media outlets, as well as numerous commercial assignments in aerospace, Erik sets out to capture the beauty and inspiration of rocket launches and space exploration to share with the world and, hopefully, inspire a new generation of innovators.

Erik co-hosts *The Grid*, a weekly photography show alongside Scott Kelby, where they share insights, discuss trends, and offer professional critiques for photographers worldwide. For those looking to learn from Erik firsthand, he leads immersive Milky Way Photography Workshops, where participants gain hands-on experience in capturing the night sky, from twilight compositions to advanced astrophotography techniques.

For more information on Erik, visit him at:

His personal website: **erikkuna.com**

His photography workshops: **milkywayworkshops.com**

His classes: **kelbyone.com/author/erikkuna**

Twitter/X: **@erikkuna**

Instagram: **@erikkuna**

Facebook: **facebook.com/erikkuna**

CONTENTS

CONTENTS

CONTENTS

CONTENTS

CONTENTS

CONTENTS

Chapter 13

Printing & Sharing   169

Bringing Your Night Photography into the Real World

Chapter 14

Wrapping It All Up   179

The Night Is Yours—Now Capture It

You're on the Verge of Unlocking the Secrets

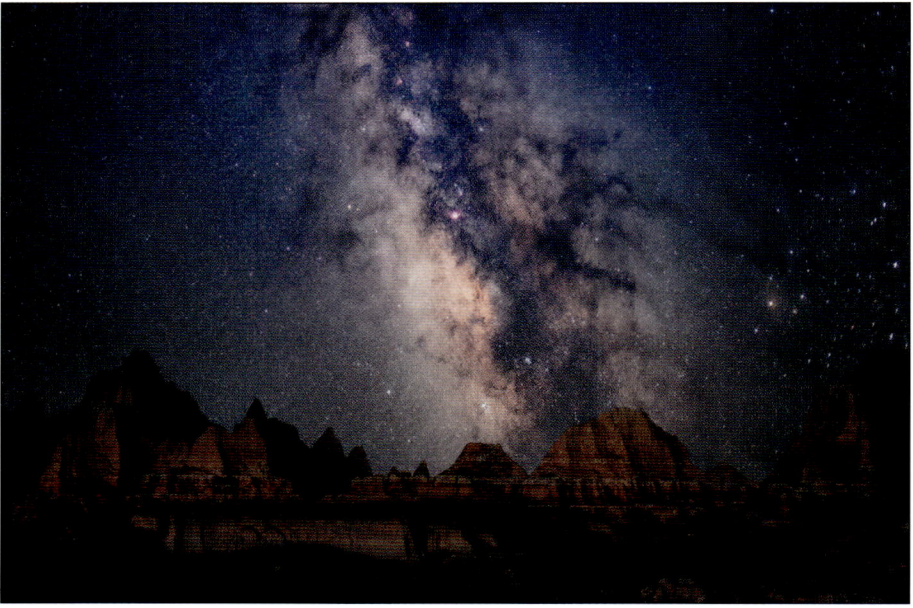

Since you picked up this book, I imagine you have a keen interest in photography and a desire to delve deeper into the mesmerizing world of astrophotography. Good news! You are on the verge of unlocking the secrets of night photography.

At first glance, the night sky may appear to be an endless expanse of darkness, but when observed through the lens of a camera, it transforms. One of the most extraordinary aspects of night photography lies in its ability to reveal the unseen; it unveils a world that the naked eye often fails to perceive. As the sun sets, the stars emerge, forming intricate patterns and constellations that have inspired civilizations throughout human history. With the right equipment and techniques—which you'll learn about shortly—you can capture these distant celestial objects and bring them closer, turning your photographs into a personal connection with the cosmos.

The challenges of night photography include handling low-light conditions and long exposure times while balancing the ever-rotating and changing sky, which can all lead to confusion. As a photographer, you already understand the importance of mastering technical skills, but when applied to night photography, these skills take on a whole new level of complexity. It requires a delicate balance between capturing enough light to reveal the night and preventing excessive noise that may diminish your image's clarity.

Why Night Photography?

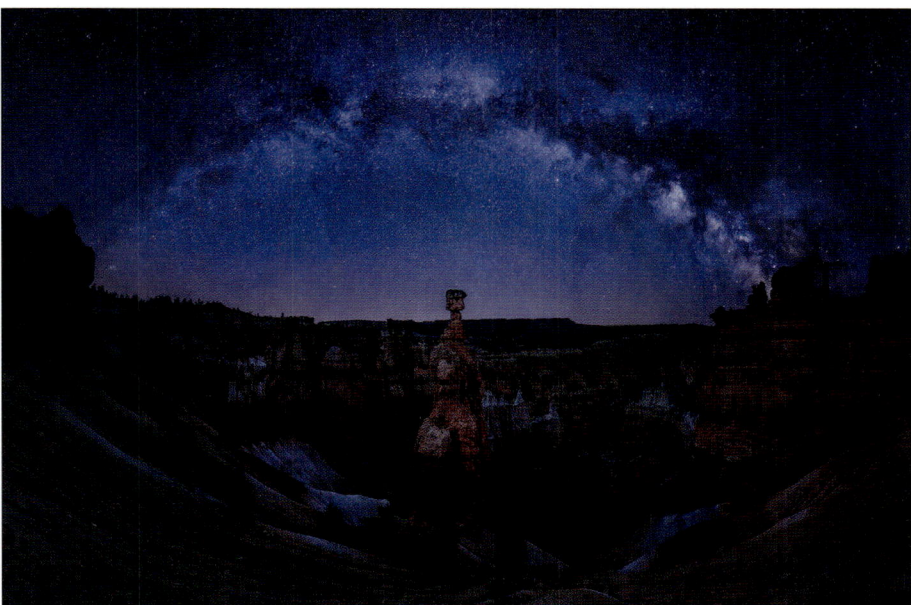

Additionally, astrophotography brings a sense of wonder and perspective. It reminds us of our place in the vast universe, humbling us in the face of the universe. While shooting the night sky, one cannot help but ponder the mysteries of the cosmos, the vastness of space, and the possibility of life beyond our planet. Night photography is not just about capturing beautiful images; it also encourages us to reflect on our existence, igniting a profound connection with the universe.

Let's face it, sunrise and sunset are like happy hours for photographers and tourists alike. It's the rush hour of the photography world, and everyone and their grand-mother are jostling for that perfect shot. But, if you stick with me here, you'll have the ultimate secret weapon up your sleeve—the night! That's right, while the world sleeps, we're capturing the universe in all its glory, and it's oh-so-awesome!

So, why night photography, you ask? First and foremost, there's the serenity and solitude. Remember those beautiful locations you always wanted to photograph without the unwanted extras photobombing your frames? Well, under the cloak of darkness, you'll find those iconic spots empty. No more dodging selfie sticks or waiting for that perfect moment when the busload of tourists finally step out of your shot.

But Wait, There's More!

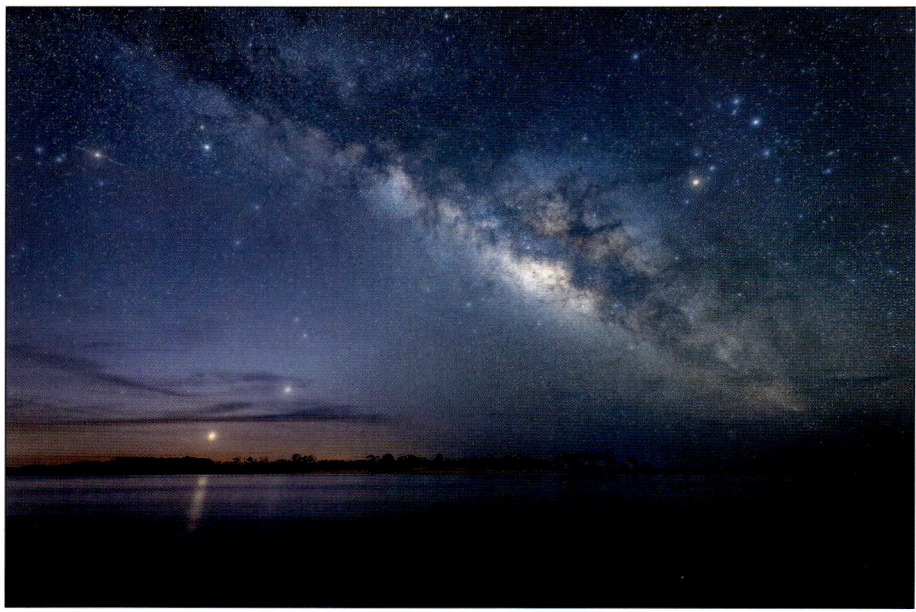

While everyone's a sucker for sunsets and sunrises, night photography has a whole different kind of magic. Did I mention the epic shots you can create? The night opens up a world of creative possibilities. Long exposures turn city traffic into streaks of gold and red, and landscapes transform into a sprawling sea of stars over your subject. With night photography, you're like a magician, conjuring up scenes that seem straight out of a sci-fi movie.

Let's not forget the gear. Astrophotography may sound intimidating, but once you embrace the dark side (quite literally), it's not that hard to master. A sturdy tripod, a wide-aperture, wide-angle lens, a low noise camera, and a little patience are your trusty companions. When everyone else shares their cliché sunset photos, you'll be the maverick who unleashes jaw-dropping shots of a star-studded sky, and trust me, jaws will drop.

It doesn't stop there. Picture this: You're in your cozy photo studio, with all that fancy lighting gear at your disposal. You can position those softboxes and strobes just right, shaping the light to your heart's content. Now, teleport yourself to a stunning outdoor location at night. Guess what? Without the sun to overpower, you can still be the lighting master. Night photography hands you the reins, giving you the power to shape the darkness with your very own lights. You've got your trusty tripod set up, your camera's ready to rock, and here comes the magic part—your portable lighting equipment. Now you can paint your scene with light, illuminating the foreground, revealing hidden textures, and adding that captivating drama that would make even Hollywood directors jealous (okay, maybe not that jealous, but you get the point).

Explore Extraordinary Worlds

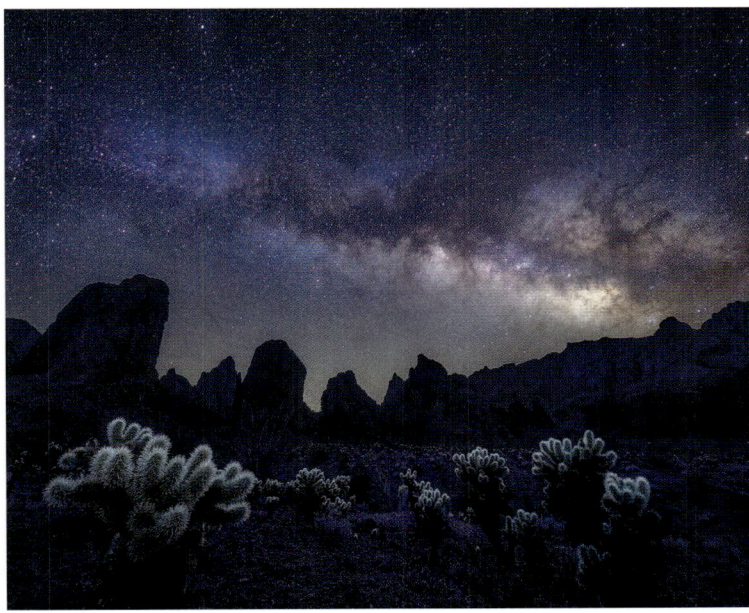

Night photography offers us extraordinary worlds to explore. From freezing stars and portraits in time to capturing the enchanting motion of star trails and streaks of light, the night is our playground of possibilities. With the power to freeze action and capture motion, your night photography will transcend the ordinary.

So, how do we freeze time in the darkness? Simple. It's all about the shutter speed. The faster, the better. Set your camera to a snappy shutter speed we can find in PhotoPills (more on this later) and watch the stars lock into place, forming a celestial masterpiece. But stars aren't the only thing we want sharp in our night frames. We've got our human models too, and we don't want them to look like blurry ghosts. No sir, we want those portraits to shine with clarity. So, the same rule applies—quicker shutter speed to the rescue.

As you go through this book, we'll flip the script and dive into the mesmerizing world of motion-blur magic. Night photography isn't just about freezing time; we've got another whole dimension to explore where we unleash the enchanting power of longer exposures and embrace the graceful dance of motion. Picture this: a starry night sky where the stars trace their paths like celestial brushstrokes, creating star trails. It's like painting with light across the heavens, and boy, does it create a jaw-dropping spectacle! To achieve this ethereal effect, we crank up that exposure time, letting the stars trail and glide across our frame. Those seemingly fixed stars reveal their true motion, and we're left with a breathtaking testament to the Earth's rotation and our artistic prowess.

Immortalize Our Place in the Universe

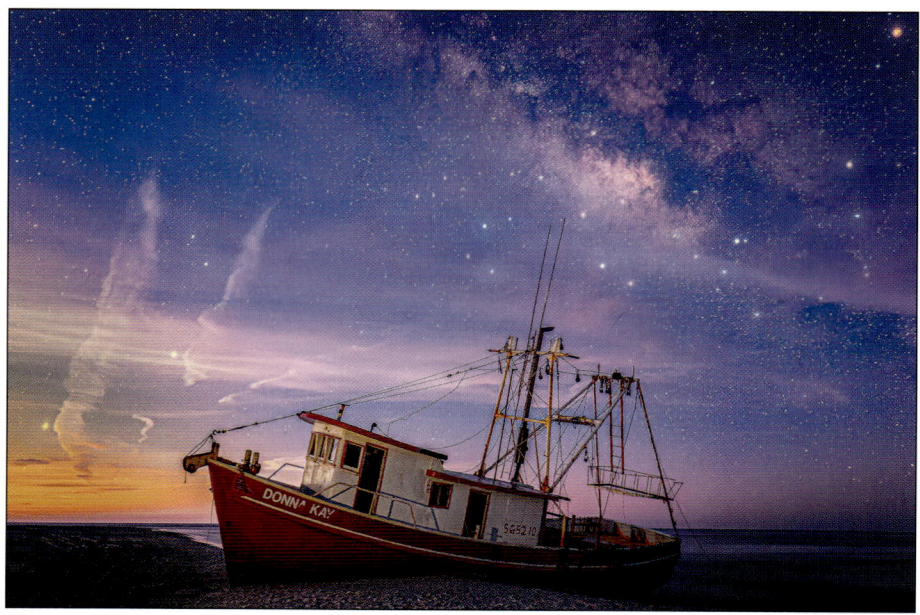

You see, as the Earth rotates on its axis, we're like passengers on a carousel, whirling around at mind-boggling speeds. Our home planet completes a full rotation in approximately 24 hours. Now, here's the kicker: the stars we see in the night sky are ridiculously far away, scattered across the vast expanse of the universe. As we spin around, it's like we're watching them from a high-speed train. They move from one horizon to the other in a long exposure.

Night photography lets us capture this perspective in a photo, immortalizing our place in the universe in a single frame. Those stars, each one a blazing sun like our own, speak to us of a vastness that stretches beyond our imagination. It's a humbling experience that puts our daily worries into perspective and reminds us of the majesty of the cosmos.

And here's the beauty of it all: when you include elements like trees, mountains, or even human subjects in your night shots, they become like tiny silhouettes against the vastness of the stars. Suddenly, the grandeur of the universe dwarfs everything else, and we are left in awe of the immensity surrounding us. But it's not just about feeling small; it's about feeling connected. Night photography unveils the interplay between us and the universe. Connecting the terrestrial with the extraterrestrial, infinitesimal beings gazing up at infinite stars. It's a moment of cosmic contemplation that brings us closer to the mysteries of the universe and reminds us of our place in this vast ocean of stardust.

Let the Universe Speak to You

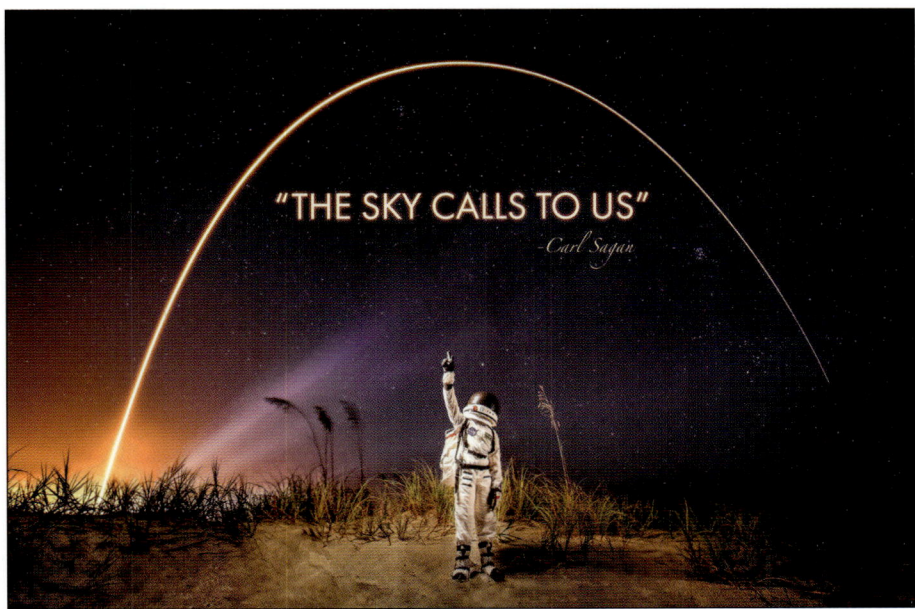

Bottom line: Remember throughout this book and your journey with night photography to embrace the power of drawing this cosmic perspective. Capture the beauty of the stars and the humbling sense of wonder they inspire. Through your lens, let the universe speak to you, and let your photography be a testament to the delicate balance between our tiny presence and the eternal beauty of the night sky.

Night photography is not just about dodging crowds and tourists, even though that's a nice bonus; it's about embracing a whole new world of mesmerizing beauty and creative possibilities. So, grab your camera, set your alarm for late-night adventures, and join us night owls as we capture the universe's secrets. It's time to show the world that the real magic happens when the stars come out to play. Keep shooting, keep exploring, and remember, in the words of the wise astronomer Carl Sagan, "The sky calls to us!"

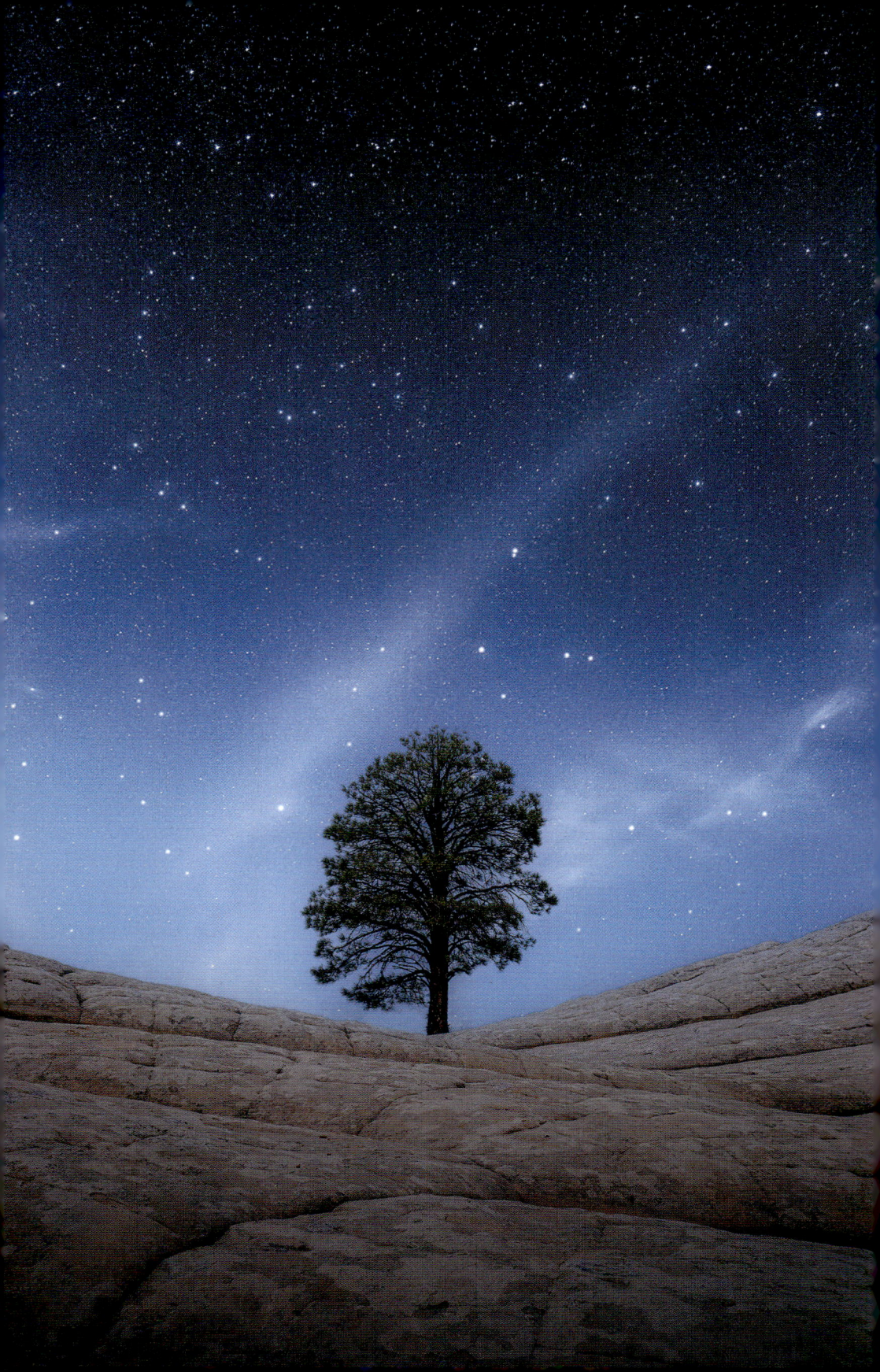

The Gear

The Tools You Need to Capture the Night

Night photography isn't just about the camera—it's about understanding how to work with the tools you have to create the best possible image. The right gear can make or break your ability to capture sharp, noise-free, breathtaking shots of the night sky. But don't get caught up in the idea that only the most expensive gear will do. The truth is that technique often matters more than price tags. We can get so caught up in the gear that we forget it's more about the image we're trying to create. It's not a specific camera body, lens, or gear that makes the picture. But, we do have to get the gear conversation out of the way here first, so that we can get to the important stuff, which is composition, technique, framing—all the elements that it takes to capture night photography. A well-planned shot with a budget setup will always outshine a poorly executed one with the best gear money can buy. Whether you're shooting with a mirrorless full-frame, a DSLR, a crop sensor, or even a smartphone, this chapter will walk you through how to maximize your setup for night photography. We'll dive into the best cameras for low-light situations, why full-frame sensors excel, and how to work around the limitations of smaller sensors. We'll break down the importance of fast lenses, tripods, and remote shutter releases, and even touch on the often-overlooked accessories that can make a huge difference—like lens hoods, dew heaters, and head-lamps with red light mode. Even the smallest tweaks to your gear setup can drastically improve your results. And for those looking to push their astrophotography to the next level? We'll explore tools like star trackers, light pollution filters, and the surprising power of computational photography in today's smartphones. The ability to stack exposures, reduce noise, and capture fine details has never been more accessible, opening up new possibilities for photographers at any level. At the end of the day, the best camera is the one that's with you. But with the right knowledge and a few essential pieces of gear, you'll be ready to capture the night like never before.

The Ideal Camera Body

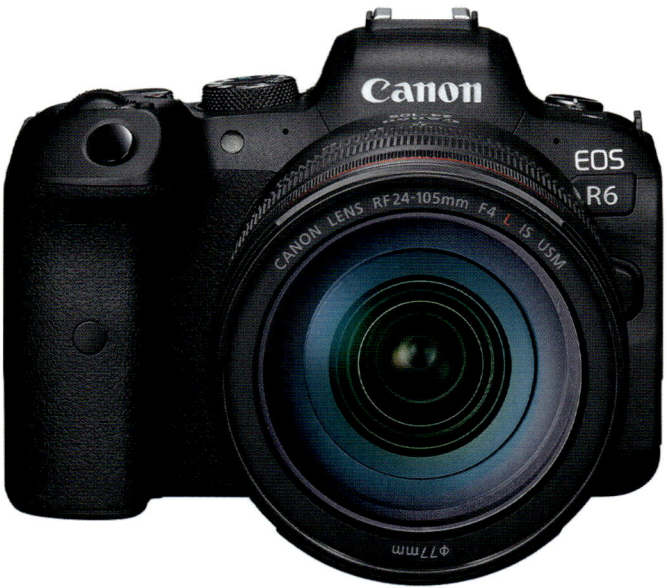

I'll keep this simple: the best camera you can get is a mirrorless full-frame sensor. With that said, you can shoot with a crop sensor, you can shoot with a smart-phone—you can shoot with any camera that works great in low-light environments because the best camera will always be the one that's with you. But, when it comes down to it, a full-frame sensor allows us to capture and absorb more light in detail than a smaller-sized sensor. This is important when we're talking about the faintest details, like stars and the Milky Way galaxy's celestial objects. We want all those details to be captured, and having that full-frame sensor helps. While a DSLR is fine too, you'll have to overcome one thing with it: a flip-up mirror. You'll need to use Mirror Lock-Up for sharp shots to take away that annoying shake that happens when you first engage your shutter. (We'll get into that more on the next page.) There's another handy feature to mirrorless technology: it offers us things like focus peaking in real-time, exposure previews, and even being able to zoom in on specific stars in live view to really nail focus (although some DSLRs have a live view fea-ture that can achieve the same results). So, what about a medium-format camera? Well, there can be diminishing returns when it comes to sensor size, and in my experience, the full-frame sensor is the best marriage of all the elements we need for night photography. Again, you'll be happiest with a full-frame mirrorless camera that performs well in low light, but any camera is better than no camera.

What If You Don't Have a Full-Frame Mirrorless Camera?

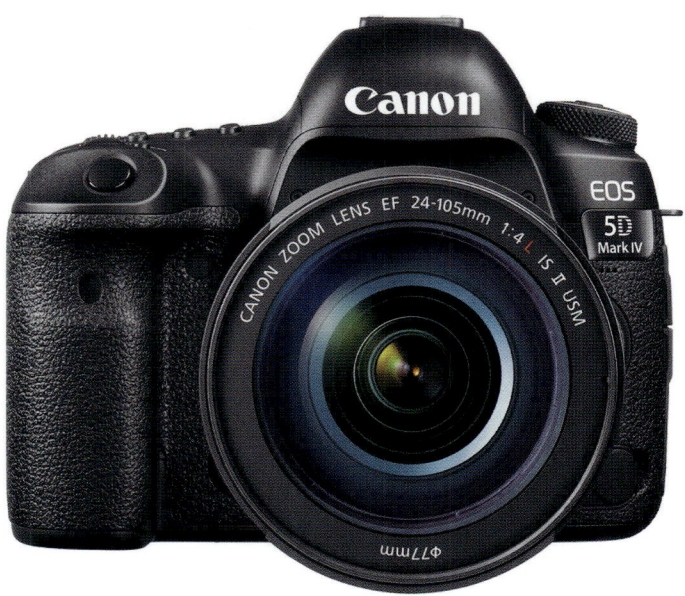

It's like I said on the previous page—there will be some limitations when it comes down to a crop-sensor mirrorless, a DSLR, or even a smartphone. The first thing is noise, the arch nemesis of the night photographer. Crop sensors or smaller sensors like those in your phone's camera have smaller pixels, leading to more noise at higher ISOs. Plus, older DSLRs struggle here because of older sensor technology. Does that mean you can't use them? Absolutely not. But you have to know how to work with them. One solution is shooting RAW because it retains more detail and allows you to remove noise better during post-processing. This is a must when it comes to night photography. The next limiting factor with a crop sensor is you will have a narrower field of view. This means you might use specialized lenses built for crop-sensors that give you a wider field of view comparable to a full-frame camera. Another technique is to use panoramic stitching with a crop sensor to get a wider field of view. This is why, for example, Canon makes an EFS lens or an RFS lens, and Nikon makes a DX lens—these lenses are built for crop sensors. Remember how I mentioned the vibration or shake that the DSLR mirror causes? This is where you'll need to use a feature called Mirror Lock-Up, along with either a remote shutter release or the camera's built-in timer to trigger the mirror to flip up, wait for the camera to stop shaking, and then take the exposure. What about phones? That's a horse of a different color (and later, there's a whole chapter on phone photography at night). The phones are leveraging computational photography, which allows us to process in-camera things that night photographers have been doing in Photoshop for years without the sometimes painful workflow. Again, more on that later.

The Lens

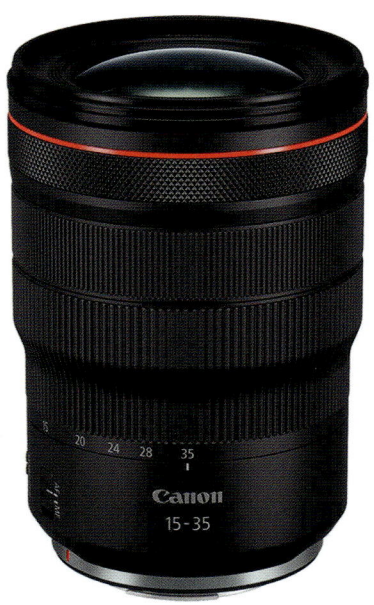

While they're both important, choosing the right lens is probably more important than choosing the right camera body. My go-to is a wide-angle. This allows
me to capture a wide field of the vastness of landscapes—including the majesty
of the Milky Way or sprawling cityscapes—all in one frame. With a focal length
from 12mm to 24mm on a full-frame sensor, a wide-angle can really embrace the
grandeur of the night sky along with the cosmos. If you're on a crop sensor, you
might use more like an 8mm to 16mm lens. Probably the most important thing, and
the thing that costs the most, is that we need a fast lens. That translates to those
low f-stop numbers—typically f/1.4, f/1.8, or f/2.8. These fast lenses are excellent in
low-light conditions because they allow us to absorb the largest amount of light
over the shortest time. That's key because absorbing more light allows us to lower
ISOs, which translates to less noise. What about zoom versus primes? While fixed
focal length primes, like 14mm or 24mm, ruled at one time, I prefer a great wide-
angle zoom. Nowadays, primes are a good way to get a decent fast lens at a good
price, but if you can afford it, I always love to have one lens that covers around
a 14mm to 30mm range. Trust me, there's nothing worse than needing to adjust a
few millimeters in your composition in the pitch dark, only to have to switch lenses.
It's also preferable to have a good manual focus mode. Most lenses nowadays have
a switch to go from manual to automatic, but the auto mode is less important to
me—at night, in low light, I'm mostly in manual mode. Putting it all together, 90%
of my photos are shot with a 15–35mm f/2.8 lens with a manual focus switch and
control. Research this online and everyone will agree they know which lens is best,
but no one will agree on which lens. My advice for finding a lens? Rent! A quality
lens is an investment. Renting makes it easier to find the right lens for your style.

A Tripod

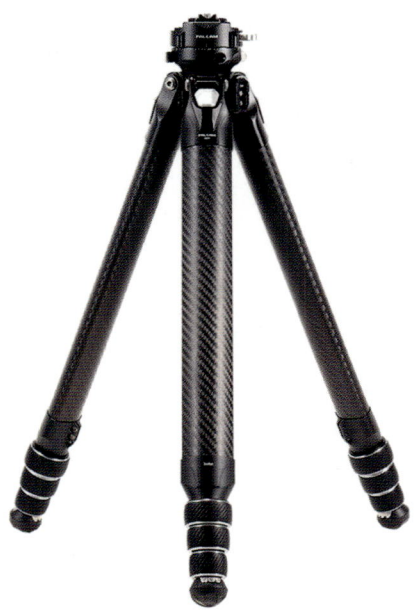

When it comes to shooting at night, a tripod is an indispensable tool for capturing stunning photos. Here's why you should always have one: First, we need stability. Night photography demands long exposure times, sometimes up to a few minutes. Hand-holding the camera during this extended exposure is a recipe for disaster, resulting in blurry shots. A tripod gives you the stability you need to keep your camera steady and free from unwanted vibrations and this will help make your shots sharp. Whether capturing starry skies, cityscapes, or even light trails, we need to have a tripod to keep the camera perfectly still while letting in what little light we have available, preventing motion blur in areas we don't want blur, yet giving us motion blur in the areas we do want to show motion. Next, composing your shot in the dark requires precision and attention to detail. A tripod keeps your camera in the desired position, allowing you to carefully frame your shot without any camera shake. So, what should you look for in a tripod? Here are a few things: First and foremost, above all else, sturdiness! We want a solid, durable, lightweight material, like aluminum or carbon fiber, that's robust enough to support the weight of our camera without wobbling or flexing. Next, for me, I want a tripod that will give me different angles than just my normal eye height—like one without a center column that can spread out to get low or extend above my head. We also need to be able to recompose easily in the dark, so a user-friendly ballhead is essential in night photography. The same goes for the legs. We want to be able to adjust the height of the tripod and the angle easily. The hardest part with this is striking a balance between stability, size, and weight. I will take a more stable yet cumbersome tripod every time.

A Platypod

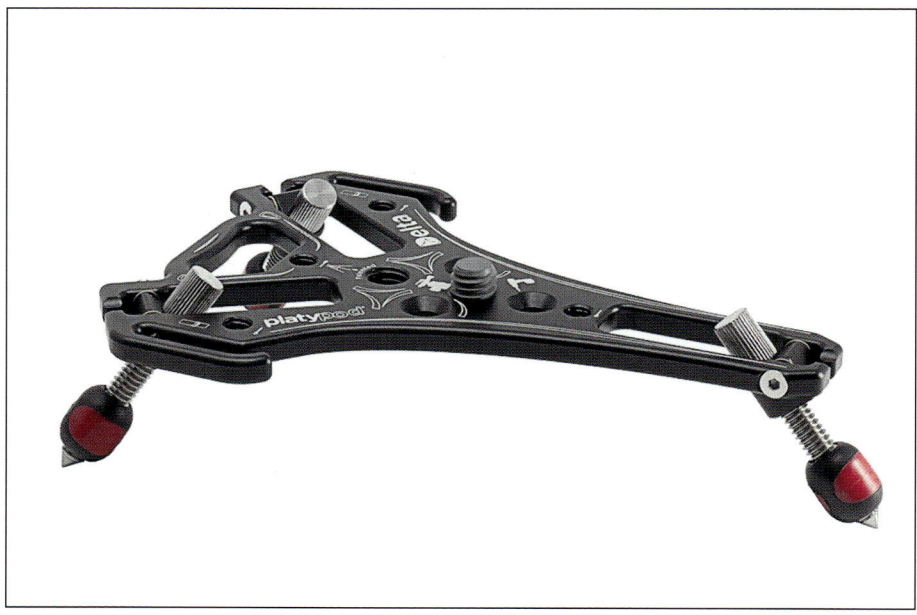

If you're shooting at night, you need stability. Period. Whether you're capturing star trails, cityscapes, or long-exposure light trails, even the tiniest bit of camera shake can ruin your shot. That's where the Platypod comes in. This isn't just a tripod alternative; it's the ultimate low-profile camera support that lets you shoot from angles most tripods can't touch. Unlike a traditional tripod, which can be bulky and frustrating to set up in tight spaces, a Platypod literally fits in your pocket while still giving you rock-solid stability. For me, the Platypod Delta is my go-to device for everything from my phone all the way up to a heavy DSLR with a large tele-photo lens. This thing is a tank in a tiny package. One of the biggest advantages of using one at night is stability on unpredictable surfaces. Rocks, sidewalks, ledges, car roofs—you name it, I've probably tried it. The adjustable fold-out feet give you a steady base, even on uneven ground, and you don't have to worry about wind knocking over a tall, top-heavy tripod. It also works in places where tripods aren't allowed, like some city landmarks or event spaces, making it perfect for capturing nighttime cityscapes. And if you're using your phone for night photography, pairing the Platypod Delta with the Platypod Grip turns it into a pro-level setup (see page 135 for more on this). It gives you the stability you need for sharp, clean shots, whether you're shooting in Night Mode, capturing light trails, or even doing astro-photography. You'll want one in your kit. It's lightweight, ultra-stable, and ready for anything. Check it out at Platypod.com and see why it's the one piece of gear I never go shooting without.

An Intervalometer

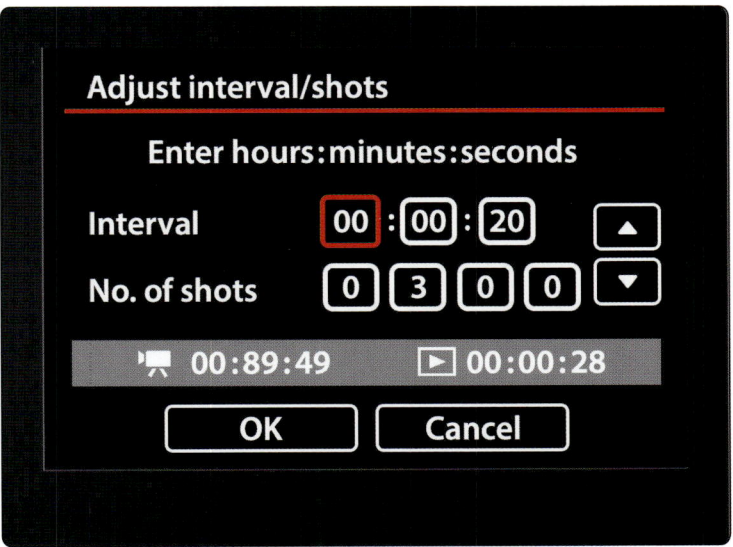

If you're serious about shooting star trails, time-lapses, or deep-sky astrophotogra-phy, an intervalometer is one of the most essential tools in your kit. Sure, you could sit there pressing the shutter every few seconds for hours, but let's be honest, that's not happening. Plus, I guarantee you'll ruin shots with the shake pressing the shut-ter introduces. An intervalometer automates the entire process, letting you focus on composition, framing, or just enjoying the night sky while your camera does all the work. So what exactly does it do? It controls your camera's shutter at set intervals, allowing you to take perfectly timed long exposures back-to-back without touching the camera. This is crucial for night photography because any camera movement ruins long-exposure shots. For star trails, the best technique is to shoot hundreds of shorter exposures (20–30 seconds each) instead of one super-long exposure. Why? Less noise, more flexibility, and no risk of a ruined shot if a stray light or plane flies through your frame. Set your intervalometer to take a shot every few seconds with no breaks, and later, you can stack them in post to create stunning, smooth trails. For time-lapses, the intervalometer controls how often your camera takes a shot, allowing you to capture the movement of stars, clouds, city lights, or even the changing colors of the night. A good starting point? Set your interval to about 15–30 seconds between shots for a smooth result. Just remember: the longer your interval, the faster your time-lapse will play back. Some cameras have built-in interval timers which are amazing too. An intervalometer isn't just useful, it's a game-changer for night photography and for me, it's a requirement.

A Trigger/Cable Release

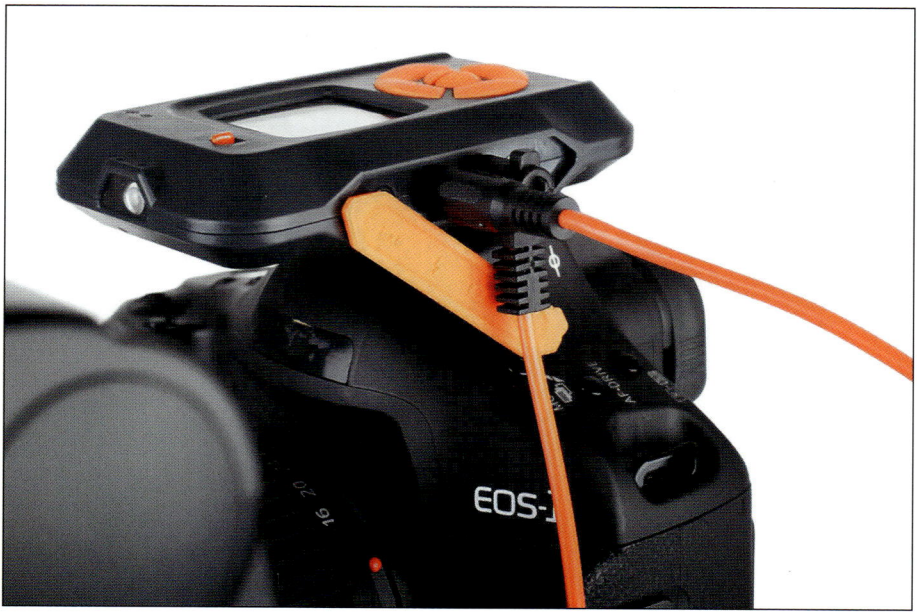

To keep your camera stable, eliminate camera shake, and achieve optimal results, you need a cable release, Wi-Fi/Bluetooth trigger, or timer delay when capturing night photos. During long-exposure shots, even the slightest movement, like pressing the shutter button, can lead to blurry images. Remote triggering offers a hands-free approach, ensuring your camera remains completely still throughout the exposure. A cable release is a simple and reliable tool that connects to your camera's remote port. By gently pressing the release button on the cable, you initiate the exposure without touching the camera. This minimizes vibrations and ensures sharp images, especially when shooting long exposures of the Milky Way, night landscapes, or while light painting. Many modern cameras offer Wi-Fi or Bluetooth connectivity, allowing you to use a smartphone or tablet as a remote trigger. By installing a camera-specific app, you can remotely control your camera settings and trigger the shutter. This wireless approach is convenient, especially when your camera is mounted on a tripod in a challenging position. If you don't have a cable release or Wi-Fi trigger, most cameras now have a built-in timer delay feature. By using your camera's timer, you can set a delay between pressing the shutter button and the actual exposure, which allows any vibrations from pressing the button to subside before the exposure begins, resulting in sharper night photos. Regardless of the method you choose, remote triggering is a must to maintain image sharpness.

A Headlamp

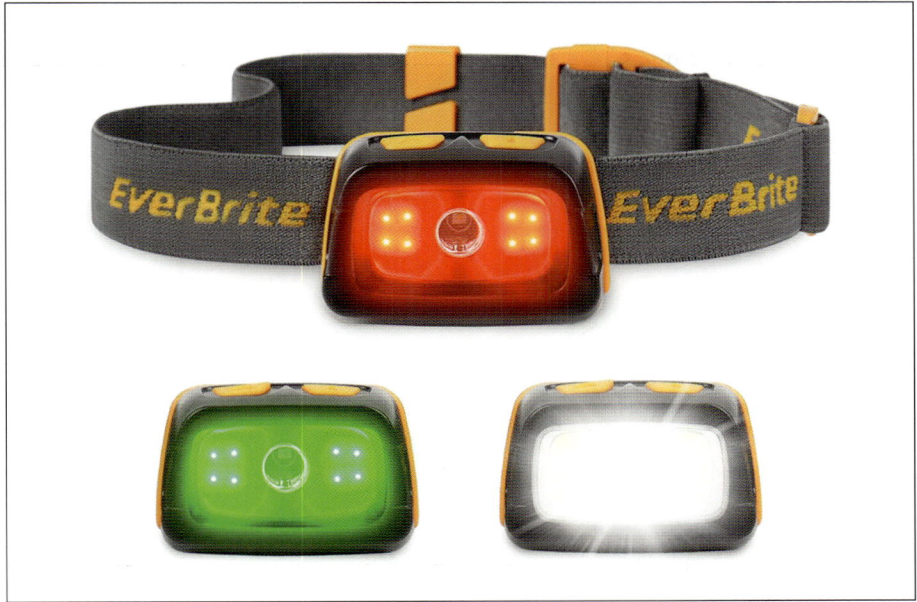

When you step into the darkness to capture those night scenes, a headlamp is essential. But not just any headlamp will do—you want one with both a regular and a red light mode. Why? Regular white light can be blinding, disrupting your night vision and making it harder to see the stars or the Milky Way. Red light mode, on the other hand, maintains your night vision by keeping your pupils dilated and sensitive to the faint celestial lights. Plus, night photography demands both hands on deck. With your camera in one hand and a tripod in the other, you need a headlamp to light your path and set up your gear without fumbling in the dark. And, if you're shooting with fellow photographers or in a peaceful night setting, the last thing you want to do is to disturb the crowd with a glaring white light. The soft, subdued glow of the red light is considerate. But, pro tip: If you're out with friends, always ask before turning on your headlamp. There's nothing worse than somebody ruining your 30-second exposure halfway through. When adjusting your camera settings or composing your shot, you need some light to see what you're doing, and a red light provides enough illumination without overexposing the scene or affecting your exposure settings. So why do you want a headlamp with a regular white light mode as well? This one's used to get to and from your destination in the dark safely. I even go one step further in getting a lamp that has a green light mode, too, since it doesn't attract the bugs as much as a white light.

Extra Batteries

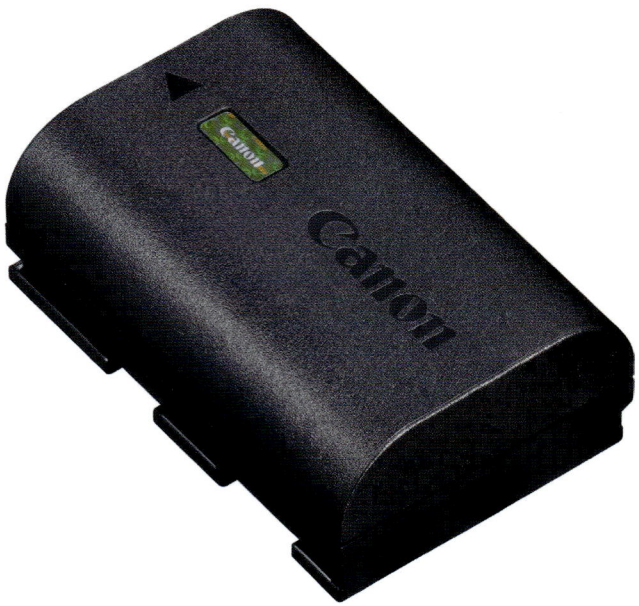

This one's important: always pack extra batteries! As darkness falls, the last thing you want is for your camera to lose power, leaving you in the dark. Night photography often involves long-exposure shots and these extended exposures consume more power than typical daytime shooting, draining your battery faster. Also, nighttime temperatures can drop significantly and the cold affects battery performance, reducing their life and capacity. Having spare batteries allows you to swap them out when one loses its charge, keeping your camera powered. Plus, in the dark, you'll use your camera's LCD or rear screen to review shots and adjust settings more than usual, which consumes additional battery power. Sometimes, the night surprises us with unexpected opportunities—a spectacular meteor shower, a once-in-a-lifetime celestial event, or a magical aurora display. When these unplanned moments unfold, you want to be prepared with extra batteries to extend your shooting session. Finally, packing extra batteries brings peace of mind. Knowing you have ample power to continue shooting, explore different compositions, and embrace the night's beauty without battery anxiety is priceless.

A Lens Hood

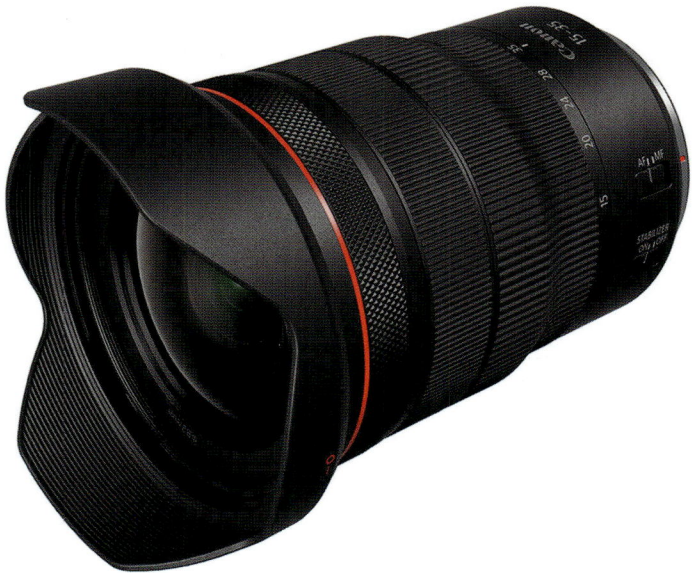

Let me share with you the lesser known secret of lens hoods and why, when it comes to night photography, these unassuming accessories bring a major benefit that will elevate your shooting experience. Picture this: You're out shooting in the dark when suddenly, an accidental bump or brush against something jeopardizes your precious lens. A lens hood, this sometimes overpriced plastic hero, acts as a guardian, shielding the front glass of your lens from accidental knocks, bumps, and even pesky raindrops. With one in place, you can focus on your creative vision without worrying about potential damage. It protects your lens without any drawbacks. Some photographers opt for clear or UV filters to safeguard their lenses. But, these filters come with their own set of issues—added reflections, potential image degradation or increased lens flare, and worst of all, a reduction of light transmission. Another big advantage of using a lens hood is it prevents dew from accumulating on your lens. That little bit of shade and insulation around the edge of the glass doesn't allow condensation to build up on the lens as quickly as it would without a lens hood. So, there you have it. It's not the sexiest piece of gear on the list, but if you embrace the lens hood, it will shield you against unforeseen mishaps, safeguarding your lens from the perils and pitfalls of damaged glass. And the best part? It protects without any pesky side effects—no added reflections, no image degradation, just pure, unadulterated protection for your precious glass.

Fill Light

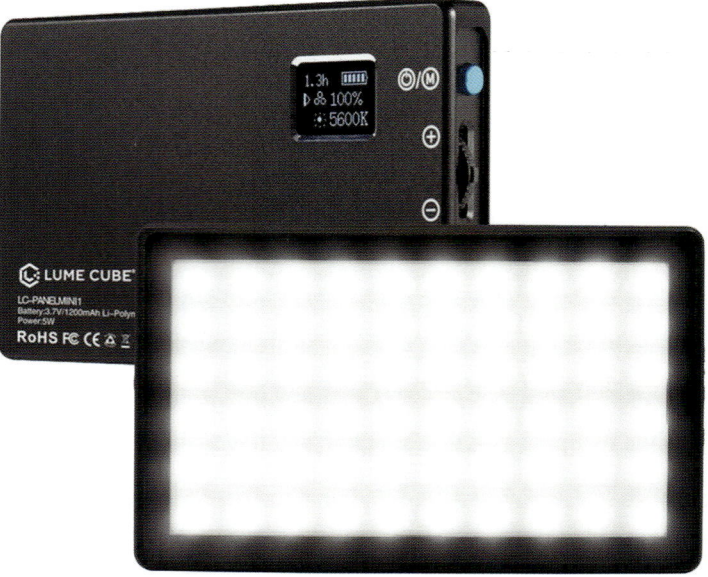

Say hello to my best friend—the dimmable LED fill light with color temperature controls. It's our secret weapon in night photography. By adding a fill light you can provide a touch of gentle light to your subjects or foreground elements. With its adjustable brightness, you can achieve the perfect balance between light and shadow, bringing out details and creating captivating compositions. But, here's the magic trick: with a dimmable LED fill light, dialing down the brightness to 1% or even lower, you can add just a subtle hint of light over a 10- or 20-second exposure without overpowering the natural darkness. This preserves the shot as a night photo while creating images that exude a sense of mystery and magic, almost like studio strobes or flash. Plus, with the ability to mix kelvin temperatures, it allows you to play with warm and cool tones, which opens up a world of creative possibilities, from creating warm, inviting scenes to bringing out the cool serenity of a starlit night. This fill light allows you to adapt to various night photography scenarios. It's perfect for capturing landscapes, portraits, or light paintings, its compact and lightweight, and it fits right into your gear bag and sometimes your pocket.

Using Your Phone as Your Fill Light

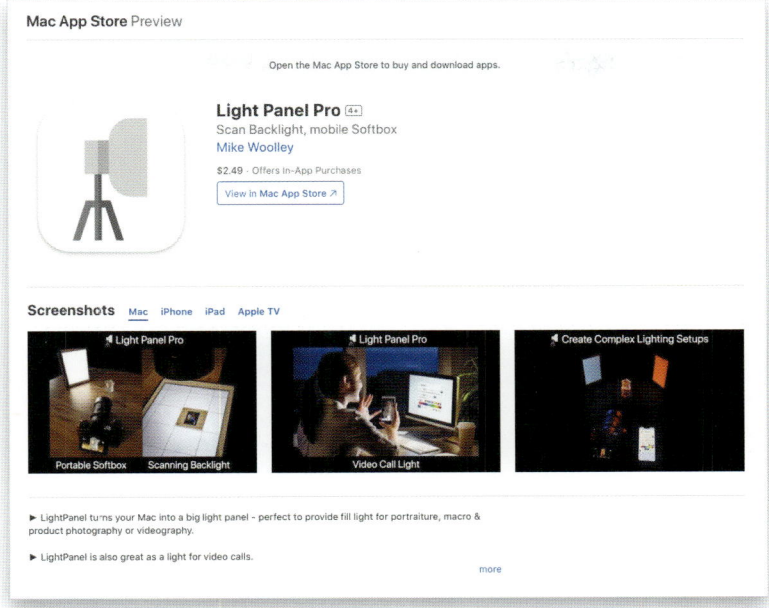

Let's say you're not ready to drop another hundred dollars on a color-changing LED light. Well, how about letting your smartphone do double duty? We can use the soft light of our phone screens dimmed down and color-balanced to act just like those fancy LED lights. Couple that with an app that adjusts the kelvin temperature of the screen and you now have another light to use to illuminate your foregrounds. Flash can be, well, flashy. And traditional light sources can overpower. But the soft dim glow from your phone screen? It's the Goldilocks of night photography lighting—just right! When dimmed down to a low power, it brings out the details of the foreground without outshining the stars. And when you add an app like LightPanel? Too bright? Swipe down. Need a touch more light? Swipe up. You've got a dimmable light source right at your fingertips. Plus, with apps like this, you can change the color temperature of your screen so you can match or contrast the ambient light. Hold it close, place it farther away, lay it flat, or prop it up. Your phone screen can be maneuvered to shed light from unique angles. And if you need a diffused glow, just pop a thin handkerchief or tissue over the screen for even softer light. Here's the kicker: Lighting equipment often means extra batteries, right? But you're charging your phone anyway. Plus, most modern smartphones come with impressive battery life. Sometimes, the best tools aren't the most obvious ones. As of writing this book, a couple apps that really help are LightPanel (for iOS) and Screen Flashlight (for Android). Both allow color mixing and dimming, which is key for this technique.

Shooting with Your Smartphone

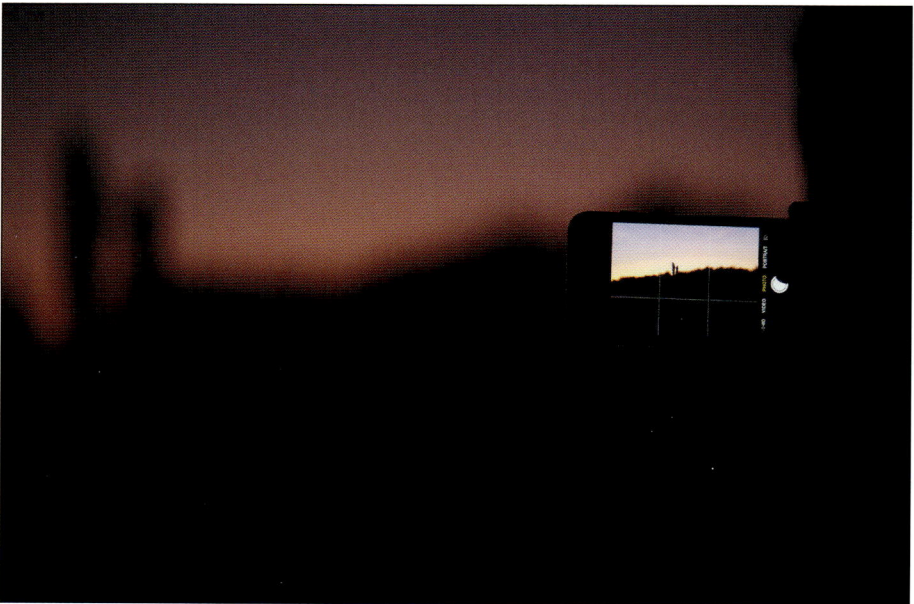

Remember when a smartphone for serious photography was laughable? Those days are gone, folks! Welcome to the era where smartphones are not just for snapping food pictures or selfies; they're your ally even with astrophotography. Now, before you roll your eyes and say, "Erik, there's no way my phone can replace my DSLR or mirrorless!" hear me out. After all, our smartphones are basically mirrorless cameras by definition. Leading players like Apple, Samsung, and Google have stepped up their game with dedicated astrophotography modes and algorithms; these smartphones optimize settings for stunning night shots. The software magic they pack in reduces noise, enhances starlight, and even auto-stacks images for clarity. Remember when smartphone photography was all "auto?" Take a look at the manual settings now—adjust ISO, shutter speed, focus, and more. On top of that, they can all shoot RAW too! With larger sensors, better optics, and advanced stabilization, today's smartphones rival some traditional cameras, especially when you factor in their computational photography modes. Not only are they awesome for shooting, but we have apps, apps, and more apps. From tweaking exposure to superimposing star trails, you've got tons of editing tools right at your fingertips. Literally. Plus, once you've edited, sharing with your community couldn't be easier. So, the next time you head out, consider leaving some of that bulky gear behind. Sometimes, the best camera isn't the most expensive one or the one with the most megapixels, it's the one you have with you. And in this day and age, that might be your smartphone. Later in the book, you'll find an entire chapter on just this topic.

Filters

The night sky might seem dark to our eyes, but it's teeming with different wavelengths of light. Picture filters as bouncers outside an exclusive club, allowing only specific light wavelengths to enter your camera sensor. First, we have the only filter I *might* use for wide-angle shots: a light pollution filter. I say "might" since I hardly ever use one anymore. Your DSLR or mirrorless camera, while a fantastic piece of machinery, struggles to distinguish between artificial city lights and starlight. A light pollution filter blocks unwanted light wavelengths, and thereby boosts the contrast and clarity of celestial bodies against the night sky. Next are astrophotography filters, which I use *all the time* when shooting just the night's sky. There are specialized narrowband Hydrogen-alpha filters, which allow the deep red light emitted by nebulae and galaxies to pass through, enhancing details that might be missed by the naked sensor. Such narrowband filters like Oxygen III are also a blessing when capturing distant galaxies and deep sky objects. If you're struggling with a lack of contrast, a multi-band filter might be what you need. This selectively allows specific colors of the spectrum through, adding depth and drama to your shots. One other must-have filter for deep sky astrophotography is a CLS (city light suppression) filter, which blocks out the common spectrums of light we use to light our towns and cities. If you're going to shoot from a polluted area, you're going to need one of these. Bottom line: filters for deep sky astrophotography are not just accessories; they enable your camera to see and capture what it otherwise couldn't. However, I may use a light pollution filter on a wide-angle shot less than 5% of the time because of the light loss. But, on telephoto shots of a nebula or galaxy, I might use a filter 99% of the time. The main difference being that those deeper telephoto shots are using a device that we'll talk about on the next page.

A Tracker

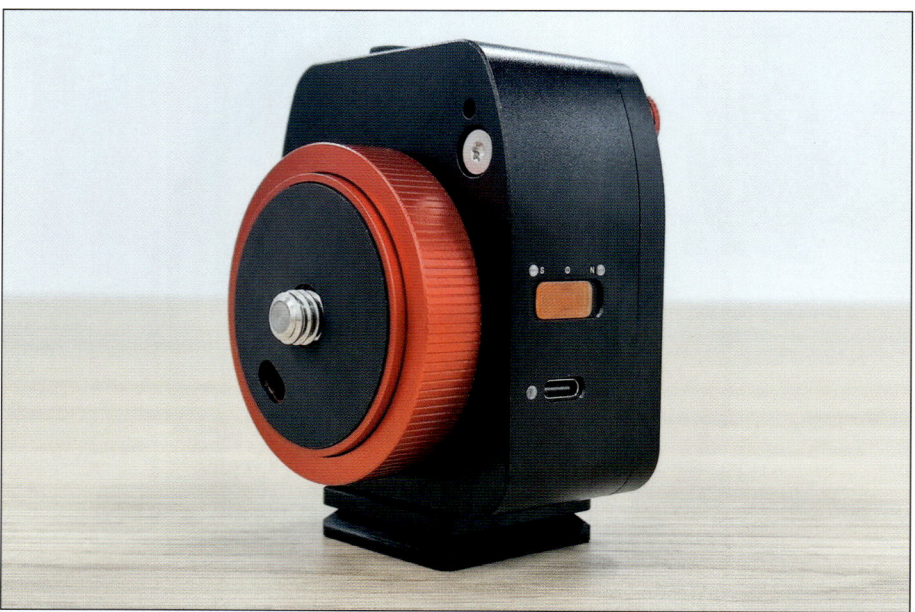

Here's where we up the game in night photography. Ever heard of star trackers? If not, brace yourself because this little tool might just blow your photography mind. But, it also comes with a huge drawback for wide-angle landscape Milky Way photos. So, here's what a tracker can do: Remember those elongated star trails in long-exposure shots that we talked about at the beginning of the chapter? They can be artsy, sure, but sometimes you want those stars crisp and sharp. As the Earth rotates, stars appear to move across the sky. A star tracker tracks this movement, slowly turning your camera to keep up. The result? Pin-sharp stars even in ultra-long exposures. With a star tracker, you can use longer exposures without getting star trails. This means you can shoot at lower ISOs and reduce that pesky digital noise. It's like giving your shots a clarity boost. Tracking the sky allows for much longer exposures, diving deeper into the universe. Capture faint stars, nebulae, and galaxies that are typically out of reach for stationary cameras. This allows for less reliance on high ISOs and faster shutter speeds, which means fewer shots ruined by noise or motion blur. You'll save on storage and extend battery life, making the most of your night out. But a quick heads-up on a couple things nobody seems to tell you: Star trackers have a learning curve. You'll need to align them with the North or South star (depending on your hemisphere), and balancing your gear on them takes some finesse. Plus, if you take shots that frame up a landscape in the foreground, you will *always* have to blend exposures. While this does require compositing skills, this means you can set optimal settings for both shots and merge them in post (you'll find more on post-processing later in Chapters 11 and 12).

Hand Warmers & Dew Heaters

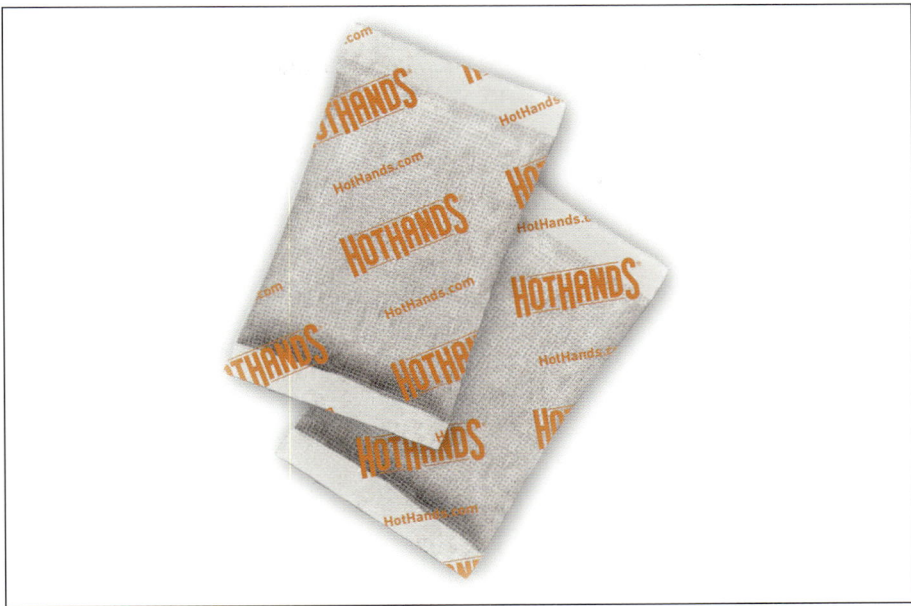

So, you're all set up, ready for the Milky Way to make its grand appearance when—ugh—dew fogs up your lens. It can happen, even with a lens hood. But fret not; there's an easy way to tackle it with dew heaters and hand warmers. As the night progresses, lenses tend to cool, sometimes below the ambient dew point. This results in moisture condensing on your lens, which is a fancy way to say it makes a foggy, un-shootable mess. Strapping on a dew heater ensures that your lens stays just above the ambient temperature, preventing dew formation. Whether battery-operated or connected to an external source, these heaters distribute warmth evenly, ensuring your shots remain crystal clear. Find yourself without a dew heater or just want an easier way so you'll never have to remember to charge it or hook it up to power? Hand warmers, typically used to warm up chilly fingers, are perfect for the job. Strap them around your lens using rubber bands and voilà! They generate just enough heat to keep fogging at bay. They're portable, widely available, and super-easy to use. A night photographer's trusty backup. Why go through all this? I speak from years of experience. Imagine the frustration: perfect composition, perfect settings, only to be thwarted by dew. Invest in a dew heater or keep those hand warmers handy.

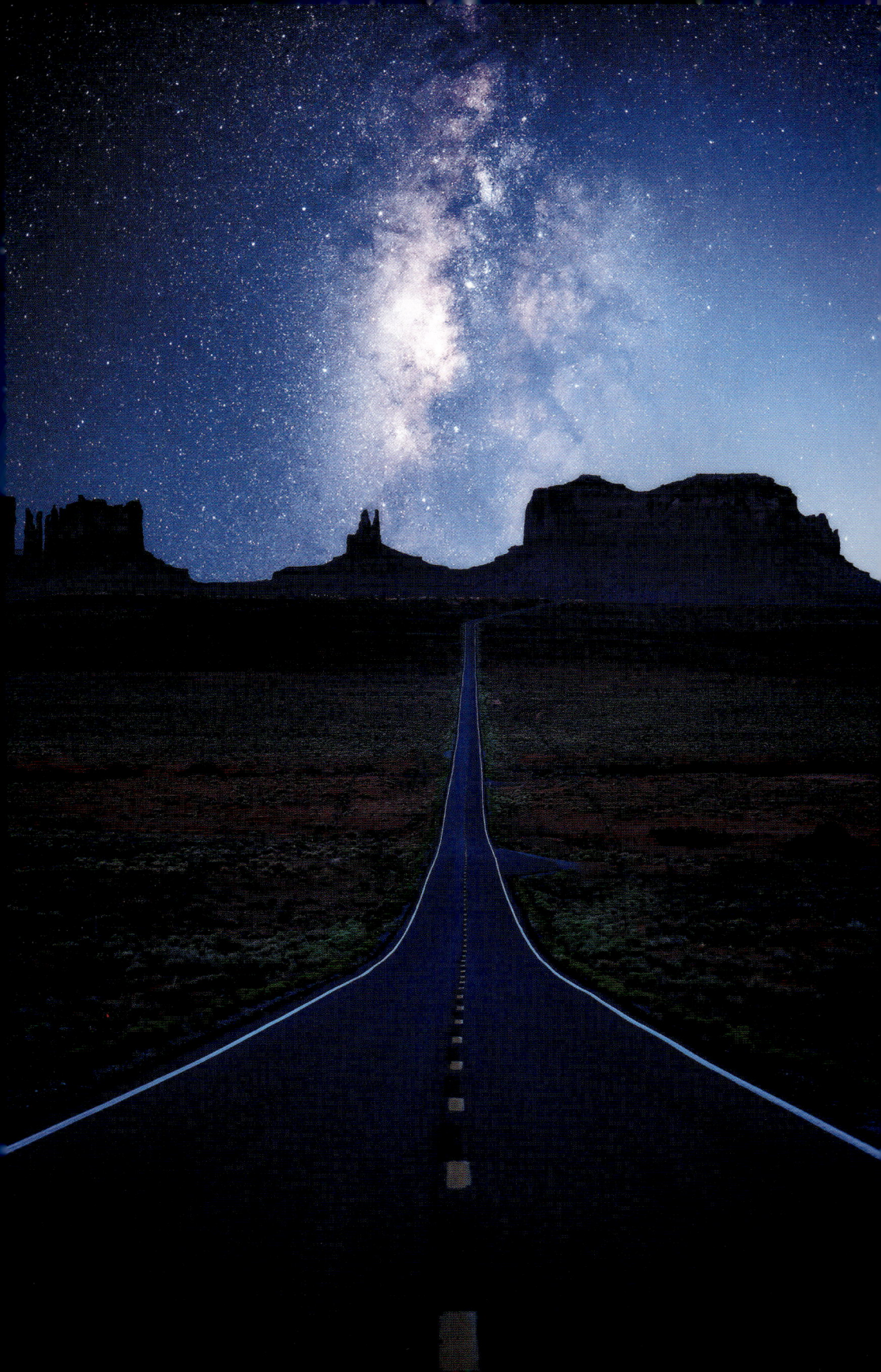

The Planning
Setting Yourself Up for the Perfect Shot

Great night photos don't just happen—they're planned. You can have the best camera, the sharpest lens, and the most dialed-in settings, but if you show up at the wrong place, at the wrong time, or under the wrong conditions, none of that matters. The night sky is constantly moving, shifting, and changing with the seasons, and if you want to capture those jaw-dropping Milky Way arcs, dramatic moonrises, or epic meteor showers, planning is everything. This chapter is all about stacking the odds in your favor before you even step outside. We'll break down how to predict where the Milky Way will be at any given time of year, how to time the perfect moon phases for your shot, and why understanding constellations and planetary alignments can help you craft better compositions. You'll learn how to scout locations during the day to avoid fumbling around in the dark later, and how apps like PhotoPills and Astrospheric can give you an almost unfair advantage when it comes to night photography. But planning isn't just about nailing the perfect alignment, it's also about avoiding disasters. We'll cover why checking weather conditions is a must, how to avoid unexpected light pollution, and why safety should always be a priority when trekking out to remote locations at night. Have you ever gotten set up for a killer Milky Way shot, only to have a sudden wave of fog roll in and ruin everything? We'll go over how to anticipate conditions like humidity, dew, and atmospheric haze, so you don't waste your night chasing a lost cause. And for those who want to take their astrophotography to the next level? We'll break down the seasonal calendar of the night sky, explaining when and where to find the best celestial events—from meteor showers to lunar eclipses—so you can capture them with precision. The difference between a mediocre shot and an award-worthy one isn't just luck, it's planning. And once you know how to read the sky like a map, you'll never miss a shot again.

Why Plan?

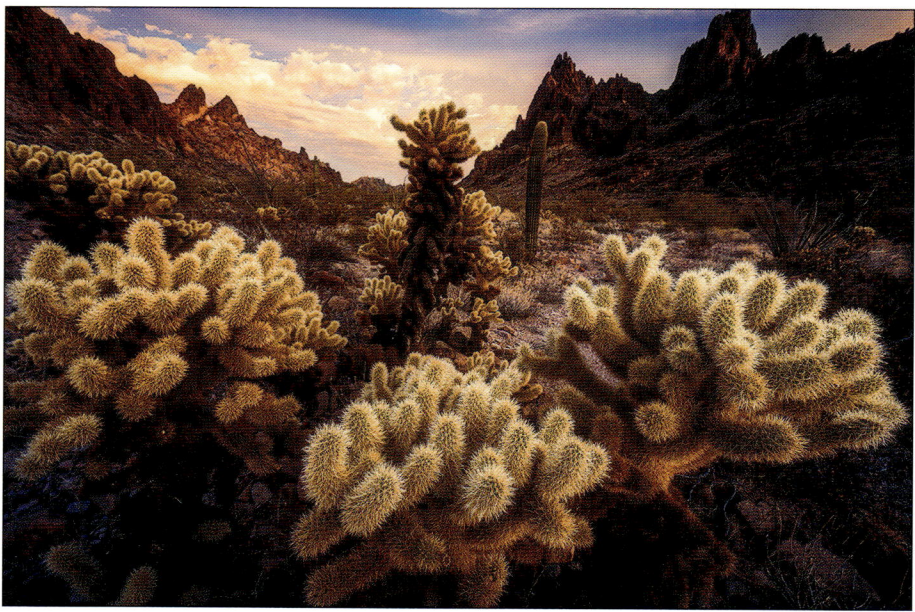

You're out in the pitch-black, tripod in hand, with the Milky Way poised perfectly above you. But, you can't decide where to stand, which lens to use, or how to frame your shot, so panic mode sets in. Can you relate? At least, that's how I felt 25 years ago. But, through the years, I've figured out the "secret sauce" to avoid this. It's called planning, and here's why it's so important: the night sky is an ever-moving canvas, with stars, galaxies, nebulae, planets, and our Milky Way shifting by the minute. Preplanning means you're set up and ready to shoot at that exact moment when the Milky Way is in the perfect position or the exact time the moon peeks over a building. Plus, the older I get, the more I put safety first. Exploring unfamiliar terrain in the dark sounds like a twisted ankle waiting to happen, and I speak from experience. Daylight scouting and planning beforehand with the tools available nowadays keep things safe. Know where to tread, where to avoid, and if that puddle is a pond of quicksand. Again, I speak from experience. Night photography requires a buffet of gear—wide lenses, telephotos, maybe even a sky tracker. Knowing your plan beforehand lets you pack smart and light. Plus, have you ever tried swapping lenses in the dark? It's a juggling act best avoided! Weather can be a fickle friend, too. Planning means you've checked forecasts, you know when cloud cover is due, or if a surprise meteor shower is in the cards. I've always believed that rather than taking a myriad of "meh" shots, planning lets me focus (pun intended) on crafting fewer, but stunningly thought-out images. Night photography isn't just an art; it's a tactical mission. Treat it as such, and I promise you it will become much more rewarding. Prep, plan, and then execute those breathtaking shots you envisioned.

The PhotoPills App

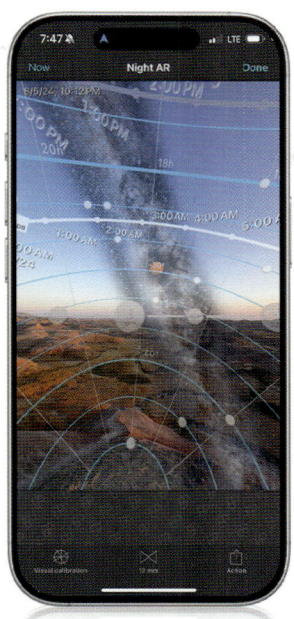

PhotoPills (for iOS and Android) is a game-changing app that makes planning and perfecting night shoots a breeze. It's like having a celestial atlas of the Milky Way, moon, sun, and even meteor showers in your pocket. Want a shot with the North Star as your anchor? PhotoPills gives you its exact position, time, and trajectory to make that happen. It offers detailed timelines on when and where you should be to get the shot you're after. No more guesswork; just perfect timing and perfect location every time. Beyond stars, the app charts the sun's and moon's phases and path. Planning a moonlit shot? It'll tell you when and where to shoot. But, it doesn't stop with just planning from home. This is where things get sci-fi cool! On location, PhotoPills' Augmented Reality (AR) feature lets you overlay celestial paths in the real world via your smartphone's camera. Want to see where the moon will rise behind that mountain? Point, tap, and voilà! Another thing I love to do on location is scout shots during the daylight. PhotoPills allows me to see exactly when and where to come back at night to get the Milky Way arching at the perfect spot in my composition. If you need to fine-tune your settings, it also offers calculators for hyperfocal distance, depth of field, and star trails. PhotoPills isn't just a tool; it's a community. Share plans, learn from fellow shooters, and even get inspired by their "Pills" of the day. This is more than an app; it's a night photographer's trusty sidekick. If there's one app I couldn't live without, it would be this one.

Where Is the Milky Way Core?

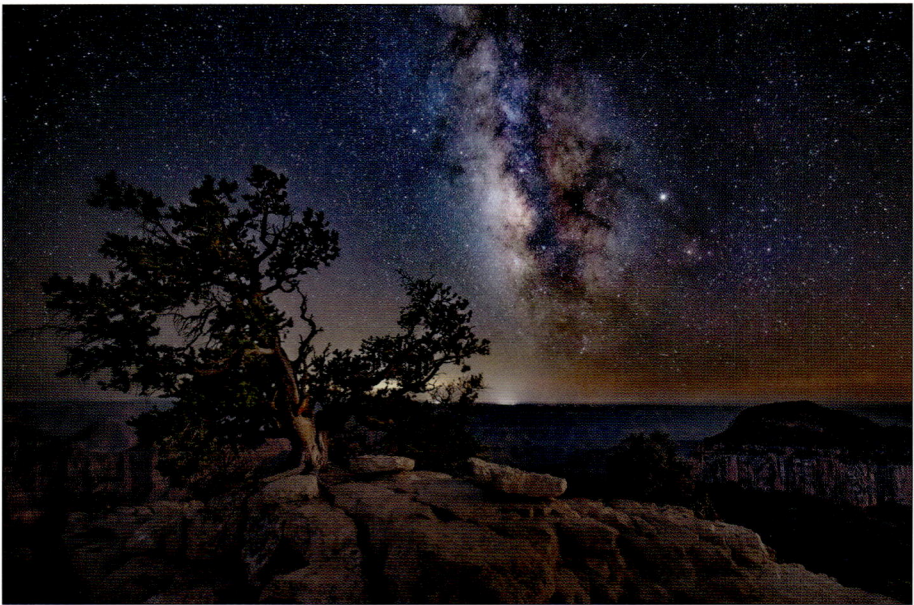

Have you ever noticed how the Milky Way core plays hide-and-seek in the skies based on the calendar? Just as Earth has four seasons, the Milky Way core follows its own celestial seasons, and depending on the month, the core appears at different angles and elevations. No matter the time of year or even what hemisphere of the earth you live in, the Milky Way core remains loyal to the southern skies. That means we're always shooting south to get the core in our shots. This makes scouting easier since we must shoot south from a north position. A great example would be the north and south rim of the Grand Canyon. If you want the Milky Way core in your shot of the canyon, you need to be on the north rim shooting south. So, how does the time of year affect us? Let's focus on the northern hemisphere here (if you live in the southern hemisphere, your seasons will differ). Come March and April, the core rises just before dawn. It's when early risers get the best view low on the southern horizon. The summer months are the Milky Way core's prime time. From June to August, it arches magnificently across the sky for most of the night. Then, as we move into September and October, the core begins its descent, setting earlier each evening. By late autumn, it bids adieu, nestling below the horizon for a short winter's rest. The closer you live to the equator, the longer you have to see the core above the horizon. One thing to note: if you see a shot of the core high in the sky in Iceland, it's fake. Those in higher latitudes in the northern hemisphere—above 55 degrees to be exact—will never see the full core above the horizon at night. During the summer, when the rest of the northern hemisphere can see it, anyone north of 55 degrees can't see it since the sun never falls low enough on the horizon, and the sky doesn't get dark enough to reveal it.

Time of Year Effects on the Night Sky

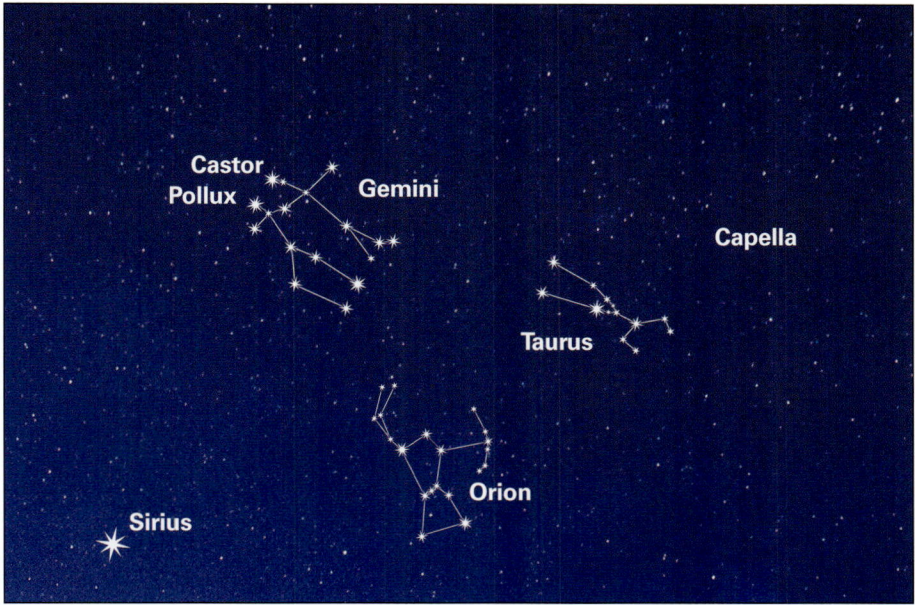

Just as trees change their leaves and moon phases shift the tides, the night sky transforms throughout the year. Ever wonder why some constellations are seasonal guests? Let's break down the cosmic calendar, so you can better understand the night sky: Earth's journey around the sun alters our night-sky viewpoint. Think of it as a merry-go-round—as we move, our view of the vast cosmos shifts, bringing new stars and constellations into focus during the night. Crisp, cold winter nights usher in iconic constellations like Orion the Hunter, the Pleiades cluster, and the brightest star, Sirius. Their high placement in the sky makes for sharp, striking captures. As winter constellations set in the west, spring introduces a parade of galaxies. It's the prime time to capture the Virgo Cluster, and the Big Dipper points us toward the North Star. Then, warm summer evenings in the northern hemisphere treat us to the Milky Way core and the Summer Triangle, made up of the stars Deneb, Vega, and Altair. The dense star fields of Sagittarius also play peek-a-boo during this time. As summer stars fade and we move toward the fall, the Andromeda Galaxy, our massive cosmic neighbor, takes center stage. The Great Square of Pegasus and the W-shaped Cassiopeia make their grand appearance, adding new shapes for us to admire. Beyond stars, each season has its meteor showers—from the Perseids in August to the Geminids in December. Knowing the calendar ensures you're ready to catch these fleeting fireballs. Basically, the night sky is a calendar, a clock, and a storybook all in one. Understanding these seasonal shifts means every venture under the stars offers something fresh for us to capture to vary our compositions. On the next few pages, we'll go deeper into the seasons since this is the area I find most people struggle with when it comes to mastering the night sky.

The Spring

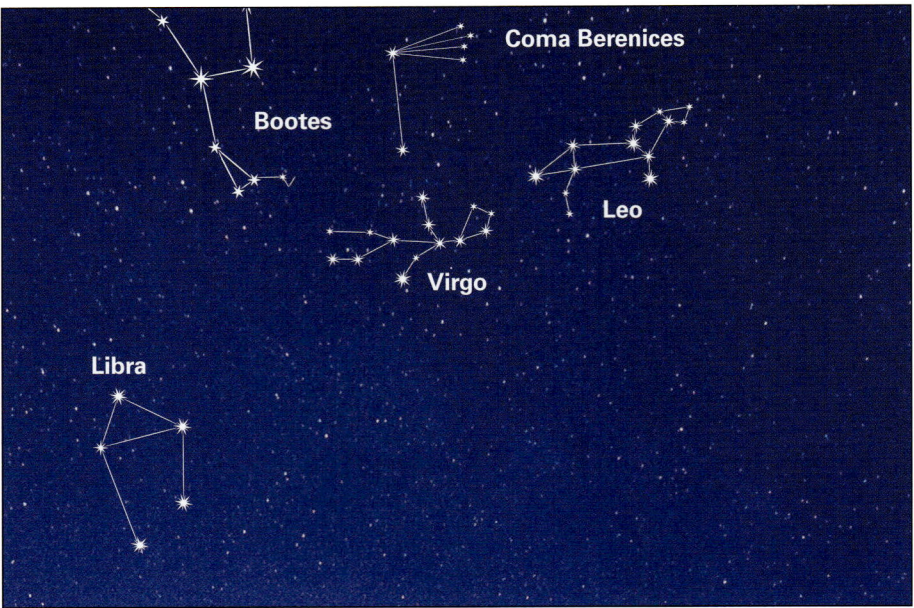

As we learned on the previous page, the seasons offer a great variety of views of our universe. (*Note:* Again, these seasons will be based on the northern hemisphere. If you're in the southern hemisphere, follow the dates for the northern seasons, and all this will apply.) Each season offers a different vantage point from which we observe the night sky. For example, in winter we see constellations and spring spouts galaxies! The Virgo Cluster becomes prominent, housing thousands of galaxies ripe for capturing. Point your lens towards Leo and Coma Berenices, too; these constellations cradle galaxies aplenty. In late winter to early spring, watch for a pyramid of faint light extending up from the western horizon called the Zodiacal light. This ethereal glow is sunlight scattering off cosmic dust in our solar system's plane. It's a rare beauty, and spring's clear skies offer the best chance to photograph it. April showers bring...the Lyrids meteor shower! Peaking around April 22nd, this meteor display can offer 10–20 bright meteors per hour, making for some dynamic night sky shots. Jupiter also begins its nightly display in late spring, while Mars and Saturn occasionally grace the dawn. These celestial giants add diversity to the star-sprinkled canvas, providing variety in our compositions. Spring's transitional weather—with mists, dew, and occasional cloud drifts—can add drama to your astro foreground. In short, spring's night sky is a blend of distant galaxies, meteoric flashes, and planetary portraits framed by Earth's own atmospheric art. It's always great to embrace the season's offerings and let every photo capture the freshness of spring, both terrestrial and celestial.

The Summer

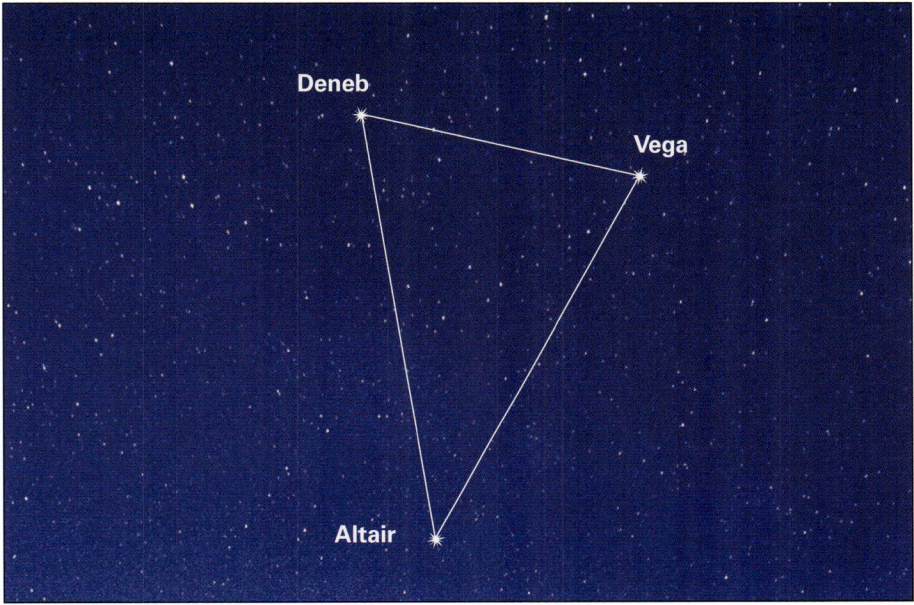

Hot summer nights aren't just for barbecues and beach outings. Summer is *the* time for the Milky Way, especially its brighter core. Around the solstice, it stretches majestically from the southern horizon, spilling across the sky. Pair that with minimal moonlight, especially during new moons, and our galaxy takes center stage in all its grandeur. The stars Vega, Deneb, and Altair form the Summer Triangle, which dominates the summer sky. It's expansive and bright and offers a guidepost for spotting surrounding constellations like Lyra and Aquila. In August, the Perseids meteor shower brings the best meteor display of the year. With up to 60 meteors per hour, it's a night photographer's dream come true. Remember, peak nights are around August 12th. Summer skies often treat us to a planetary waltz. Venus appears post-sunset, Jupiter dominates most of the night, and Saturn, with its iconic rings, makes its appearance. Their dance can bring a sprinkle of dynamic contrast to your images. Speaking of contrast, nebulae and star clusters, like the Lagoon Nebula and the Wild Duck Cluster, pop out in summer. These require longer exposures, trackers, and a telephoto lens, but oh, the rewards! We'll have a whole chapter later just about this deep-sky astrophotography. While one might think we want a pristine sky, summer's atmospheric haze can act as a natural diffuser, softening stars and adding a dreamy glow to our images. Plus, the occasional thunderstorm, with its lightning streaks and broken clouds, can amplify the drama. Even smoke from those dreaded wildfires can, in small doses, diffuse the sky nicely. Summer nights are filled with opportunities for interesting images. From our galaxy's core to shooting stars to the bright dance of the planets, there's never a dull moment.

The Fall

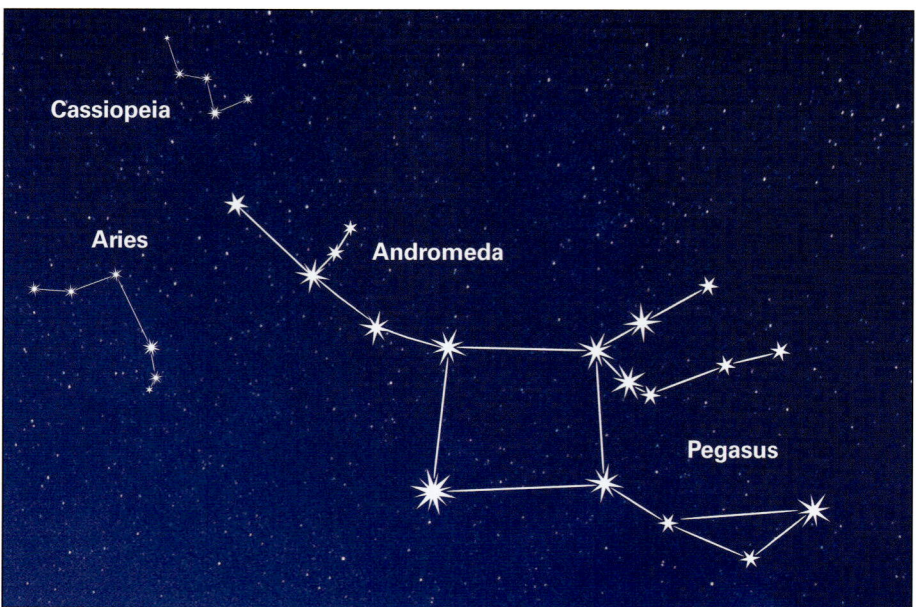

As the leaves turn and the air crisps up, the night sky dons its own array of changing colors. First up, the Andromeda Galaxy, our massive spiral neighbor, becomes a highlight. It's the best time to capture this behemoth, the galaxy nearest to our own, floating just 2.537 million light years away (give or take)! Just like spring, the ethereal glow of the zodiacal light makes a brief encore. This time, it's seen pre-dawn, extending from the eastern horizon. It's like nature's own flashlight illuminating the cosmos. Plus, the distinct W-shape of the Cassiopeia constellation graces the zenith. Its placement, along with its bright stars, makes it a brilliant focal point in night captures. A gift from the iconic Orion constellation, the Orionids meteor shower peaks around October 21st. Its radiant meteors are remnants of Halley's Comet, providing a celestial show with historical echoes. The cooler nights of fall often deliver sharper planetary views. Look out for Mars, which often showcases itself prominently in the fall, and Uranus is at its brightest. By fall, the bright core of the Milky Way starts its descent, setting earlier each evening. However, the outer arm remains, offering a more subtle, but equally mesmerizing, capture against the autumnal night. Just know that in northern latitudes, visibility of the core will be almost impossible by this time. Fall's shorter days mean earlier golden and blue hours—those magical times right after sunset and before full darkness. The hues blend perfectly with emerging stars, offering a transient but splendid shot of astronomical twilight. So, as we prepare for winter's embrace, the autumn sky unfolds with a mix of galaxies, meteor showers, and early evening hues.

The Winter

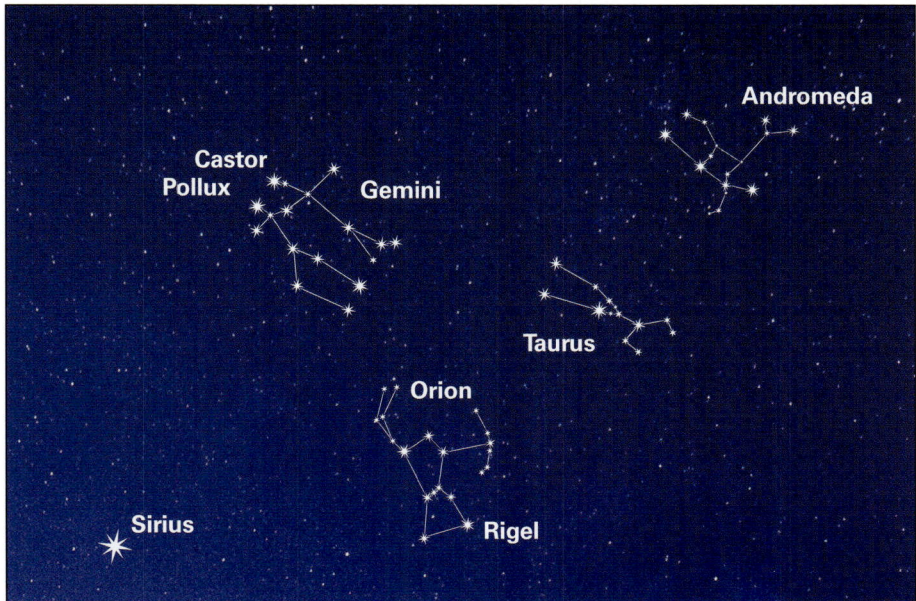

Winter isn't just about the cold. The season's chill brings with it some of the clearest and starriest skies. Orion, the Hunter, rises. This iconic constellation, with its three-star belt, becomes the jewel of winter nights. It also boasts the radiant Orion Nebula, a stellar target just waiting for your lens's attention. Given the size and time of year, this is the nebula to start with when learning telephoto tracker astrophotography (more on this in Chapter 5). Touted as December's starry spectacle, the Geminids meteor shower peaks around December 14th. With up to 150 meteors per hour, it's one you don't want to miss. Winter nights can sometimes present a planetary trio—Jupiter, Saturn, and Mars, creating a beautiful planetary alignment. With the crisp winter air minimizing atmospheric distortions, they shine brighter and clearer. Sirius, the brightest star in our night sky, takes center stage. Its twinkling radiance offers a stable and brilliant point of focus, especially on the coldest of nights. While the Milky Way core is hidden by daylight, the outer arms of the Milky Way stretch across the sky. The contrasting darker winter backdrop lets these fainter stars shimmer in prominence. Winter solstice gifts us the longest night, giving photographers an extended canvas to experiment with—more night means more opportunities. Just keep warm and stock up on hand warmers for both hands and lenses (see page 17 for more on them). The brightest stars of six constellations form a celestial pattern, including Sirius and Rigel (Orion's knee). This stellar polygon is a winter exclusive, offering a grand expanse of the winter sky to frame in your shots. Winter's cold brings out clarity—the air is cleaner, the stars twinkle sharper, and the nights unveil a celestial tapestry that's both vivid and vast. As you hear the crunch of snow under your boots and see your breath fog up, remember that your lens has a date with the stars.

Solar Eclipse

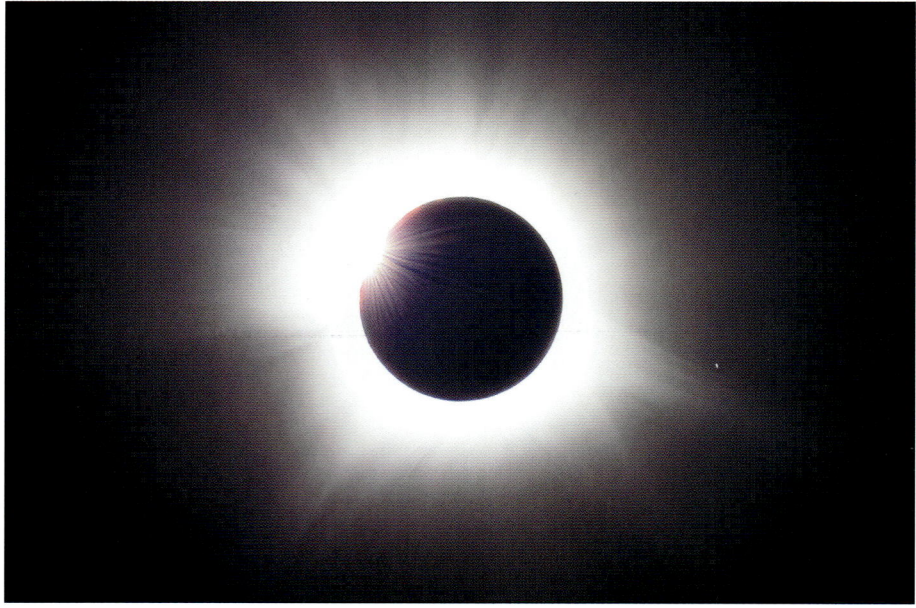

When our brightest star, the sun, decides to play a game of peekaboo, we get the mesmerizing spectacle called a solar eclipse. Whether it's a fleeting partial or a breathtaking total, each solar eclipse tells a unique story:

Total Eclipse: The sun is entirely masked by the moon, which plunges us into day-time darkness (as seen here).

Partial Eclipse: The moon obscures only part of the sun, like a cosmic bite mark out of the sun.

Annular Eclipse: The moon is just a tad too far from Earth, leaving a luminous ring of the sun.

Always use a solar filter or eclipse glasses for your lens. It's vital for safeguarding your eyes and your camera's sensor from the intense solar rays. You can use ND filters stacked up to 18–20 stops, but I'd always recommend a solar filter to be safe. Heck, you can even use welding glass. A telephoto lens captures the sun's details, especially during moments like the "diamond ring" in total eclipses. Just make sure you don't point your telephoto lens at the sun until you have a proper solar filter over it. The slow progression of a solar eclipse necessitates a solid tripod to mini-mize shake and maximize clarity. Start around ISO 100 at f/8. Your shutter speed will vary based on the sun's brightness. As the eclipse progresses, continually adjust. Bracketing shots will ensure a range of exposures, crucial for capturing this dynamic event. Research times and stages of the eclipse. Scout locations with clear horizons and practice your shots. Be ready for that fleeting moment of totality. Photographing a solar eclipse is about preparation and respect (mainly for our powerful sun), but with the right gear, settings, and patience, you'll have a shot for the ages.

Lunar Eclipse

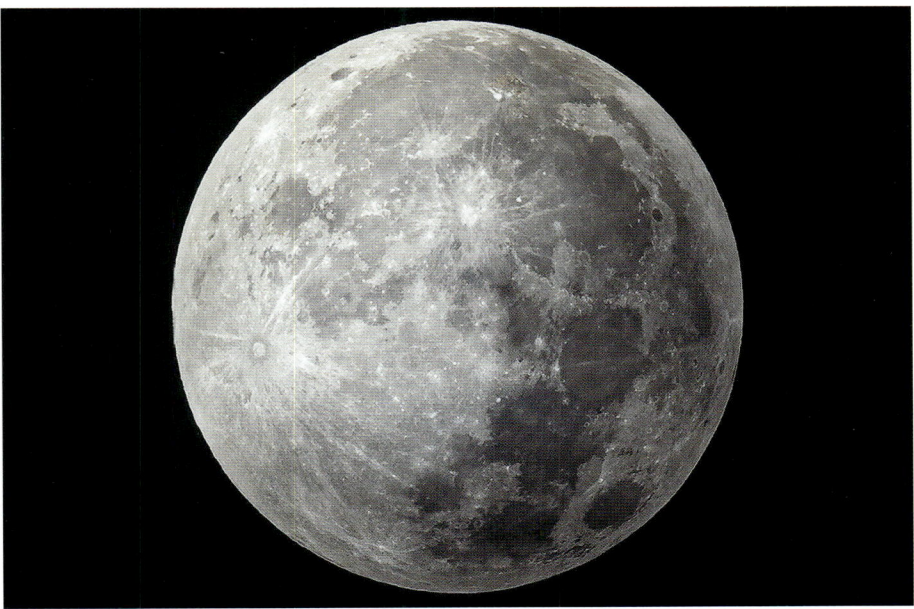

A lunar eclipse isn't just Earth casting its shadow on the moon; it's a slow dance of cosmic proportions, with hues and phases over hours. Ready to capture the moon's metamorphosis? Here's what you need to know:

Total Eclipse: The moon dives deep into Earth's shadow, sometimes glowing a deep red or copper.

Partial Eclipse: A segment of the moon gets cloaked in shadow, which creates a celestial crescent.

Penumbral Eclipse: Subtler, with the moon passing through Earth's outer shadow. It's a play of light and faint shadow and can add a lot of depth and dimension to the moon (as seen here).

No special filters are needed here. A telephoto lens, though, enhances the moon's features, especially during a blood-red total eclipse. These eclipses span hours, so a robust tripod is non-negotiable. For extreme telephoto shots, think about a tracker with a moon mode to help your sanity. Begin with ISO 800, f/8, and a shutter speed of 1/125th. The moon's luminescence varies across the eclipse, so stay flexible and adjust accordingly, never fearing a little ISO to keep that shutter speed quick enough to freeze the moon in place, especially with a telephoto lens. Know your eclipse—research its phases, timing, and the expected color palette. Test shots will help you hone your settings before the main event. Lunar eclipses offer a buffet of tones, phases, and moments. From the first shadowy depth to the deep red totality, each phase is different.

Meteor Showers

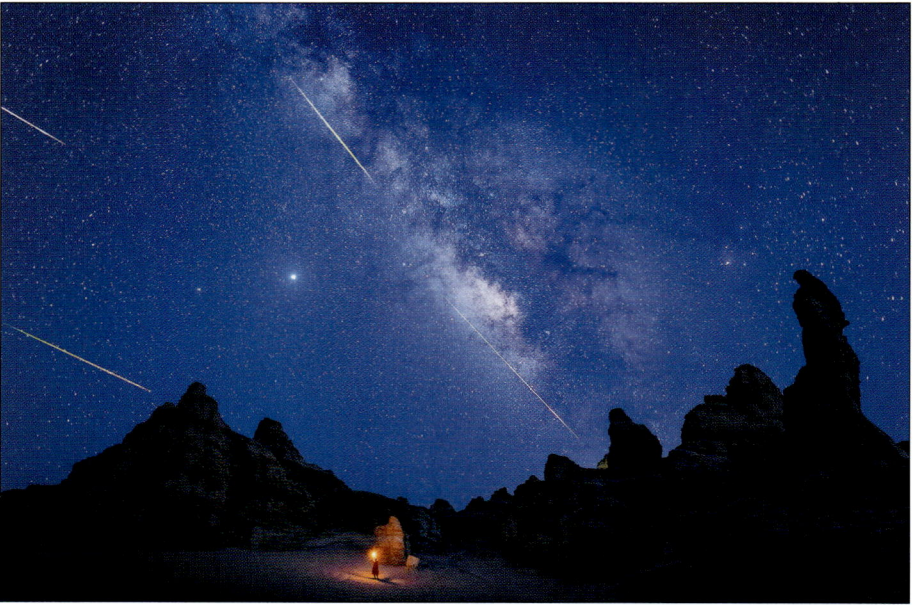

The night sky occasionally likes to put on a light show, courtesy of meteor showers. These celestial spectacles, where streaks of light dash across the night sky, offer moments of fleeting beauty. But first, what are meteor showers? They arise when Earth passes through the debris left behind by comets. These particles burn up in our atmosphere, creating brilliant streaks of light. As you learned on the seasons pages earlier in this chapter, each meteor shower has a peak night where maximum meteors can be seen per hour. A wide-angle lens—ideally between 14mm and 24mm—captures these streaks perfectly by capturing a broad swath of the sky, increasing your chances of getting those meteors. With that said, a sturdy tripod is a necessity—you'll be doing long exposures to capture the streaks, so stability is key. To capture a meteor shower, start with a wide-open aperture (like f/2.8) to capture as much light as possible. ISO should hover between 3200 and 6400, but be ready to adjust based on ambient light. Shutter speed? Aim for 15–20 seconds, avoiding star trails but long enough to capture meteor trails. Dark skies matter here, too. Head away from city lights—a place with a broad, unobstructed view of the sky is golden. Finally, meteor showers are unpredictable. There might be bursts of activity followed by quiet spells. Stay patient, keep shooting, and enjoy the show. Trust me, be patient—I speak from experience here. There's nothing worse than packing up and heading back to your vehicle only to see eight meteors streak across the sky in less than a minute on the hike. Meteor showers are a blend of preparation, the right gear, and a dash of luck. But when that brilliant streak lights up your frame, it's pure magic.

The Moon

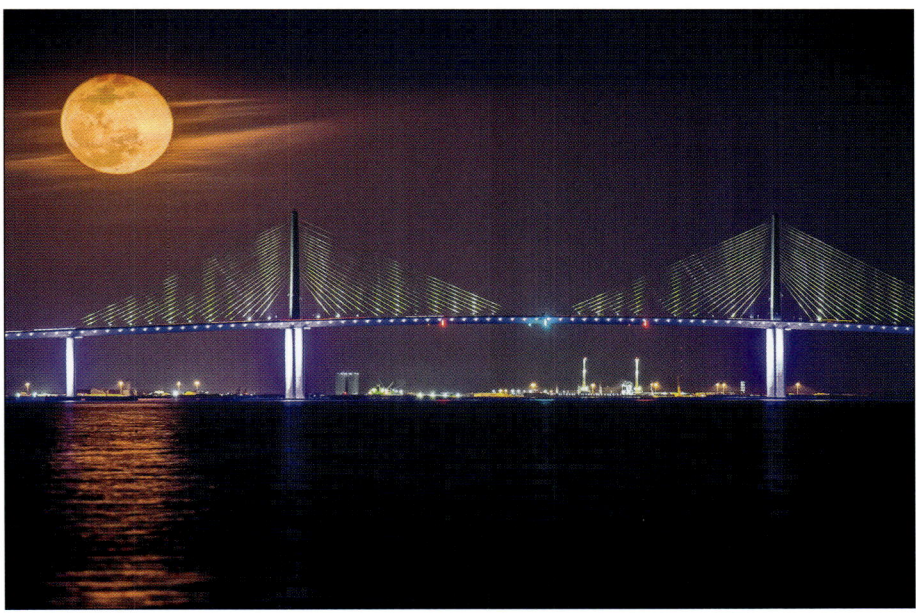

Our moon is not just Earth's loyal sidekick but a celestial body that's mesmerized humans for all time, including photographers! From slender crescents to grandiose full moons, it offers us some fantastic opportunities to photograph:

New Moon: Invisible to us, as it's between Earth and the sun.

Crescent: A charming sliver, thin and delicate in the sky.

Quarter: Half illuminated, half shadowed. Perfect balance.

Gibbous: More than half, but not fully lit.

Full Moon: A radiant circle, bright and magnificent.

Zoom or telephoto lenses are ideal—something in the range of 200–400mm (or more) will magnify the moon's details, or if you want a tight shot of it, or a shot of it along the horizon. Given its brightness, you might shoot at faster shutter speeds and could argue you don't need a tripod. However, for consistency and sharpness, a tripod is always recommended. With a bright moon, start around ISO 100, f/8, and a shutter speed of 1/125. Adjust based on the moon's brightness and your environment. I'd even recommend a higher shutter speed, going to ISO 800 and increasing your shutter speed to 1/1000. Why? The number one complaint I hear is "my moon shots are blurry" and every time I look at their settings, the shutter speed is too low for a sharp shot, even on a tripod. For crescents or dimmer phases, you'll need to increase the ISO to 800 or 1600 or open the aperture a tad more. The key is to keep that shutter speed up and remember that if you have a DSLR, you absolutely want to use mirror lockup. Shutter speed and camera shake are the things that keep people from those moon shots that they want—not their lens, camera body, tripod brand, etc.

Light Pollution & the Bortle Scale

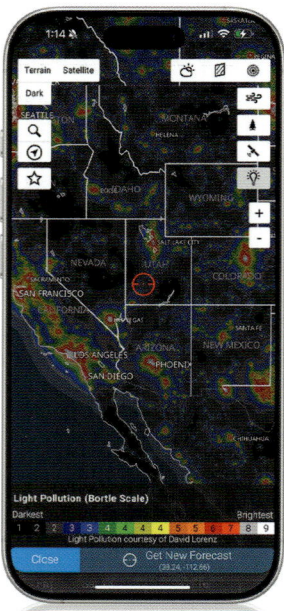

If you've ever planned a night shoot only to find the sky drowned in an orange glow, you've met the astrophotographer's enemy: light pollution. The artificial brightening of the night sky caused by city lights, street lamps, etc. Great for keeping us from tripping, but terrible for seeing (or photographing) stars. But, it does more than just dim the stars—it reduces contrast, washes out details, and makes astrophotography nearly impossible in some areas. That's where the Bortle scale comes in. Created by astronomer John E. Bortle, this nine-level scale helps measure the night sky's brightness from pristine dark skies (Bortle 1) to bright inner-city conditions (Bortle 9). Here's a quick look: Bortle 1–2: Perfect dark skies—no light pollution. The Milky Way is insanely detailed and casts a visible shadow, so you're probably out in the middle of nowhere—this is the dream. Bortle 3–4: Suburban and rural skies. The Milky Way is still visible, but some artificial glow is present near the horizon. It's an excellent compromise and usually accessible within a couple hour's drive of 80% of the population. Bortle 6–7: Urban skies. The Milky Way is almost completely gone, and only the brightest stars and planets remain visible. It's still okay, but not ideal. Bortle 8–9: Inner city skies. Forget about anything but deep-sky photography with serious narrowband filters or basic star trail shots. The sky is a dull orange from the glow, and only a handful of stars are visible. You can find good locations using apps and websites—like Astrospheric, Light Pollution Map, and Dark Sky Finder—to check Bortle ratings on a map, so you can scout locations before heading out. When reading a Bortle scale map, look for the darker areas in blue and black—those are your best bets. Areas in green and yellow are okay, but orange and red mean moderate to heavy light pollution. Just get as far from city lights as possible, use maps to plan, and when all else fails, use light pollution filters to help cut through the glow.

Using Light Pollution in Your Favor

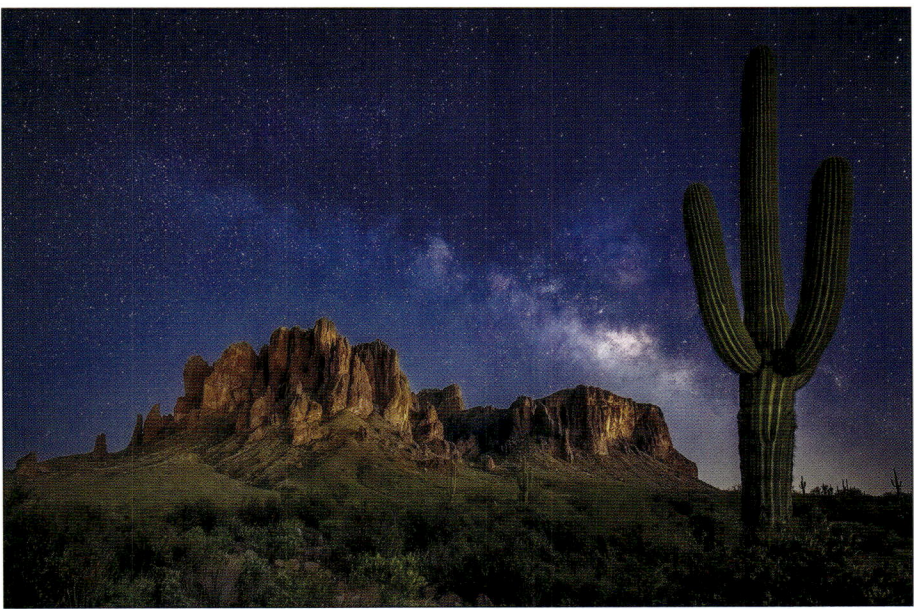

Light pollution gets a bad rap in astrophotography, and for good reason—it drowns out stars, washes out details, and can turn a deep-sky masterpiece into a murky mess. But here's the thing: Light pollution doesn't have to ruin your shot. In fact, when used creatively, it can add depth, drama, and mood to your night photography. A perfect example? Imagine shooting a landscape where a distant city casts a soft glow on the foreground while the Milky Way rises behind a mountain range untouched by artificial light. The city glow acts like a giant fill light, revealing details in the foreground without overpowering the stars behind it. This balance creates an image that feels both grounded and celestial—a perfect blend of Earth and sky. To pull this off, position yourself so the artificial light is working for you, not against you. If you're near a city, use its glow to softly illuminate your foreground while making sure your skyward view remains dark. Apps like Astrospheric (see page 35 for more on this one) or Light Pollution Map help you scout locations where there's a clear divide between light-polluted and dark skies, allowing you to compose a shot where the two blend naturally. Another trick: Use long exposures to smooth out and soften city light. Instead of fighting it, let it fill in shadowed areas, adding texture to your scene while keeping the sky crisp. If the city glow is too strong, you can use a light pollution filter to reduce its intensity without killing the mood. Think of light pollution as a secondary light source—one that can add atmosphere and warmth to your shot, as long as you control where and how it appears in your frame. Master this technique, and you'll turn what most see as a limitation into one of your most powerful compositional tools.

The Weather

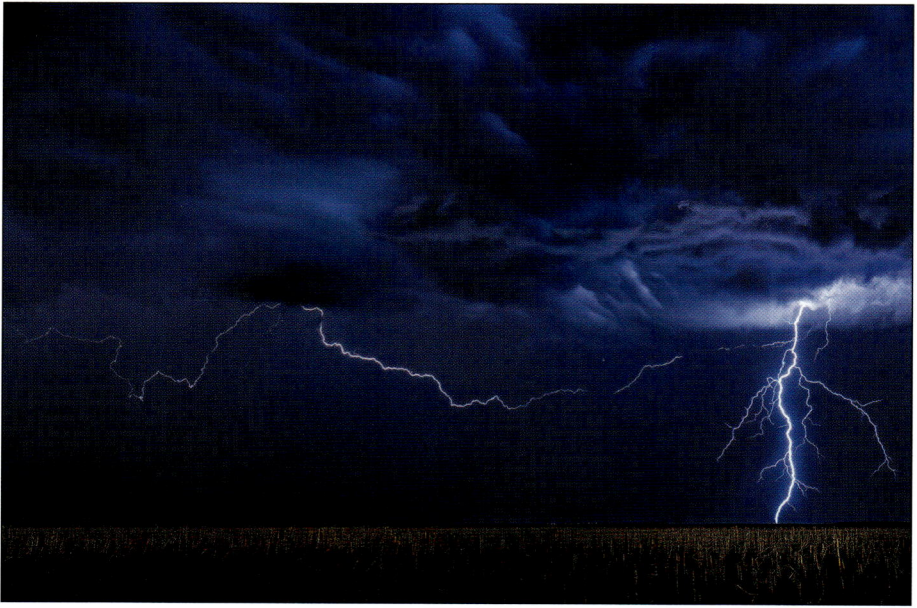

Ready to capture the stars, but there's a cloud looming? Night photography has its unique set of weather challenges. So, let's talk about tailoring your night shots based on the weather. Clear skies are the jackpot! They're perfect for astrophotography and Milky Way shots. But, while cloud cover might obscure stars, clouds can reflect city lights, creating a unique, moody ambiance. Going further, fog and mist can lend an eerie, ethereal feel, especially when lit by ambient sources. Then there's light pollution, which is not exactly weather, but city lights can haze up the sky. Sometimes it's a hindrance, sometimes it's artsy, and other times we can use the light pollution to light up our scene. The worst thing for a night photographer, though, is the dreaded dew point. If your lens is going to drop into this zone, you need a lens warmer or dew heaters. Cold or humid nights can cause lens condensation and a lens warmer or dew heater can save your night. Speaking of dew, a weather-sealed body and lens hood can protect your gear from a sudden shower or built-up condensation (see Chapter 1 for more on gear). Weather apps tailored for astronomers and night photographers really help (we'll look at one of them on the next page). They'll predict cloud covers, meteor showers, even aurora possibilities—all before you even leave the house. This can be a lifesaver, so you don't drive three hours just to be faced with cloudy skies. But, maybe you aimed for stars and got clouds. Don't pack up! Change your composition. Use what you're dealt. Some cloud patterns, especially if moving swiftly, can be intriguing in long exposures. Night photography is as much about embracing uncertainties as it is about planning. Every weather pattern can create a unique canvas for your photos.

The Astrospheric App

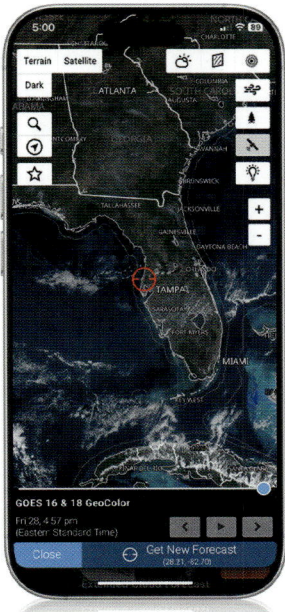

Ever had one of those nights when you've driven miles, hauled your gear, and just when you thought the Milky Way was about to pop, a pesky cloud ruined your plans? Enter the Astrospheric app. Like PhotoPills (we looked at it on page 21), this is the ace up your sleeve. Here's the scoop: Astrospheric doesn't just provide any generic forecast; it dishes out a detailed astronomical weather prediction. So, instead of a simple "clear skies" tag or icon, you're looking at cloud cover percentages, transparency ratings, and seeing conditions. It's like having an astrophotography-focused meteorologist with you. I do have to mention: This tip is designed with the North American night photographer in mind, as it offers expansive coverage within North America. If you're outside North America, there are a few other apps that will work, but nothing on this level. Whether you're planning to shoot the deserts of Arizona or the rugged terrain of the Rockies, Astrospheric has got you mapped. Plus, let's face it, sometimes it's not just clouds obscuring our view. With the increasing wildfires and atmospheric changes, Astrospheric's smoke and aerosol data come to the rescue. You get real-time data, ensuring you know what's hanging between you and the universe. The app isn't just about what might obstruct your view, it also clues you in to moon phases, planetary positions, and even potential meteor showers. This isn't just forecasting; it's night sky storytelling. It will even show when and where the International Space Station will pass over a given location. It's not just another weather app; it's a specialized tool for night photographers. Think of it as your astrophotography weather app, ensuring you're in the right place at the right time. So, while you're packing that lens and tripod, do yourself a favor and download Astrospheric on your iOS or Android device or go to www.astrospheric.com.

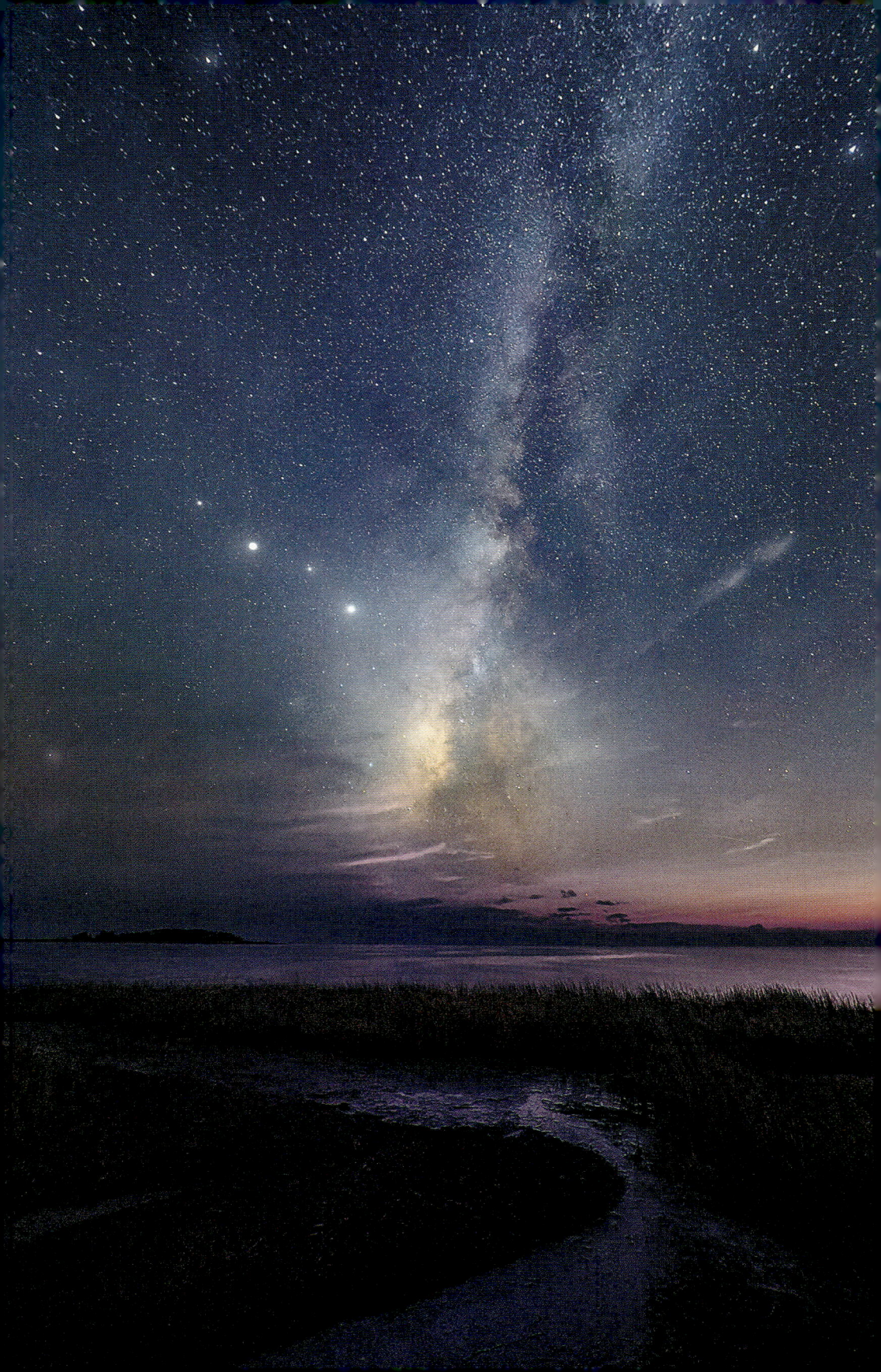

The Settings

Mastering Exposure for the Night

If night photography was just about pointing your camera at the stars and pressing a button, we'd all be doing it. But the truth is, nailing the perfect night shot is a delicate balance between three key settings: shutter speed, aperture, and ISO. Get one of them wrong, and you're left with star trails when you want crisp points, noisy shadows that swallow your details, or a scene that's just way too dark to work with. The right settings don't just capture what you see; they bring out details the naked eye can't even perceive. This chapter is all about taking full control of your camera's settings to ensure your night shots turn out exactly as you envisioned. We'll start with why manual mode is non-negotiable for night photography—your camera's auto settings simply can't handle the darkness. Then, we'll dive into shutter speed and how to freeze the stars in place or stretch them into dramatic light trails. Aperture plays a major role, too, controlling how much light hits your sensor and balancing sharpness across your scene. And, of course, ISO—the setting most photographers are afraid of cranking up. Spoiler alert: ISO 6400 isn't the enemy, and we'll talk about why it's actually your best friend when shooting in the dark. We'll also demystify white balance and color temperature, ensuring your images don't come out with an odd tint that ruins the mood. We'll cover RAW files (because if you're shooting in JPEG at night, we need to talk), plus essential tricks like test shots at high ISOs to nail your composition without wasting time. And if you've ever struggled to focus at night, I'll walk you through my foolproof method to lock onto the stars with pinpoint accuracy—even in pitch-black conditions. It's not luck that separates a stunning night photo from a disappointing one; it's knowing your settings inside and out. Once you do, you won't just take night photos—you'll make them!

Choosing Your Shooting Mode

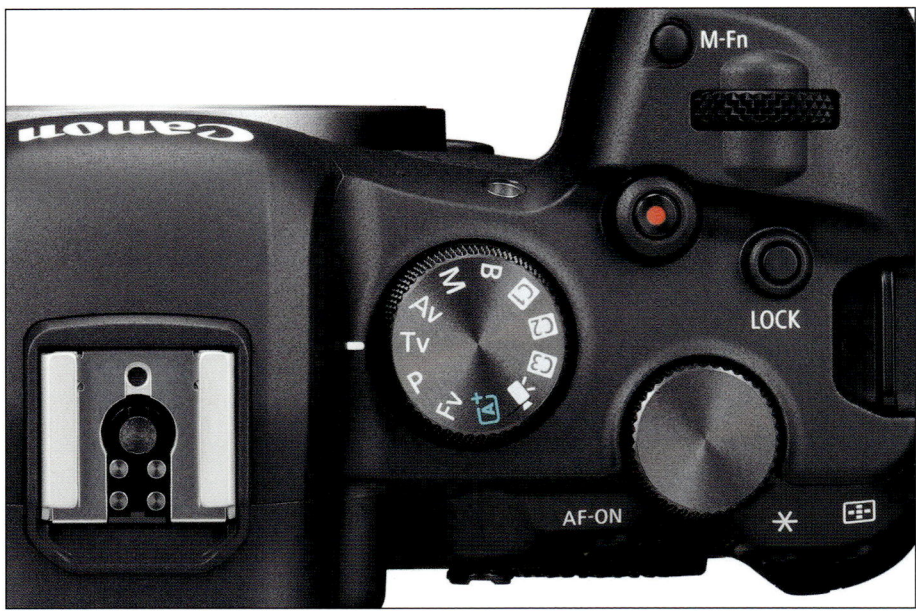

Night photography isn't just about stars; it's about light (or lack thereof). So, you'll need to know when your camera needs to be in certain modes. Let's break it down: Manual (M) mode is the holy grail for most night photographers and is where a majority of my Milky Way and night photos are taken. In this mode, you're the boss. You adjust shutter speed, aperture, and ISO independently. Want a starry sky with crisp stars? Opt for a wide aperture, slow shutter speed, and moderate ISO. Is there a learning curve? Absolutely! But the creative control? Unparalleled. This is the one genre of photography where I'm in manual mode the majority of the time (I can't say the same for my landscape, travel, aerospace, and aviation work). With aperture priority (Av/A) mode, you set the aperture and the camera decides the shutter speed. This is perfect for when there's some ambient light. Set a wide aperture to let in more light, or narrow it for less light and let the camera do its thing with the other settings. But again, this mode only works best when there's a lot of ambient light since we're relying on the camera's metering, which isn't accurate at night. With shutter priority (Tv/S) mode, you dictate the shutter speed, and the camera chooses the aperture. It's great for capturing movement, like car trails or moving clouds against the night sky, but we are, again, relying on the camera's metering, which isn't great at night. Bulb (B) mode is basically manual mode, but for those shots that need exposures longer than your camera's longest manual setting (often 30 seconds)—press to start the exposure and release to end it. Ideal for deep sky objects and extended star trails. In the end, remember this: Modes are just starting points. Each night scene is unique, and sometimes, breaking the rules can lead to unexpected results. Experiment and practice. There's no wrong mode or wrong setting to try. But, for me, at night, I'm usually in manual mode.

Shooting in Manual (or Bulb) Mode

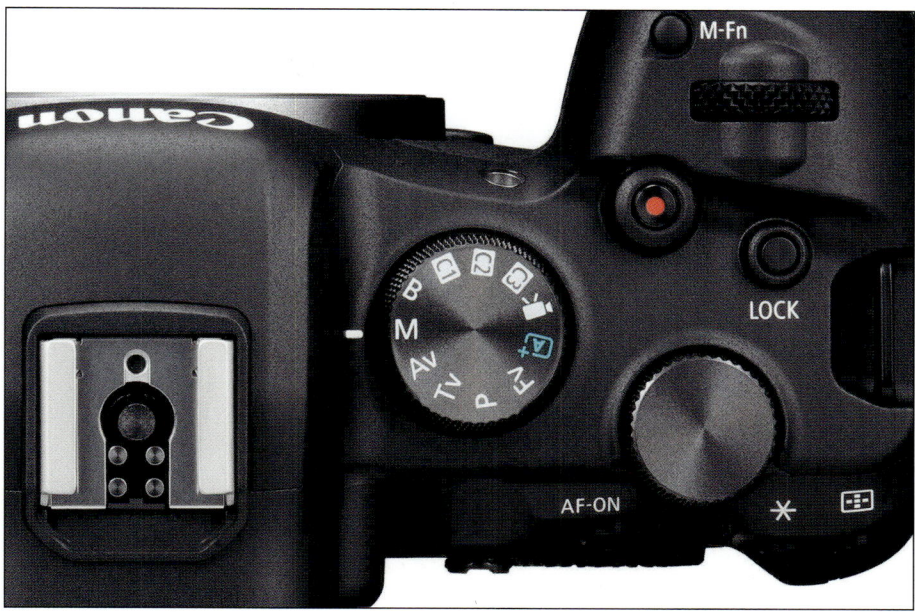

While the twilight and midnight hours present their challenges, one thing to know about nighttime is that light is usually more consistent. With full control over f-stop, shutter speed, and ISO, we can conquer the night with manual mode. Here's why: The night sky isn't your average subject—it's dark. Auto settings? They can get confused in low light. Manual mode, though, hands you the reins. Control your ISO for noise management, your aperture for depth, and your shutter speed to capture everything from star points to star trails. But what happens if you need more than 30 seconds (most manual mode settings max out around 30 seconds for exposure)? Enter bulb mode. It allows you to open the shutter for as long as your battery (and patience) permits. Using bulb mode, you can experiment with different exposure lengths based on available light. Manual mode also allows you to adapt to the unpredictable. Clouds rolling in? Meteor shower suddenly blazing across the sky? Manual mode lets you pivot on the fly. Adjust settings in real time to meet the whims of the night without your camera's internal metering getting fooled. We can also tame the noise in this mode. Night photography often craves high ISO settings to get those electric Milky Way skies. With manual mode, you can fine-tune it. Balance sensitivity with noise levels to get the lowest ISO night shot possible. So, while the night may be full of mysteries, manual and bulb modes demystify the process of capturing it. Embrace these modes, and you're not just taking a shot in the dark, hoping a camera that's designed for a bunch of ambient light will meter properly. Your exposures at night won't change too much frame to frame. So, it's better to find the right mixture of f-stop, shutter speed, and ISO. What are those right settings? Flip the page to find out.

How Wide Your Lens Is Open: F-Stop (Aperture)

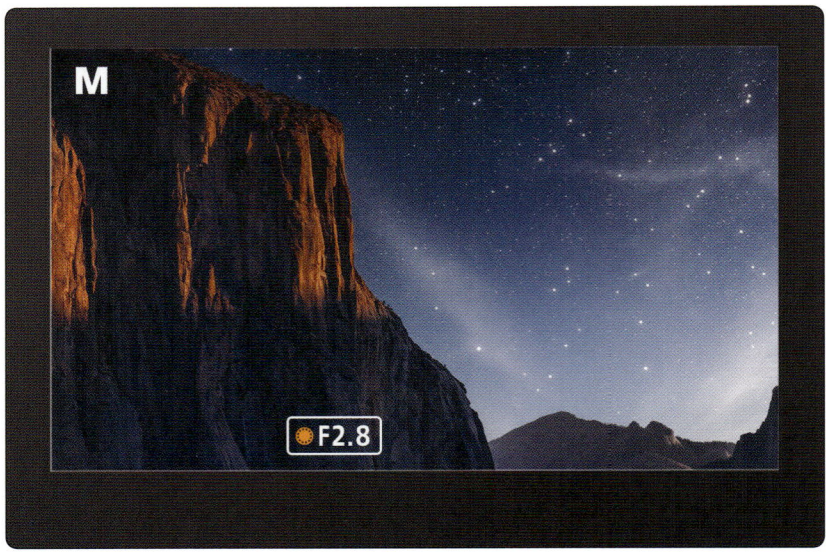

When selecting the right f-stop for night photography, you might think, "Open wide and let the light flood in!" And often, you'd be right. Set your lens at f/2.8, and that's all there is to it. But, let's break it down when it comes to night photography: The f-stop (aperture) determines how wide your lens opens. A lower number like f/2.8 means a wider aperture, which lets in more light. Higher numbers, like f/16, indicate a narrower aperture. We want it open wide. But, the challenge with night photography is the lack of light. The stars, though bright, are mere pinpricks in the vast cosmic canvas. To capture their brilliance, your camera needs to absorb every photon it can. This is where a wider aperture (like f/2.0 or f/1.4) comes in, acting like a vacuum for starlight. A wide-open aperture also provides a shallower depth of field. For astrophotography, where the subjects (stars) are light years away, this isn't as much of a concern. But if you have a foreground element—a majestic tree, a tent, or rocky terrain just feet away from the camera—you'll need to balance your aperture to achieve sharp focus on both the stars and the foreground. Next, every lens has a sweet spot—an aperture where it performs its best, delivering peak sharpness. While f/1.4 for a fast lens might be optimal for light intake, sometimes stopping down a bit (say, to f/2.8) can yield sharper results—especially at the edges of the frame since you're getting closer to those sweet spots, which usually reside around f/8 or f/11. Remember, the aperture is just one third of the exposure triangle. A wide f-stop might let in more light, but it could introduce lens aberrations. By understanding how aperture, ISO, and shutter speed balance, you'll master photography. So, while f/2.8 is a fantastic starting point (and often the best choice) for many night scenarios, understanding your scene and lens can guide you to even more stunning captures.

How Long Your Shutter Is Open: Shutter Speed

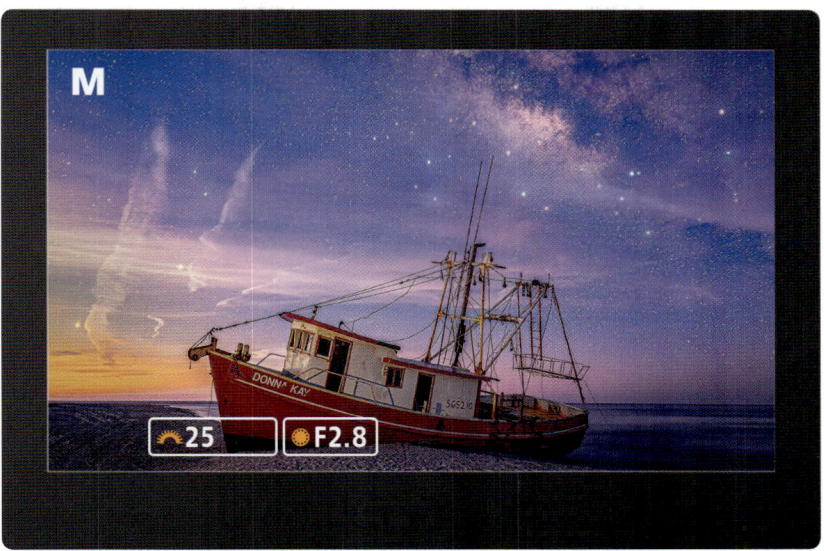

Think of shutter speed as the amount of time your camera's sensor gets a peek at the scene. A fast shutter speed, like 1/500, is a quick peek. A slow one, like 30 seconds, is a prolonged gaze. At night, we lean toward those longer gazes to soak in the sparse light. But, it's also about controlling motion in your frame. Stars might seem static, but thanks to the Earth's rotation, they're moving fast across the sky. Go too long with your shutter speed and stars become streaks. This phenomenon gives rise to the 500 rule (or the 400 rule for crop sensors): take 500, divide it by your lens's focal length, and the result is the longest exposure time (in seconds) before stars blur. For example, a 20mm lens would give you 25 seconds (500/20). We also have the better NPF rule, found in the PhotoPills app (see page 21) that'll tell us exactly how long we can keep our sensors exposed before the stars blur (it's shorter than you think). Again, it's all a balancing act! By optimizing shutter speed to be just long enough to avoid star trails (but not too long), you can often use a lower ISO, reducing noise. Digital noise becomes more apparent at higher ISOs, so shorter, crisp captures paired with lower ISOs mean cleaner, clearer star shots. But, not too low! Say you're shooting a foreground element under the Milky Way, or wind rustling through trees. A shorter shutter speed might preserve those elements without blur, adding sharp contrasts to the ethereal sky, but a longer exposure will blur the trees. Or, by contrast, with a car moving through your scene, a short exposure will freeze the headlights while a longer exposure will blur them throughout the scene. So, while long exposures are synonymous with night photography, the key is to find that sweet spot—short enough to maintain the clarity you want, yet long enough to capture light, all while keeping ISO in check.

How Sensitive Your Sensor Is to Light: ISO

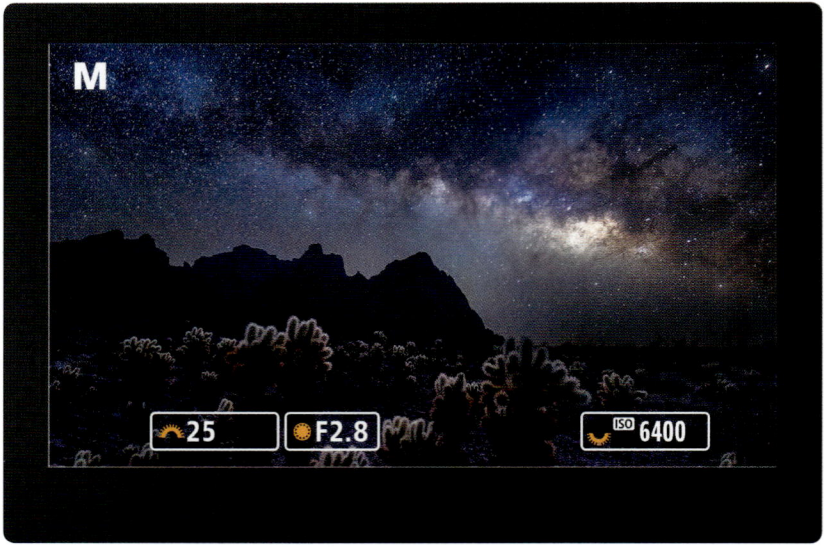

ISO is like the volume knob on an amplifier—turn it up and the signal becomes louder, but turn it up too much, and you'll hear that pesky sound distortion. So, how do we hit that ISO sweet spot? In the simplest terms, ISO, in digital cameras, determines your camera sensor's sensitivity to light. Lower values (like ISO 100) mean less sensitivity, but less noisy shots. Crank it up (ISO 6400 and beyond), and you'll grasp fainter lights, but you'll also introduce digital noise or grain. That's the dilemma. The Milky Way's faint glow requires a sensitive setting to capture, plus it's moving at hypersonic speed. The biggest mistake I see people making when they start out with Milky Way photography, specifically, is a lack of ISO. They don't want to crank up the sensitivity of their sensor enough. ISO amplifies the weak light of the distant stars, allowing us to photograph the galaxy's full splendor. So, I recommend starting at ISO 6400 for Milky Way photography. But, again, the catch-22: while high ISO brings out those elusive star details, it also adds noise, making photos grainy—the equivalent of that static on a loud radio. And just like too much static can ruin a song, too much noise can obscure the Milky Way's delicate details. But, we'll do things in post later in the book to almost remove this noise even at ISO 6400. Why ISO 6400? It's "The Goldilocks Zone" nowadays. For many cameras, especially newer models, ISO 6400 can be the sweet spot. It offers a blend of sensitivity and clarity. You get enough amplification to reveal the galaxy's grandeur without drowning in digital noise and at that sensitivity, what we can do in post, will take that ISO 6400 shot and make it look like ISO 800. While ISO 6400 might be a general guideline, every camera sensor has its own strengths and quirks. Always test out different ISO levels to find the best balance for your gear, but the point is: don't go too low, as it will limit the light gathering ability of your camera.

The Exposure Triangle: It's Just Math

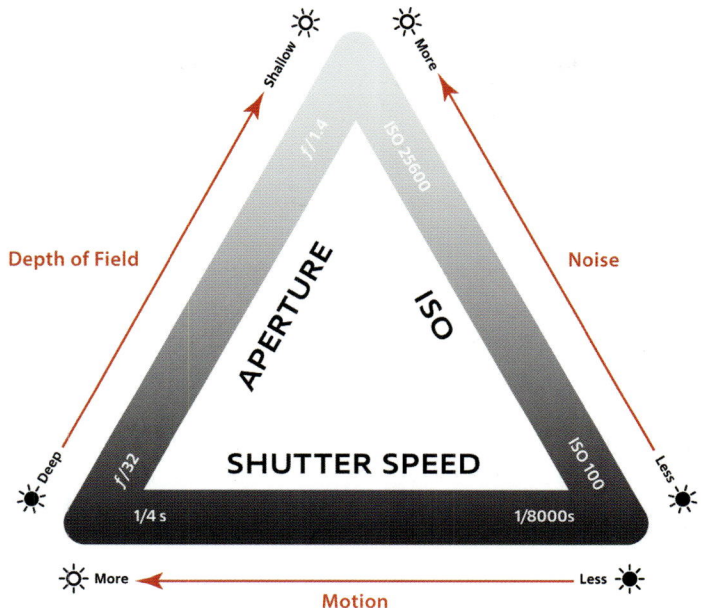

Understanding the interplay between aperture, shutter speed, and ISO truly elevates your photography. And, understanding the exposure triangle is at the heart of night photography. On each corner, we have aperture (how wide your lens is open), shutter speed (how long your sensor is open), and ISO (how sensitive your sensor is). Together, they control the light hitting your sensor. In night photography, you often crave a wide-open aperture (like f/2.8) to pull in as much light as possible. But remember, this also affects depth of field. You want your shutter speed long enough to capture the glimmers of the night, but not so long that stars blur into trails. This is the balance between exposure and motion. You need your ISO high enough to amplify the faint light, but not so high that your images drown in noise or ambient light. It's a delicate balance. Here's where math comes in: Doubling or halving any setting is often referred to as moving by "one stop," and this is the key to understanding the balance. Increase your ISO from 3200 to 6400, and you've increased your exposure by one stop, letting in twice the light. But, let's say that makes things too noisy. Compensate by reducing your shutter speed by one stop (halving its duration). That's it! You've balanced the equation. As you adapt your settings, remember that ISO is the flexible friend in this equation. It can step up or down in sensitivity, compensating for adjustments in aperture or shutter speed. So, by understanding stops, you can juggle these three elements in balance. The exposure triangle might seem daunting, but with a bit of practice, it becomes second nature. For me, the equation to capture the Milky Way in one exposure is usually f/2.8, 20 seconds for an ultra-wide lens (around 15mm), and ISO 6400. Want it brighter? Add in ISO. Darker? Remove it, one stop at a time. For less blurry stars, I might drop the shutter speed to 10 seconds, but that means I have to increase the ISO or open up the aperture. It's as simple as that!

Choosing Your White Balance

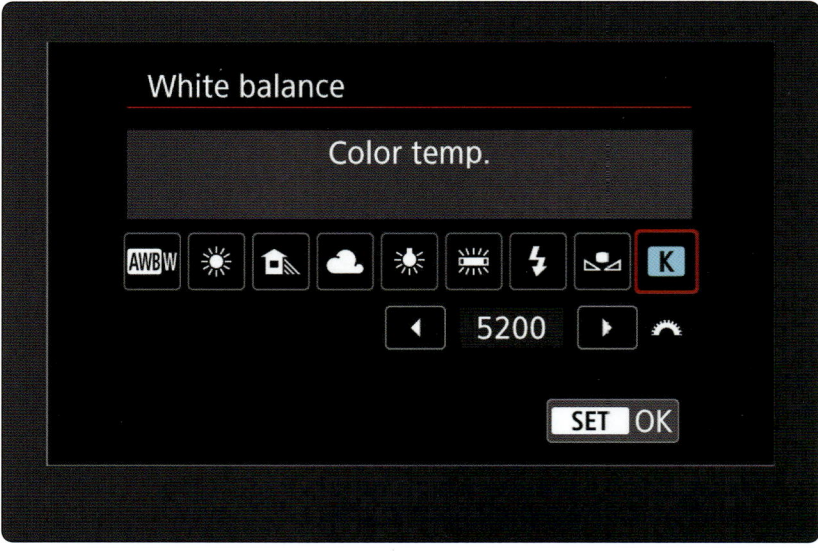

The sometimes overlooked, yet utterly transformative aspect of night photography is white balance (WB). Ever captured a night scene and thought, "Why does it look so...weird?" Chances are WB is your culprit. At its core, WB adjusts colors so that white looks white. Different light sources (like streetlights or moonlight) cast different color tints. By tweaking the WB, you ensure your photos' colors are true to the scene. Where most people fall into a trap is with Auto White Balance (AWB) mode. It's like the camera's best guess for the scene. It works great during the day, but at night, with so many mixed light sources, it can get perplexed. Relying solely on AWB might not always produce the results you want. For me, in manual mode, I'm in kelvin white balance at night, where I'm manually picking my WB on the Kelvin scale. For example, for starry landscapes, a kelvin WB around 3200K–4200K can render stars and the Milky Way beautifully. But, at twilight, you might capture blue hour best in the 4200K–4800K range. Remember, there's no strict rule—tweak to your taste—but, you need to know your main light source. Some photographers swear by the Tungsten WB setting for night skies, which is around 3200K. It adds more blue tint to the scene, emphasizing the cool vastness of the cosmos and adding blue to the sky. We humans really like blue in the sky, so it tends to be a pleasing start. How do you make sure you never miss with the WB? Easy! Shoot in RAW. That's your golden ticket. With RAW files, you can adjust WB in post-processing without degrading image quality. The beauty of night photography is its flexibility. Feel free to experiment with the WB settings—swipe through them to see what feels right or just look around to see where the main light source is coming from. If it's warm light, go lower, like 2700K–3200K. If it's cool light, go more toward 5200K–6500K. I'll break down the Kelvin scale more on the next page.

Understanding Kelvin Temperature

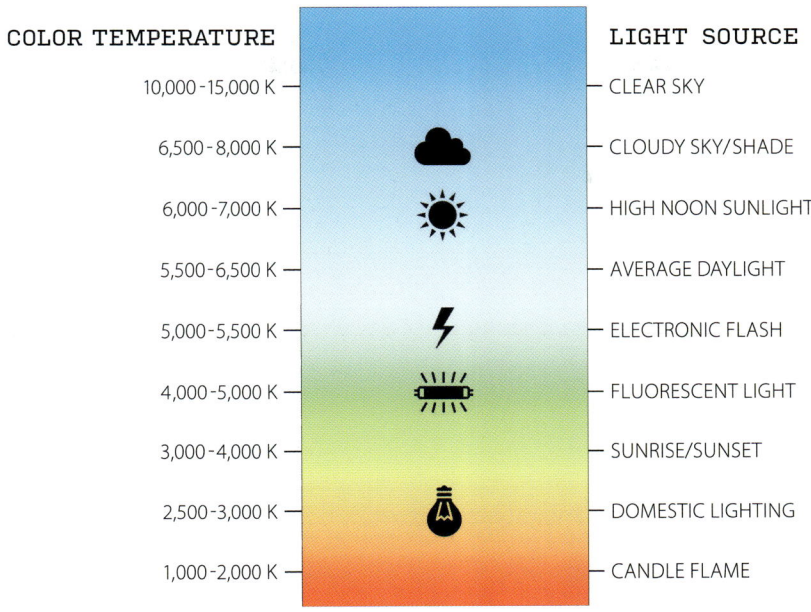

COLOR TEMPERATURE		LIGHT SOURCE
10,000-15,000 K		CLEAR SKY
6,500-8,000 K		CLOUDY SKY/SHADE
6,000-7,000 K		HIGH NOON SUNLIGHT
5,500-6,500 K		AVERAGE DAYLIGHT
5,000-5,500 K		ELECTRONIC FLASH
4,000-5,000 K		FLUORESCENT LIGHT
3,000-4,000 K		SUNRISE/SUNSET
2,500-3,000 K		DOMESTIC LIGHTING
1,000-2,000 K		CANDLE FLAME

Okay, okay, I know this isn't the sexiest subject. However, I have to dedicate a whole page to this because nailing your white balance is crucial to getting the best detail, tone, color—heck, even emotion—out of your shots. I can't tell you how many shots I see where the white balance is so off that it's distracting. Maybe not even distracting, as it's more tinted with some color so egregiously that it just sucks the life out of the image. My white balance goal, especially with night photography, is to balance—yes, that's the key word—balance the white levels of the image to a neutral tone. From there, we can color mix or color grade, but without having a spot-on white balance, you're leaving so much of your image's detail, clarity, and tone on the table. This is why, for me, I push more toward just dialing in a kelvin temperature. At first, you're going to have to train your eye to see kelvin temperatures. How do you do that? Look at the light. There's a reason why light bulb packages say "warm white," and then next to that is "2750K", or maybe 3200K for a tungsten warm white bulb, or 6500K or 5600K for a cool white bulb. Or, even the dreaded fluorescent lights with a green tone to them in that 4500K. It's because the names describe the light source and the color of the light. If you perfect your understanding of the kelvin temperature of a scene, you'll get more detail out of that scene (at least this is what has worked for me over the years). Then, you'll start understanding where your light source falls along that Kelvin spectrum. It does seem more complex than it is, but I promise you that with practice, you will get perfect, or maybe even, as my wife might say, "annoying," like when I walk into a room and say, "Oh, that's nice—a 3000 kelvins light."

Use Manual Focus

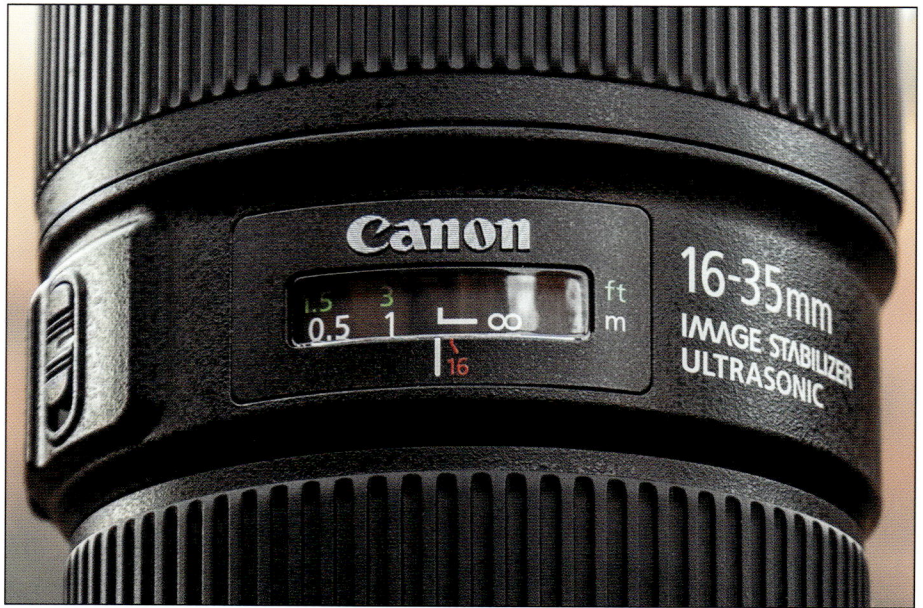

Have you ever tried capturing the night sky only to discover later those twinkling stars look more like blurry blobs? Dialing in that perfect focus for stars can be tricky, but with some know-how, you'll have sharp stars. Manual focus is your friend (I hope you're noticing a trend by now). While I'd hardly use Manual focus during the daytime or even at blue hour, I'm almost always in Manual focus at night. Auto focus often struggles in low light, and you don't want your lens hunting for focus in the dark. Not to mention that pesky AF illuminator will sure annoy anyone out there shooting with you. So what do I do? First, I start with infinity—but not quite. Many lenses have an infinity (∞) mark. While it's tempting just to turn your focus ring to infinity, it's often not spot-on for stars. Instead, start slightly before the infinity mark as your baseline. Next, here's where the magic happens: Most modern cameras, especially mirrorless and DSLRs since 2008, have a nifty feature allowing you to zoom in on your LCD screen in Live View mode. Find a bright star, then press your zoom button. First, you might go 5x, and then 10x or more. This magnified view allows for ultra-precise manual focusing right on your Live View display. With that star magnified on your LCD, slowly adjust your focus ring. Your goal? Make that star as tiny and pinpoint sharp as possible. As you tweak, you'll see the star's shape change from a blob to a speck. Finally, once focused, snap a test shot, then zoom in on the playback and inspect those stars. If they're crisp and clear, you're set. If not, refine and test again. But, don't just trust it all night—keep an eye on your focus. Lens focus can drift as temperatures change or with just a slight bump. So, if you're out for a long night, periodically recheck your focus. There you have it! With a dash of patience and the magic of LCD zoom, your stars will shine with razor-sharp clarity.

Shoot in RAW

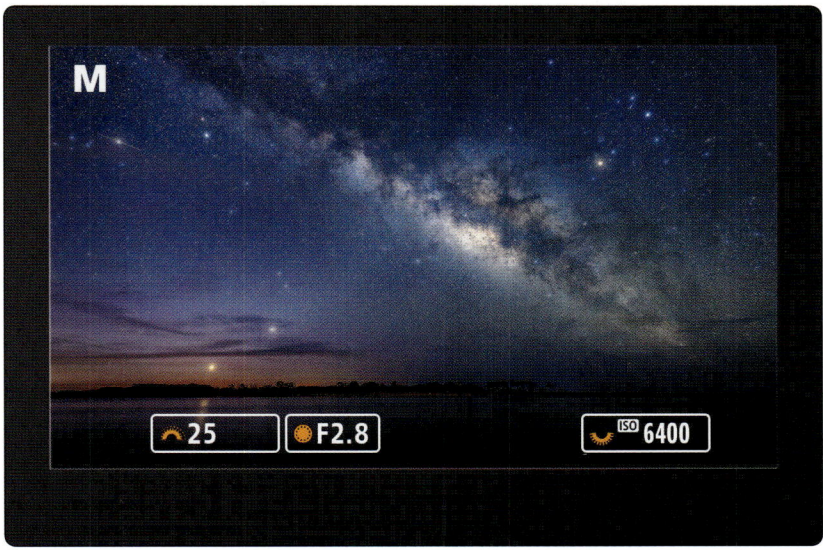

Have you ever wondered why every seasoned night photographer swears by RAW? Well, it isn't just a preference, RAW is a game-changer for night shots. Think of RAW as the photo world's equivalent of getting all of the raw ingredients to cook a meal. RAW captures all the data your sensor sees without compressing or altering it. Unlike JPEG, which trims and processes data based on the camera and manufacturer's processing. There are advantages to that, but you might end up with a meal like you'd get at a chain restaurant—it's cooked, but it's not amazing. It's a consistent, good, everyday meal. But, with a RAW file, a master chef can make a 5-star meal. However, just like with making a 5-star meal, if you don't know what you're doing, it can turn out terrible. RAW files are what we call "flat"—they will need post-processing or "cooking" in post. This leads us to the biggest benefit of RAW processing: You see, night photos often need some TLC in editing. Are the shadows too dark? Are the highlights too bright? With RAW images, you've got a wide spectrum of details saved. This flexibility means you can adjust exposure, tweak shadows, recover highlights, add selective sharpening, and even remove RAW-level noise more effectively than with a JPEG. Plus, remember our chat about white balance (back on page 44)? If you've shot in RAW, you can change the white balance in post without a hitch. Suddenly, that overly orange campfire or too-blue Milky Way can be fine-tuned. Not to mention, editing software is ever-evolving. A RAW file ensures that, as software improves, you can revisit and re-edit with the latest tools. It's the gift that keeps on giving! Shooting in RAW is like having a safety net for your night photography—it forgives minor missteps and lets your post-processing truly shine. So, bottom line, shoot RAW! You'll thank me later.

Using Long Exposure Noise Reduction

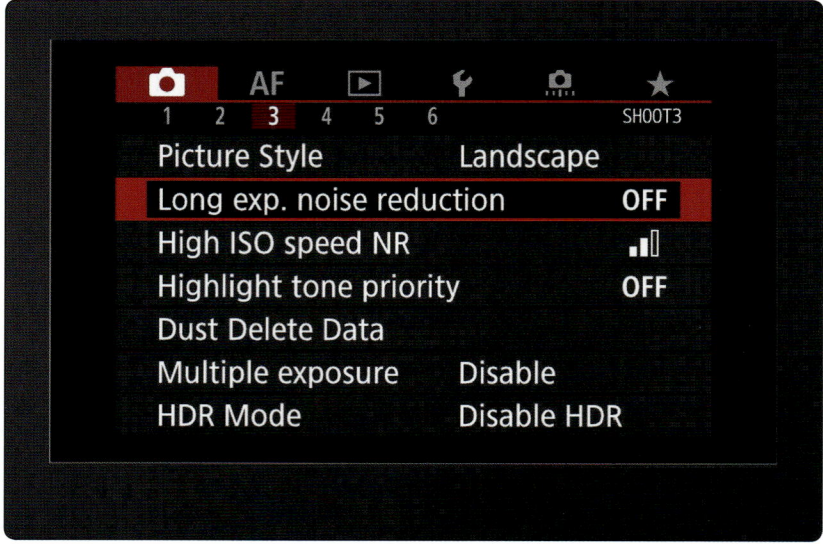

If you've ever taken a long exposure and wondered why your camera just sits there processing for what feels like an eternity, congratulations, you've met Long Exposure Noise Reduction (LENR). It's supposed to clean up your image by taking a second dark frame right after your shot, mapping out noise and hot pixels, and then subtracting them. Sounds great in theory, but in practice? It depends. Here's the deal: If you're only taking a few long exposures, LENR can be helpful, especially on warm nights when sensor heat adds extra noise. It works well for single exposures where you just want a clean shot straight out of the camera without worrying about post-processing. But if you're shooting star trails, time-lapses, or stacking multiple images later, turn it off. The problem with LENR is that it literally doubles your exposure time because your camera is stuck processing the dark frame before it lets you take another shot. Shooting a five-minute exposure? You're now waiting another five minutes before you can take the next one. Not ideal when time matters. If you're shooting a sequence of star trails or need back-to-back shots for a time-lapse, that delay is a deal-breaker. Most astrophotographers prefer to shoot without it and handle noise in post with stacking or AI-based noise reduction. Stacking multiple exposures naturally reduces noise, and modern editing tools do a way better job than your camera's built-in processing ever could. So unless you're just taking a couple of long-exposure shots and want an easy in-camera fix, LENR is usually more trouble than it's worth. The best move? Test it out. If you're shooting a single long exposure, give it a try. But if you're planning to shoot multiple frames in a row, skip it, keep shooting, and clean things up later. Just know that you can use it, plus you can also use LENR and stacking and AI-noise reduction together—there are no limits other than time. But, for me, AI-based noise reduction is where it's at.

Take Test Shots

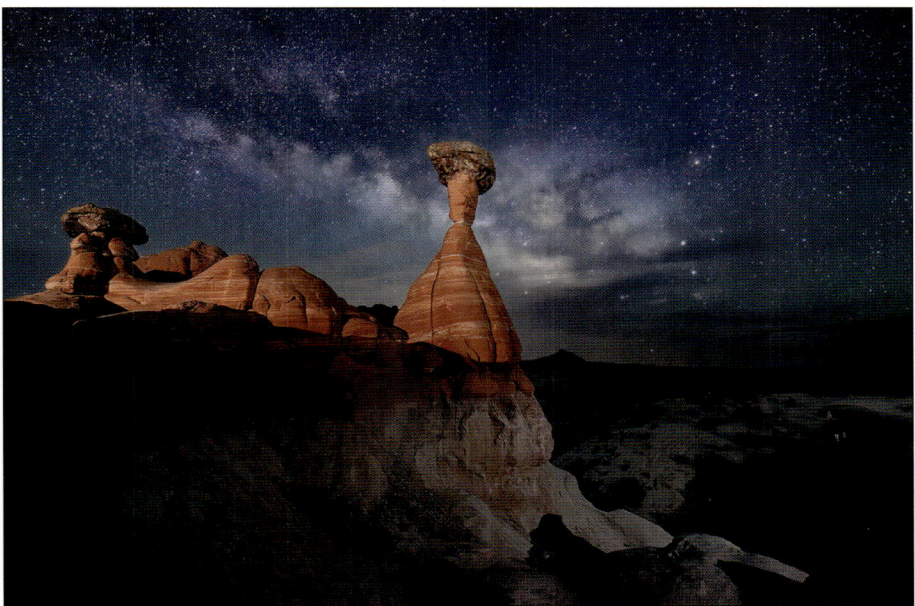

Ever felt like composing a shot at night is akin to finding a needle in a haystack? Darkness can be disorienting, and waiting for long-exposure test shots can feel like forever. Enter the power of cranking up your ISO for rapid composition checks. Night landscapes are tricky. Stars are above, shadows are below, and you're squinting to discern that tree line or rock formation. Pushing your ISO to extreme highs, like 25600 or even 51200, is like temporarily giving your camera night vision goggles, so you don't have to wait 20–30 seconds for a shot. Again, let's go back to the basic math of that exposure triangle (we looked at it on page 43). Bumping your ISO from 6400 to 25600 lets you capture the same amount of light in a quarter of the time! So, that means a test shot, which took 20 seconds, now takes just 5 seconds. It will feel like cheating. You'll get what feels like instant feedback when you go from a 20-second exposure to a 5-second one. With this high-ISO, super-fast test shot approach, you can quickly gauge if that tree is off-center, if the mountain silhouette doesn't align with the Milky Way in the right place, or if you're too close to that foreground. Spot something off? Adjust and reshoot. However, a word of *warning*: these extreme ISO test shots are purely for composition. They'll be noisy and grainy, but that's okay. Embrace the noise in these test shots; it's a small price to pay for speedy composition. *But*, and that's a huge *but*, once you've nailed the frame, dial back to your desired ISO (like that sweet spot at 6400) for the actual shot. Plus, there's a bonus we get from this technique: faster shutter speeds mean less time with the shutter open, which can be a tiny battery saver during those lengthy night sessions. In a nutshell, using super-high ISOs for framing is like the quick sketch before the masterpiece. It saves time, reduces guesswork, and lets you iterate on the fly. Once you find the frame, lower the ISO and change the exposure time accordingly.

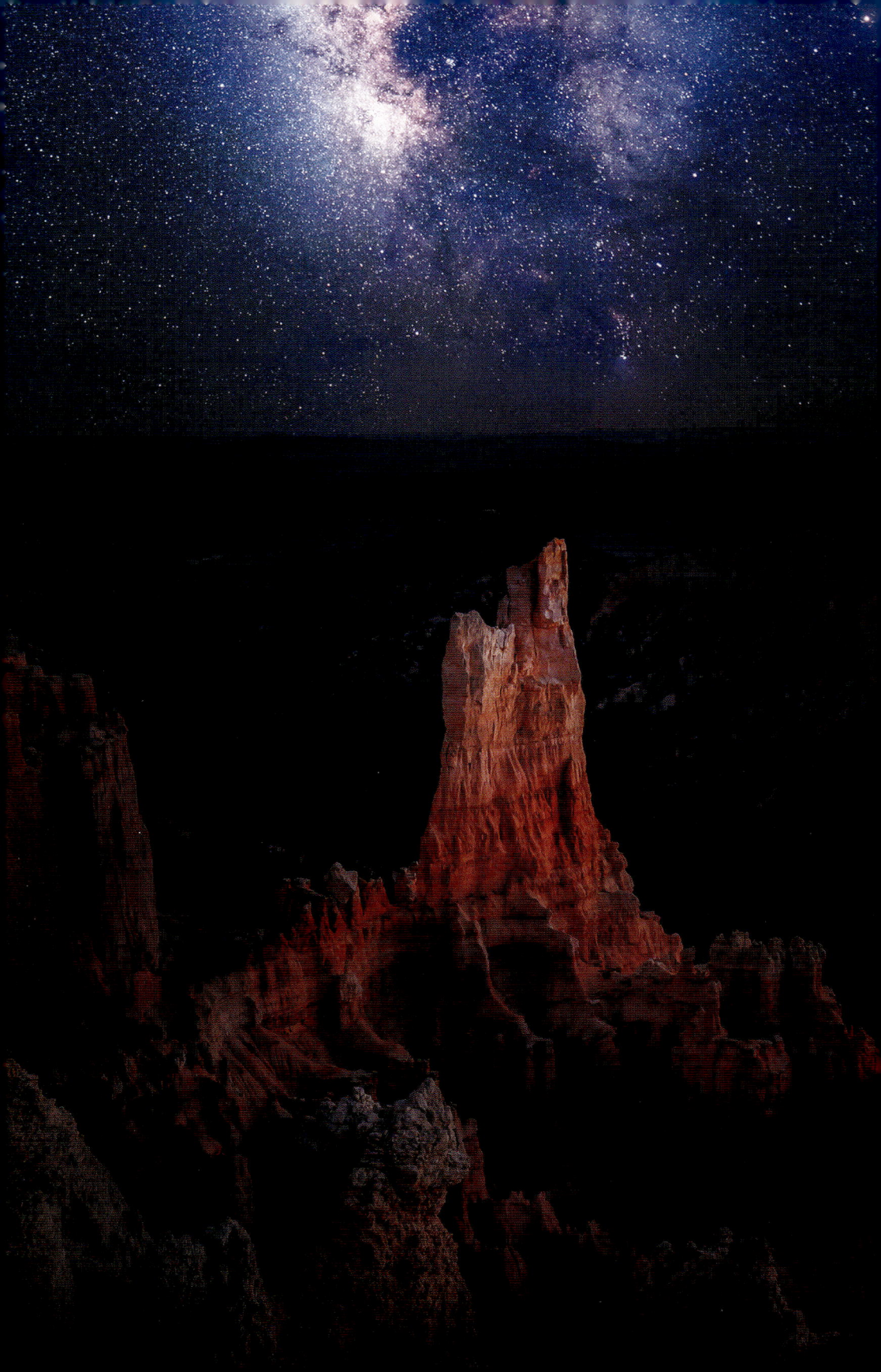

4

Shooting in Low Light

Controlling Exposure When Light Is Scarce

Shooting at night is a whole different beast. Everything you know about photography in the daytime—where to focus, how to expose, what settings to use—gets flipped upside down the moment the sun dips below the horizon. Suddenly, your camera's autofocus is useless, your metering system is confused, and your LCD screen is lying to you about how bright your image really is. If you've ever taken what looked like a perfectly exposed shot at night, only to get home and realize it's way too dark, you know exactly what I mean. This chapter is all about making sure your camera works for you, not against you, in low-light conditions. We'll cover why your LCD screen can't be trusted at night and why your histogram is the real MVP when it comes to dialing in the perfect exposure. We'll talk about high-ISO test shots, a secret weapon for quickly composing in the dark, and how to manage noise so your final image is clean and sharp. And if you're still struggling to get tack-sharp stars, we'll go over manual focusing tricks, including why playback zoom is your best friend in the field. But it's not just about exposure and focus; it's about knowing how to navigate your gear in the dark without fumbling around like you're trying to solve a Rubik's Cube blindfolded. I'll walk you through why mastering your camera buttons in total darkness is crucial, how a simple red headlamp can protect your night vision (and how knowing your buttons and dials keeps you from being "that guy" who ruins a long exposure with a flashlight and headlamp), and why dimming your LCD and covering tiny indicator lights can make all the difference when shooting with others. Shooting in low light takes patience, precision, and a bit of strategy, but once you get the hang of it, it opens up a whole new world of creative possibilities. With the right approach, you won't just take night photos, you'll take control of them. Let's dive in.

Again, Take Test Shots

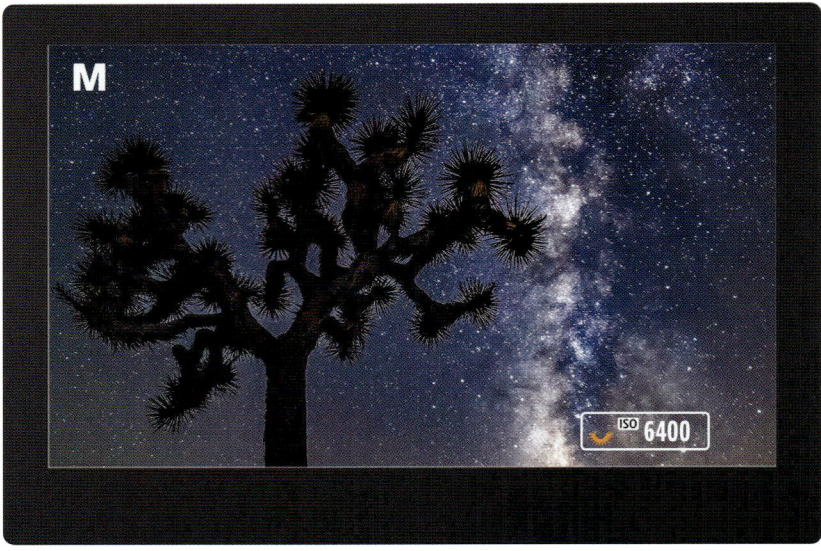

I know we talked about it earlier, but I see so many friends struggling with this one and they get so frustrated seeing me get a composition and setting dialed in quickly. Have you ever wondered how to nail that Milky Way landscape shot without spending hours in trial and error? Or wondered how friends can capture a dozen different compositions when you're trying to find your first one? The magic trick is high-ISO test shots. At night, time becomes a luxury. Every moment matters! First, the Milky Way is moving, and second, we want to go to bed. Instead of long exposures (which are time-consuming), switching to an extremely-high-ISO shot gives you a sneak peek into the final image. By ramping up the ISO, your camera essentially gets "night vision." Now when I say "high ISO," I mean high, like 25600 or 51200. While this introduces noise (which we don't want for the final shot), it lets us view the Milky Way's position, the foreground elements, and potential obstructions lightning-fast without having to wait 20 seconds. It's challenging to frame a shot in the dark, but by doing this, you can tweak and perfect your composition on the go—adjust your foreground, align a tree with the Milky Way core, or simply ensure you aren't cutting off anything important in your frame. Test shots aren't just about composition; they're invaluable for settings, too. Check your focus and gauge if you need a wider aperture or if your shutter speed needs adjustment. They're your litmus test before you commit to the longer, noise-free exposure. Night photography is part technique, part race against time. These quick shots maximize your efficiency, ensuring you capture the cosmos right in the position you want before it shifts, clouds roll in, or light conditions change. High-ISO test shots are quick, insightful, and the key to capturing the night sky. Just remember: once you're done, adjust your settings back to reasonable noise levels, like ISO 6400 or lower.

Don't Rely on Your LCD Screen

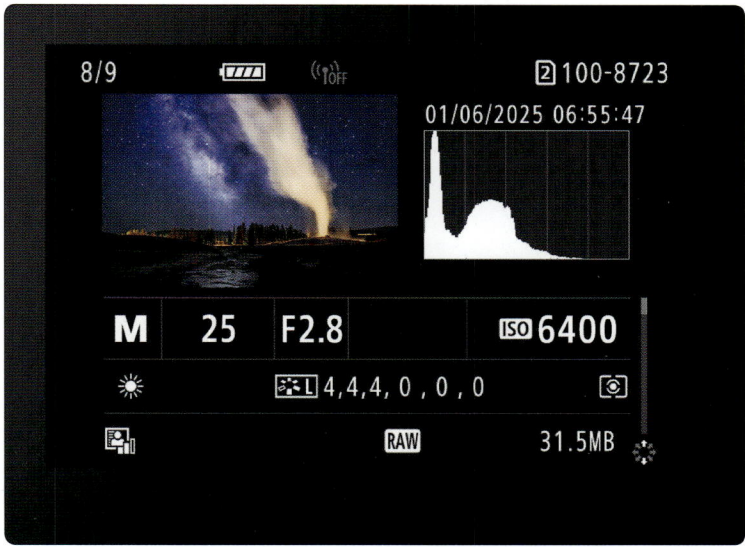

Ever shot what you thought was the perfect nighttime photo only to later discover it was way darker on your computer? Here's the thing: In the pitch-dark, your camera's LCD screen is like a mini flashlight—it seems super-bright, potentially making your image look well-exposed even when it's not. You'll want to trust your camera's histogram, not your eyes! I will never say that about any other genre I shoot, but this little graph plots the brightness of your image and it can't fool your eyes. Peaks on the left mean shadows; peaks on the right are highlights. Ideally, for a balanced exposure, you want those peaks toward the center. No more guessing games! (We'll talk more about this on the next page since it's so crucial.) Next, tone down your screen's brightness at night. While this won't change your exposure, it'll give you a more accurate representation of what you're capturing (we'll look at this one more on page 60). Remember, it's just a reference; the histogram remains the ultimate truth-teller. Finally, activate your camera's highlight warning (often called the "blinkies"). Overexposed parts of your image will blink, ensuring you don't blow out those precious details. Plus, an added tip: After your shot, zoom in, and check the details, especially in the shadows and highlights. If something's off, adjust and reshoot. The aim is to ensure details aren't lost in pure blacks or washed out whites. Night photography is a beautiful challenge, but your LCD can be deceiving. Lean on the trusty histogram.

Let Your Histogram Guide You

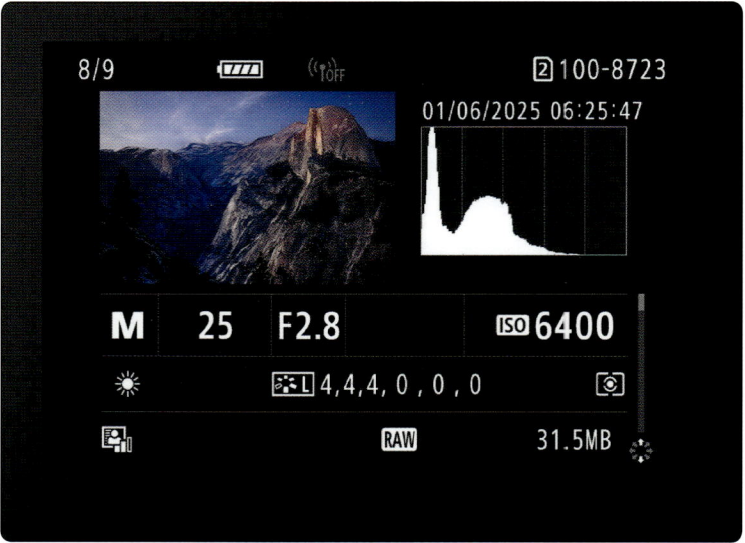

As you just learned on the previous page, one of your most valuable allies when shooting the night sky is the histogram. If you've overlooked it during the day, at sunset, or twilight, I don't blame you—I do as well. But, at night, you have to embrace it because your LCD's brightness might be deceptive. The histogram is essentially a graph that maps out the tones in your photo, from pure black (left) to pure white (right) and peaks show where most of your image's tones lie. For night photography, a majority of the data will lean left (as seen here), but you don't want it all squished against the edge—that means lost detail! If your histogram's data is shoved against the left edge, you've got clipped shadows, which are regions of pure black. Too far right? Clipped highlights. The beauty of the night sky lies in its subtleties, and clipping erases them. When you're capturing the Milky Way, you'll want a slight peak bump toward the left middle of your histogram. This indicates those gorgeous mid-tones—the heart of our galaxy. While you aim to avoid extreme darks and lights, the night sky isn't about a "balanced" histogram like daytime shots—it's darker by nature. However, ensuring details across the spectrum is key, and that's where the histogram guides you. Make adjustments, reshoot, and refine. Think of the histogram as letting you see the unseen in your images, and it's a great way to not be fooled by your LCD screen's brightness. Just make sure the majority of your histogram falls below 50% on the brightness; if not, it's not going to be a night shot anymore. That's a problem with metering at night. The camera always wants to properly expose the shot, and at night, that means overexposing. Night shots should be dark, but they shouldn't be so dark that they have no detail in the shadows and no pop in the highlights. To ensure that happens, we have to add some ISO.

Dealing with Noise

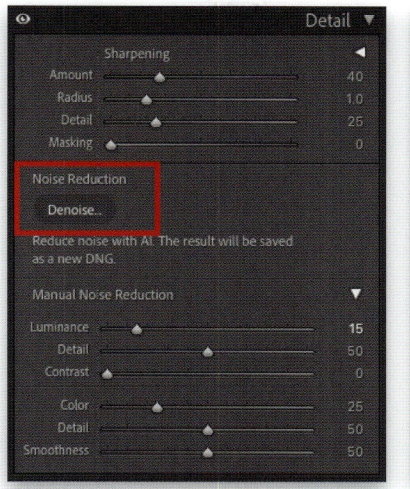
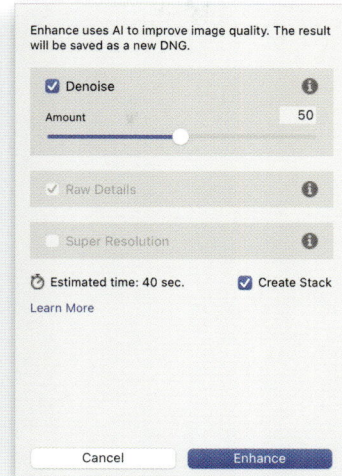

Ah, the ever-elusive quest for the perfect night shot without the grainy interference of noise. Those tiny, colorful, grainy specks tend to crash our party for a couple of reasons: First, high ISO settings, which we often resort to when the lights dim, amplify the camera sensor's sensitivity up to ISO 6400 or ISO 12800, but this also adds noise. Second, long exposures, though fantastic for catching every photon of starlight, can cause sensors to heat up, producing heat noise. But fear not, for there are ways to handle this challenge, starting with in-camera noise reduction. While this feature can be a tad slow, as it usually takes a second dark frame to subtract noise, the results can be impressive if you're not doing any noise reduction techniques yet. However, keep in mind that this method can sometimes soften the image and is done all in-camera, so I'd rather go with option two. Post-processing tools like Lightroom and Photoshop have noise reduction features that target and smooth out the noise and grain, even using AI on your RAW files. This eliminates half or more of the noise in your files. There are also plugins like ON1 NoNoise AI or Topaz Denoise AI noise reduction. These tools are next-gen level, leveraging artificial intelligence to wipe out the noise. The trick is to balance noise reduction with detail retention and these programs allow us to remove it at the RAW level and even selectively on the image through layers. Another trick is stacking, which thanks to ON1 and Topaz, I don't do much of anymore. But, by taking multiple shots of the same scene and stacking them in post, random noise gets averaged out, leaving behind a cleaner image (we'll look at this more in Chapter 12). You must embrace noise reduction. A bit of noise won't overshadow the awe of a perfectly composed Milky Way or a shimmering aurora, but we have to mitigate it.

Avoiding Noise

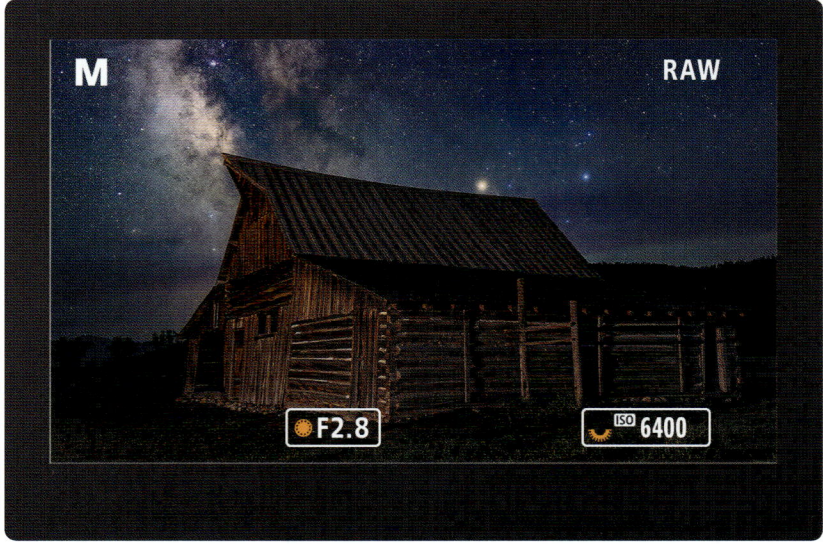

We can remove noise with noise reduction tools, but there are ways to reduce it from the get-go: First, know your camera's sweet spot. Each camera has an ISO level where it performs best in low-light conditions and this doesn't always mean the highest available ISO. Familiarize yourself with your camera's noise threshold. That is, the highest ISO setting where noise isn't overwhelmingly apparent to you. This might be ISO 1600 for some models and ISO 6400 for others, or with some of these new sensors, that can be as high as ISO 25600. But, for many modern mirrorless cameras that number is north of ISO 6400. Next, the sharper your image, the less apparent the noise. I hope you've picked up by now that a sturdy tripod is a must in night photography. Any shake or blur can accentuate noise, turning what could've been minor grains into glaring distractions. Next, shoot RAW! JPEGs are compressed, and this compression can enhance the appearance of noise. RAW files keep all the data from the sensor, giving you a cleaner starting point and allowing for better noise reduction in post. Also, using a lens's widest aperture, like f/2.8, allows more light onto the sensor in a shorter amount of time, which can reduce the need for super-high ISOs. Underexposing is a common mistake in night photography. While it might seem logical to shoot darker scenes darker, underexposed images tend to have more noise when brightened in post. It's often better to capture a scene brighter, and then dial it back during editing. Finally, camera sensors don't love extreme temperatures. Heat can increase noise, so if you're shooting in warmer conditions, limit the duration of super-long exposures. Remember, the objective isn't to eliminate noise completely; it's a natural part of digital photography, especially at night. Instead, the goal is to manage and reduce it, allowing the stars, landscapes, and celestial events to shine without noisy interference.

Use a Red Headlamp

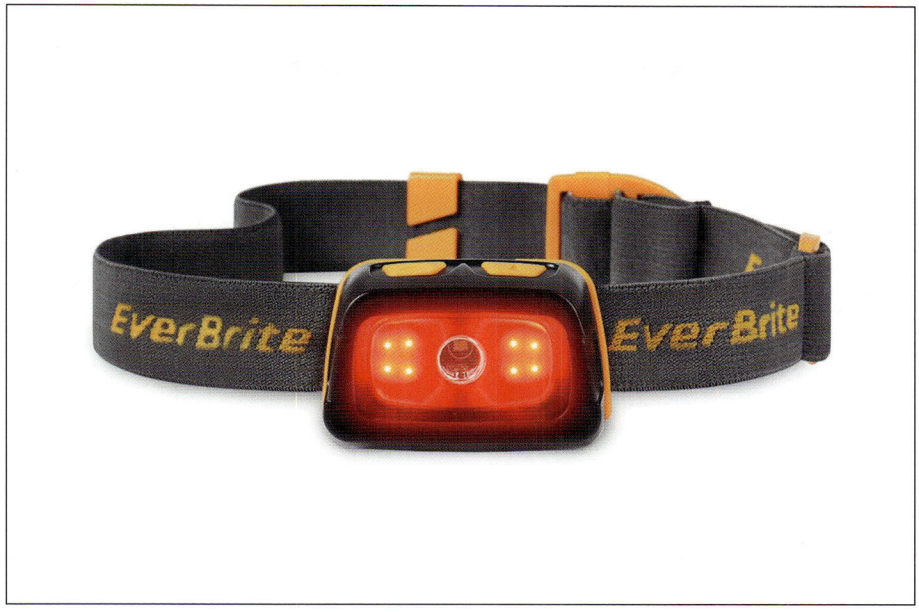

Diving into the depths of night photography, you'll find that preserving your night vision becomes paramount. Enter the unsung hero of the night photographer: the red headlamp (we also looked at headlamps back in Chapter 1). Our eyes have two types of photoreceptor cells: rods and cones. Cones help us see color in well-lit conditions, while rods handle our low-light vision. These rods are super-sensitive to light, and—fun fact—they don't perceive the color red well. This quirk is where the magic of the red headlamp comes into play. When you're out capturing the beauty of the night, the last thing you want is for a bright white light to flood your field of vision. It can take your eyes anywhere from 20 to 30 minutes to fully adjust to the darkness, but mere seconds of white light can reset that clock, forcing you to start the adjustment process all over again. Using a red headlamp lets you see your gear and settings without blasting your eyes with brightness. The red light is dim enough that it doesn't mess with your rod cells, so your eyes remain adjusted to the dark. It's all about preserving that night vision. Beyond your personal vision, consider your fellow stargazers or photographers. Nothing can ruffle the feathers of a night sky enthusiast faster than being inadvertently flashed with a white light during a crucial observation or long-exposure shot. The red headlamp ensures you're not "that guy" ruining everyone's eyes when out with a group. With that said, when shooting in groups you should *always* ask if anyone is shooting before turning on your headlamp, *even* a red one. The red headlamp is more than just a tool—it's a saver of night vision.

Finding Focus

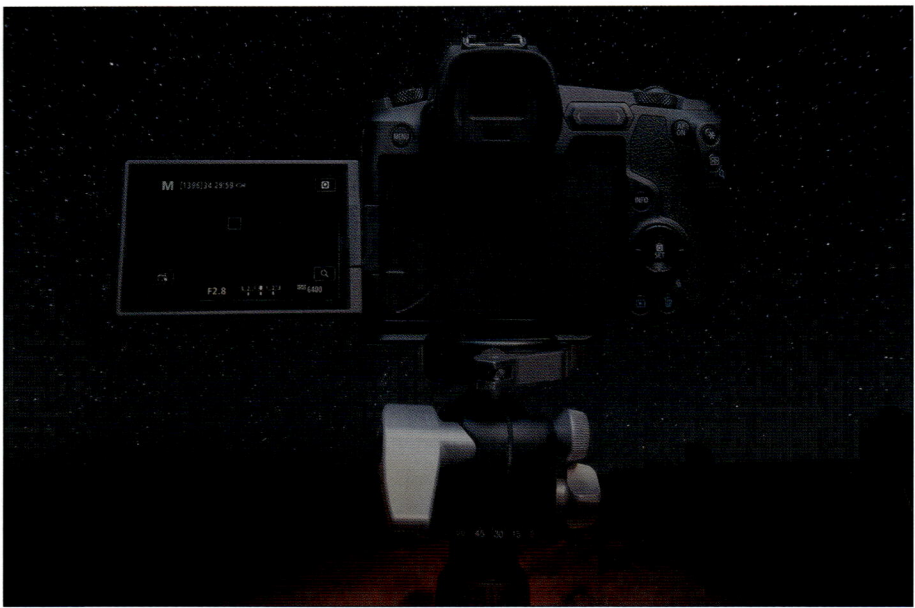

We talked about it in Chapter 3, but this is a big one and the number one frustration people have when they come to one of my in-person workshops. If you've ever tried to tell your camera to "focus on that star right there," you know it isn't always cooperative at night. Achieving razor-sharp focus is one of the trickiest parts of nighttime photography. During the day, your camera's autofocus system is a champ. But at night, it can often feel like it's fumbling in the dark. It's tempting to crank your lens to its infinity focus point, but here's the catch: true infinity might not be precisely where your lens indicates. Manufacturing discrepancies or temperature changes can shift this point ever so slightly. So, switch to manual focus, which gives you complete control and eliminates the camera's desperate hunt for focus in low light. Most modern DSLRs and mirrorless cameras have a Live View feature—use it! Zoom in (digitally, on your LCD) to 5x or 10x magnification, or even 30x if you have it. This magnified view helps you adjust the focus ring on your lens until those stars become tight, tiny pinpoints. To set focus, aim your camera at one of the night's brighter stars or even a planet—their increased brightness makes them easier to focus on. Once sharp, lock your focus. Now, you might be thinking, "If I focus on the stars, my foreground won't be sharp." If you're incorporating a landscape or other elements into your shot, remember the rule of hyperfocal distance. There's the sweet spot where you achieve maximum sharpness both near and far. There are apps and charts that can guide you on this based on your camera and lens, but because we're using wide-angle lenses, this tends to be a few feet away from the camera. Plus, we can also focus stack shots if we want. Lastly, take a test shot, adjust as necessary, and then start shooting. Focus isn't just about clarity here; it's about capturing the ethereal, the distant, and the otherworldly in all their celestial glory. Trust me, you don't want to miss focus on that!

Zoom In to Check Focus

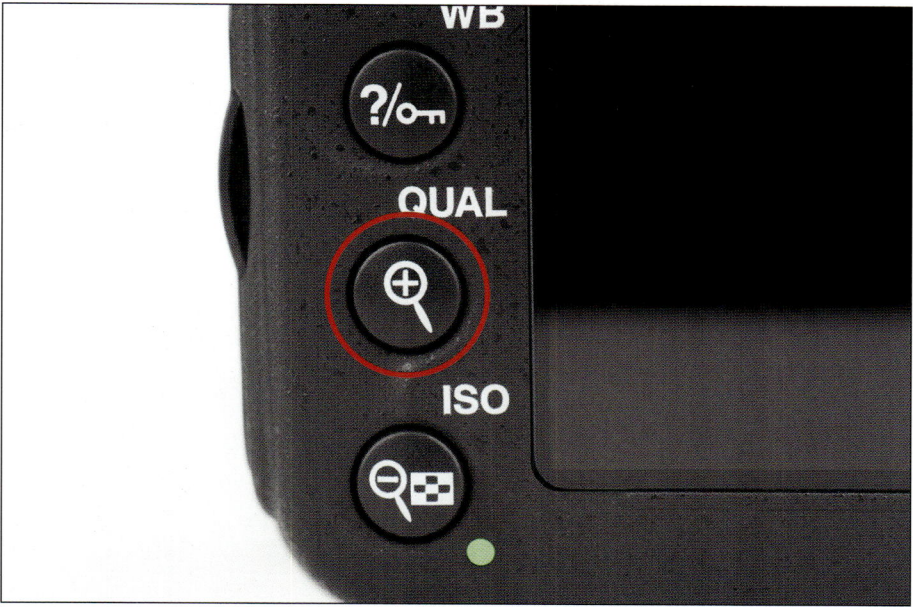

One of the biggest challenges we face in night photography is ensuring our shots are in razor-sharp focus. While your eyes may deceive you, especially in dim lighting, there's one tool you've got that always tells it like it is: the playback zoom feature on your camera. After you've just snapped what you believe might be your masterpiece, don't just take your camera's tiny LCD at face value. Those stars might look crisp at a quick glance, but the devil is in the details. By zooming into the playback of your image, you're able to make sure every star is sharp. This is where you can discern the difference between a star that's a clear pinpoint and one that's just a smidge blurry. The closer the inspection, the better, and often, your camera will let you magnify an image several times its original size. This allows you to see if you genuinely nailed the focus or if adjustments are needed. Imagine the frustration of capturing what you think is the perfect Milky Way shot, only to get home and discover it's slightly out of focus on your larger computer screen. The field is pitch-black, the Milky Way is in position, but the stars? They're just not as crisp as they should be. By checking on-location, you're not just verifying focus, you're giving yourself a chance to correct and reshoot immediately instead of doing what I did for years starting out. I'd think it was sharp only to return home to blurry dots in the sky. Remember, the night sky is fleeting—conditions change, clouds roll in, the Earth rotates, and the Milky Way drifts. The playback zoom is your friend, ensuring that when the stars align—literally and figuratively—you've got the shot in all its tack-sharp detail.

Your EVF, LCD & Those Pesky Little Lights

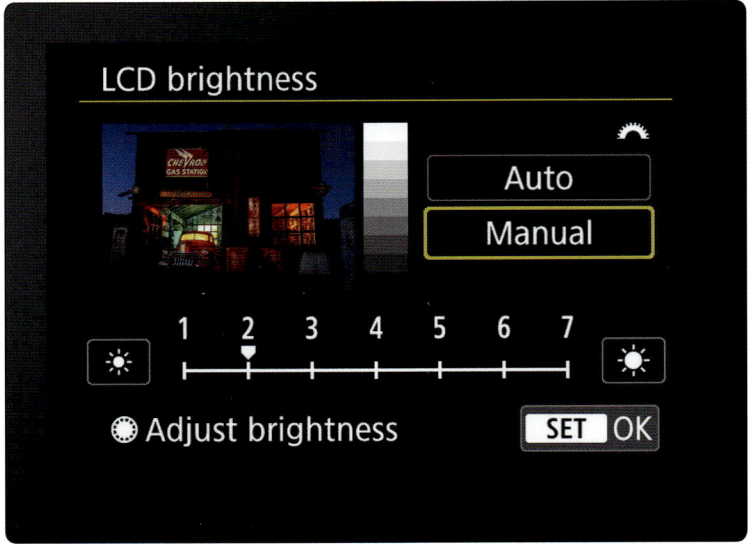

Our cameras sometimes need a little guidance to ensure they don't add unwanted light to our nighttime photos. In the daytime, the EVF (electronic view finder) and the LCD screen are your best friends, displaying vivid previews and reviews of your shots. But at night they can turn into glaring spotlights illuminating the scene. Having them too bright can be blinding, throwing off your night vision and making it challenging to see the stars. It'll also skew your perception of the exposure, making images appear brighter than they truly are. So, first, get into your camera settings and dial down the brightness of both the EVF and LCD. Most cameras offer manual control over the screen luminance. By toning down the brightness, you not only preserve your own night vision but also get a more accurate representation of how your shots will appear in a normal viewing condition. But it's not just about the screens. Those teeny indicator lights on your camera, like the red recording light, the AF assist lamp, or the countdown timer, may seem insignificant, but in the pitch-black, they can shine as bright as a beacon, which might ruin your shots. They're also terrific at attracting the annoyed glances of fellow photographers vying for the same unspoiled darkness. If you're out shooting with friends or with a group, a simple piece of gaffers tape over these lights can hide them. It's courteous, it's easy, and trust me, your group will appreciate your thoughtfulness. Even better, pack some gaffers tape in your bag, so you can offer it to your friends when they ruin everyone's shot with those annoying lights.

Know Your Buttons & Dials

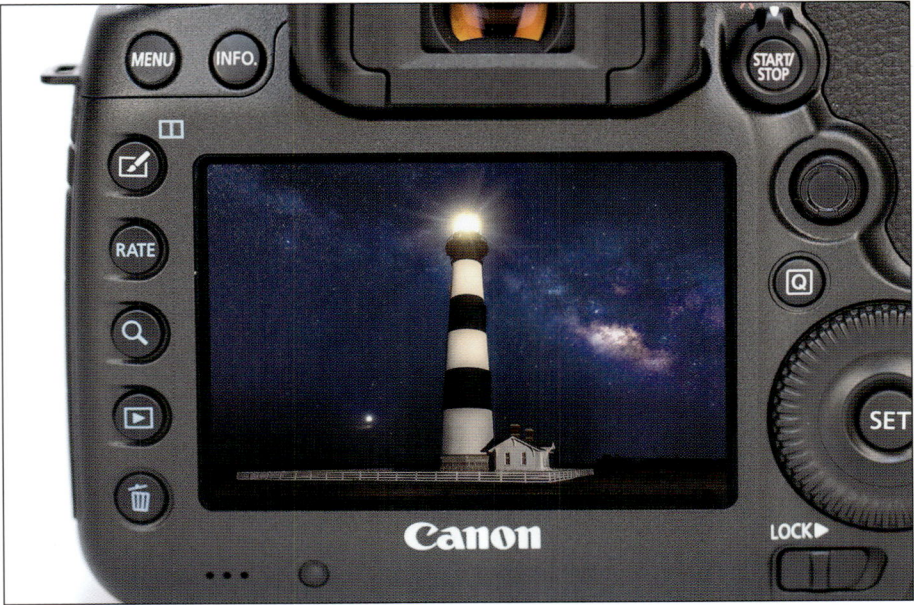

Dive into night photography, and you'll quickly realize that while the universe unveils its marvels, your trusty camera suddenly feels a bit...mysterious. In the golden hour, those buttons and dials were all so familiar, almost second nature. But at night, they morph into elusive little riddles. The first thing I teach my workshop students before they go on location is to go into a dark room and master every button on their camera and lens. Why does this matter so much at night? In low light, every moment is fleeting. It's all on nature's clock, not yours. Fumbling around, remembering where the ISO dial is or which button controls the focus, can cost you that once-in-a-lifetime shot. Not only that, but when you have to rely on your red light headlamp (see page 57), you'll constantly be messing up your friends' shots. And if you take my advice and wait to turn on your headlamp until you confirm with everyone they're not taking a frame, you'll realize quickly why I suggest knowing your camera in the dark. Mastering your camera's controls will translate to confident adjustments when the lights are low. It's like learning the keys on a piano—when your fingers know where to go, you can make music without looking. Similarly, when your fingers remember the layout of your camera, you can adjust settings seamlessly, letting you focus on the important things. This familiarity also preserves the ambiance of the setting. Avoiding the frequent need to illuminate your camera with a flashlight ensures that you maintain optimal night vision and don't disturb fellow photographers with sudden bursts of light. Lastly, confidence in your controls means more time to immerse yourself in the experience.

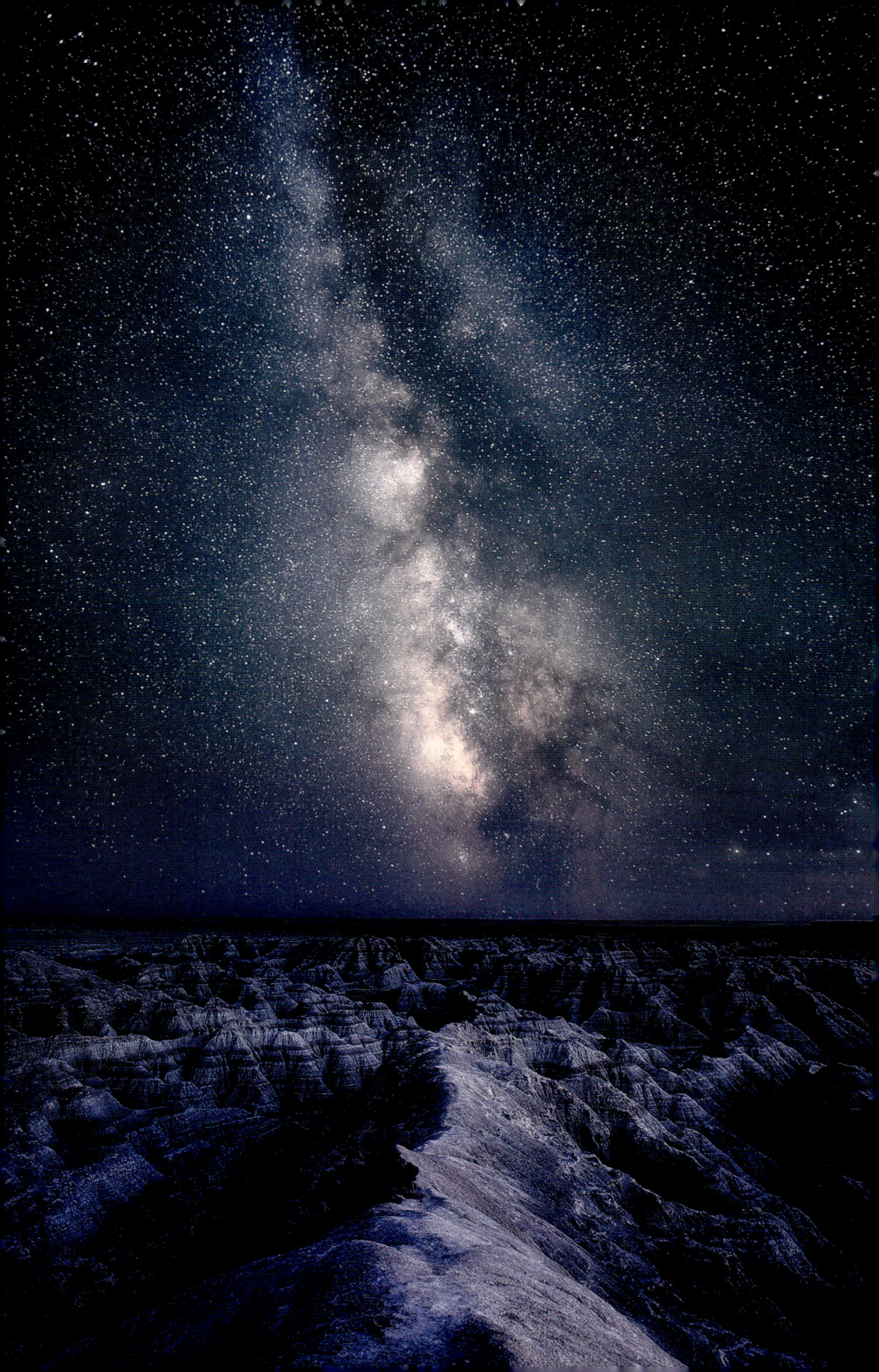

5

Astrophotography

Capturing the Deep Sky
& Beyond

If you thought night photography was tricky, welcome to astrophotography, where we take the challenge, crank it up to 11, and throw in a little chaos for good measure. This isn't just about snapping a few stars and calling it a day (or night). This is about capturing light that's traveled for millions of years just to land on your camera's sensor. Think about that—some of the photons hitting your lens started their journey before humans even figured out fire, and here you are, about to make them part of your composition. No pressure. This chapter is all about going beyond basic night photography and diving into deep space—the realm of nebulae, galaxies, planets, and pinpoint-sharp stars. We'll break down the two main styles of astrophotography and focus on deep sky imaging, where it's just you, a telephoto lens (or telescope), and the mind-blowing realization that you're capturing celestial objects millions of light-years away. Now, before you panic about needing a PhD in astrophysics, relax. We'll take it step by step. You'll learn how to track the stars like a pro, why stacking images is basically noise reduction magic, and how to not completely break your brain while focusing on a tiny dot in the sky. And if you've ever wondered how to photograph Saturn's rings or the swirling clouds of Jupiter, I've got you covered. But here's the thing: Astrophotography isn't just about having the right gear. It's about timing, location, and patience. Finding dark skies away from light pollution is key, understanding how the moon affects your shots is a game-changer, and knowing what's visible in different seasons will save you from looking for the Andromeda Galaxy in the wrong part of the sky. Trust me, I've been there. So if you're ready to level up, embrace the waiting game, and take your night photography from "cool" to absolutely jaw-dropping, you're in the right place. Let's shoot some stars—literally.

Astro-Landscapes vs. Deep Sky

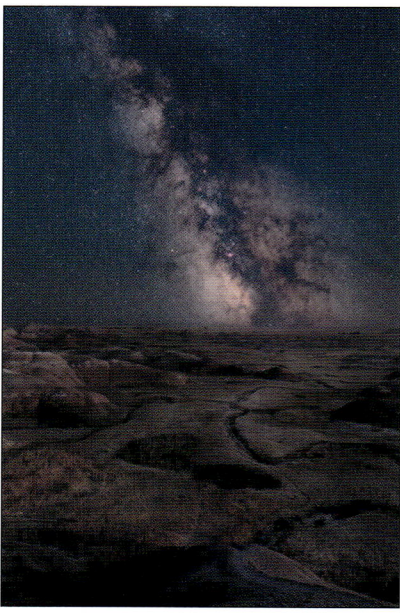 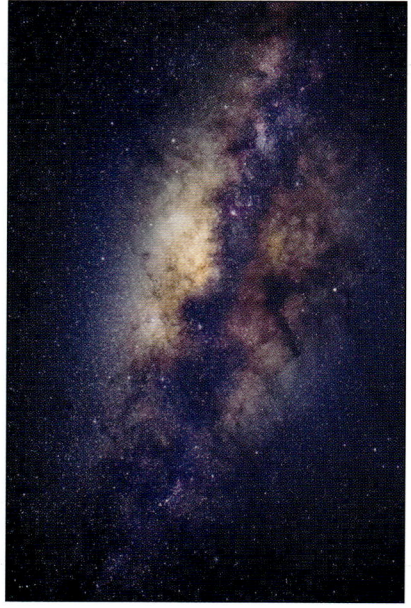

Astrophotography isn't a one-size-fits-all genre; it has distinct styles, each with its own allure and challenges. On the one hand, there's the world of astro-landscapes (seen above left). This is where the majesty of the night sky meets the beauty of the Earth. Imagine capturing the ethereal glow of the Milky Way as it arches over a tranquil desert landscape or the dance of the Northern Lights mirrored in a serene Arctic lake. Here, the aim is to create harmony between the terrestrial and the celestial. Wide-angle lenses, a sturdy tripod, and a bit of patience are often all you need to work this magic. But remember, your composition should bring together both land and sky. This is the dominant form of astrophotography most photographers start out capturing since the barrier to entry is low. Then there's the deep sky domain (seen above right). It's less about where you are or connecting the terrestrial with the extraterrestrial and more about just what's light-years away. This is the space of nebulae, galaxies, star clusters, and planets—the distant wonders that require more than just the naked eye. Here, telephoto lenses, specialized mounts, and trackers become necessary. These trackers follow the rotation of the Earth, ensuring that even during prolonged exposures, those distant cosmic entities remain sharp. It's a whole different ball game, one of precision and meticulous setup. But the rewards? They're out of this world—literally. Just expect a larger learning curve and a hefty tax on your wallet.

The Magic of Astro-Landscapes

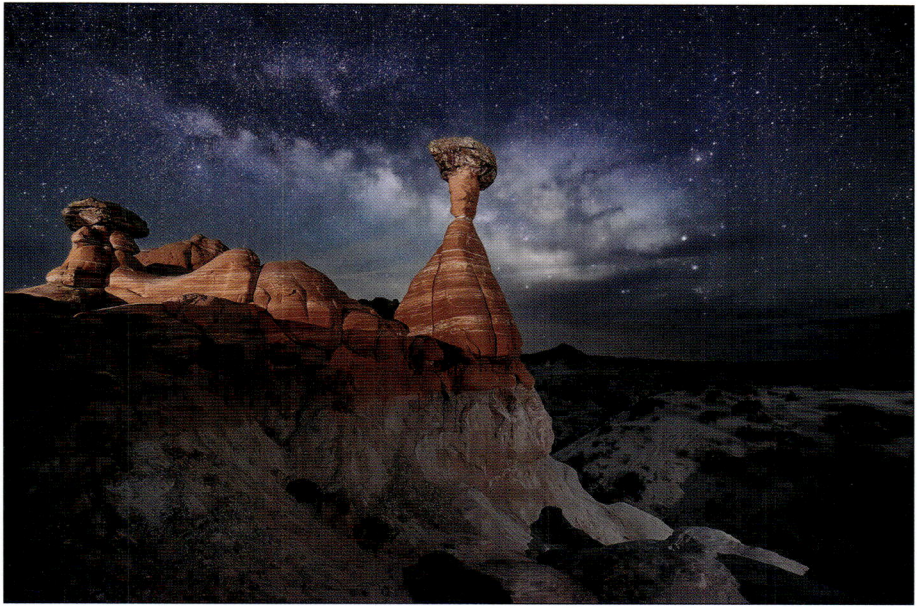

Astro-landscapes, or Milky Way nightscapes, offer a unique blend of the ethereal and the tangible. They're where a frame intertwines the vastness of the cosmos with Earth, and at the heart of every compelling astro-landscape lies a balance. The Milky Way stretching over a desolate canyon isn't just about the stars or rocks but their relationship. It's about juxtaposition—how the ageless constellations complement the ancient erosion of the Earth, or how the fleeting streak of a shooting star contrasts with the steady lighthouse on a cliff. With this style, your choice of location is paramount. While the stars are universal, how they interact with your environment will dictate the narrative of your photo. A desert might speak of isolation and vastness; a mountain range might emphasize majesty and height, reaching up toward the sky; a serene lake could offer a mirror, doubling the celestial wonder. But it's not just about picking a picturesque spot. Remember, the less light pollution, usually the better. This style requires you to venture out, away from city lights, where the skies are darkest. That's where stars shine brightest. Equipment-wise, wide-angle lenses are the go-to. They capture a broader swath of the sky and the land. As usual, a sturdy tripod is a must—the slightest movement during a long exposure can turn your stars into streaks. And always be patient. The Earth rotates, the clouds move, and conditions change. But in that perfect moment, when the land and the sky align just right, you'll capture a slice of magic that's both grounded and celestial.

Deep Sky Wonders

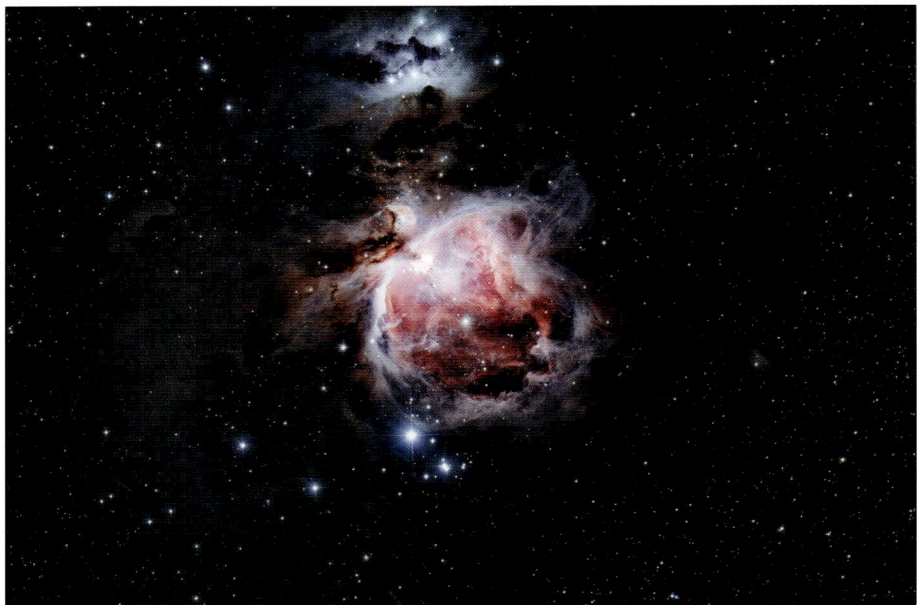

Deep sky astrophotography is like embarking on a celestial adventure. While astro-landscapes paint a harmonious blend of the heavens and Earth, deep sky astrophotography is all about transcending our planetary bounds and reaching straight into the heart of our universe. At its center is precision and patience. The tools of the trade are high-magnification telephoto lenses or telescopes, which allow you to zoom into those distant wonders and showcase their complexities (see page 74 for more on them). Then there's the mount—specifically, a tracker (we looked at this on page 16). It compensates for Earth's rotation. Without it, your long exposures would capture star trails instead of pin-sharp stars and galaxies. This is key! Location is still critical, just as it is with astro-landscapes, so you want the least light pollution to ensure that the faint light of distant galaxies isn't drowned out by artificial light—the darker the sky, the deeper you can gaze. But you don't need complete darkness if you use those filters we discussed earlier (on page 15). Because we're not concerned about the earthly foreground, we have more leeway with specialized filters and longer exposures (more on that soon). While astro-landscapes rely on wide-angle lenses, deep sky is all about the zoom. You're zeroing in, focusing on a celestial object, and making it the centerpiece. The story here isn't a dialogue between land and sky; it's a focused monologue of the universe, narrated by a single celestial object, nebula, or cluster at about 200–800mm. And then there's post-processing. Deep sky images often benefit from stacking—a technique where multiple shots are overlaid to highlight the best details and reduce noise (more on that in a minute, as well). Deep sky astrophotography is about exploration and patience. It involves gradually building up signal—or what some would call "data"—to reveal celestial objects that are often too faint to see with the naked eye.

The Unique Milky Way Landscape

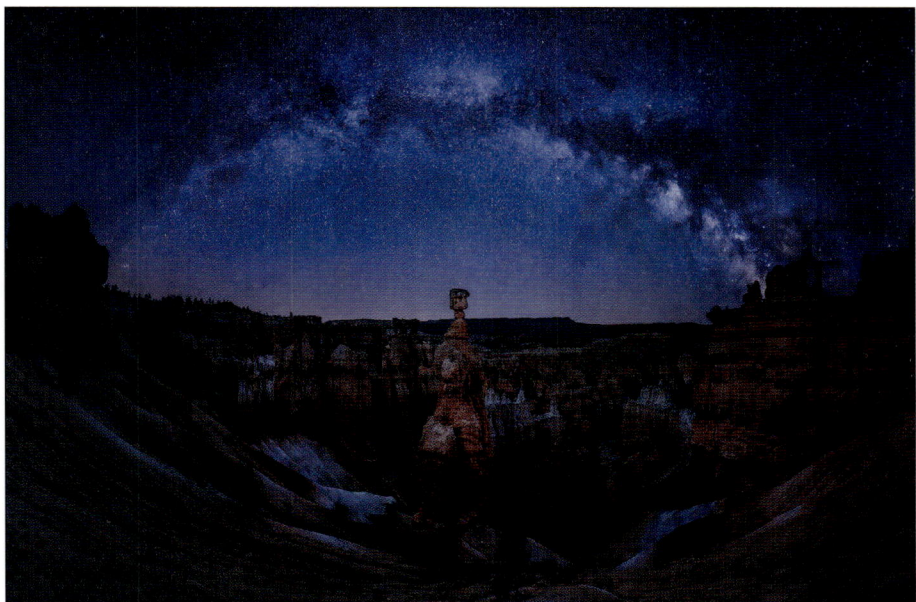

Milky Way landscapes hold a unique allure, blending the wondrously celestial and the deeply terrestrial. With its band arching across the night sky, the Milky Way is a sight. But it's not just about the stars; it's about context. It's the arc of the galaxy over a tranquil desert, the soft glow juxtaposed against jagged mountain peaks, or the Milky Way's core reflecting in a still alpine lake. The story is told in these contrasts and juxtapositions. When choosing a location, remember that the Milky Way is dim. Light pollution, even from distant cities, can drown out its delicate details. Seclusion is key, not only for clarity but for immersion. Being in a remote location, under a canopy of stars, enhances the connection to the vastness above, and if you embrace it, I guarantee it will show in your work. The better you know your subject, the better your photography. Plus, depending on your hemisphere and the season, the core might hover near the horizon or arch overhead (you learned about this in Chapter 2). A fast wide-angle lens, often between 14mm and 24mm, is ideal because it lets you capture a generous portion of the sky and the landscape. Wide apertures, like f/2.8, gather more light, revealing the galaxy's intricacies, and don't skimp on stability—long exposures demand sturdy tripods. Compositionally, think harmony. How can the land lead the eye to the stars? Maybe it's a winding river pointing to the galaxy's core or trees framing the stars. Processing Milky Way shots requires a gentle touch and balance is vital, ensuring the stars shine brightly without overwhelming the earthly elements.

Capturing the Milky Way Landscape in a Single Exposure

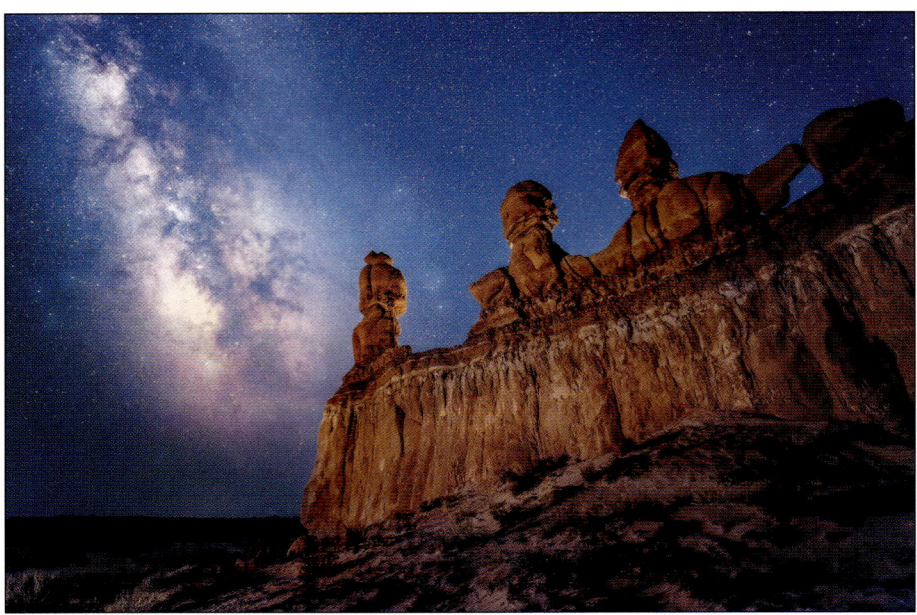

Capturing the Milky Way's majesty in one frame is my passion. It always feels like catching lightning in a bottle. But, here's the secret: with some know-how and a bit of practice, anyone can nail that awe-inspiring image in a single exposure. Start with the basics: timing and location. Familiarize yourself with when the Milky Way's core will be most visible, using apps like PhotoPills (see page 21). Location-wise, distance yourself from the lights of urban areas. Darkness is your best ally in Milky Way landscapes as it will allow the Milky Way's intricate details to pop against the landscape. Now, we have to gear up. A full-frame camera paired with a fast wide-angle lens—preferably in the realm of 14mm to 24mm with a wide f/2.8 aperture or wider—is a combination that gathers a lot of light in a short time, which is vital for capturing the galaxy's brilliance. Anchor everything with a sturdy tripod—at long exposures, even tiny shakes can result in a blurry image. How about settings? An ISO between 3200 and 12800 ensures clarity without excessive noise, and a shutter speed of around 20 to 25 seconds hits the sweet spot between capturing ample light and avoiding star trails. Open that aperture wide, aiming for f/2.8 to allow maximum light in, and since nailing focus can be tricky, manual mode's your friend here. Use Live View to focus on a bright star and zoom in on it to guarantee sharpness. Composition is key, so incorporate earthly elements that naturally guide the viewer's gaze toward the Milky Way's splendor. Once you've taken your shot, check the histogram on your camera and ensure your capture is balanced, and not too dark or overexposed. With a RAW image, you have ample wiggle room in post-processing to bring out the best in your single-shot masterpiece.

Blue Hour Blending

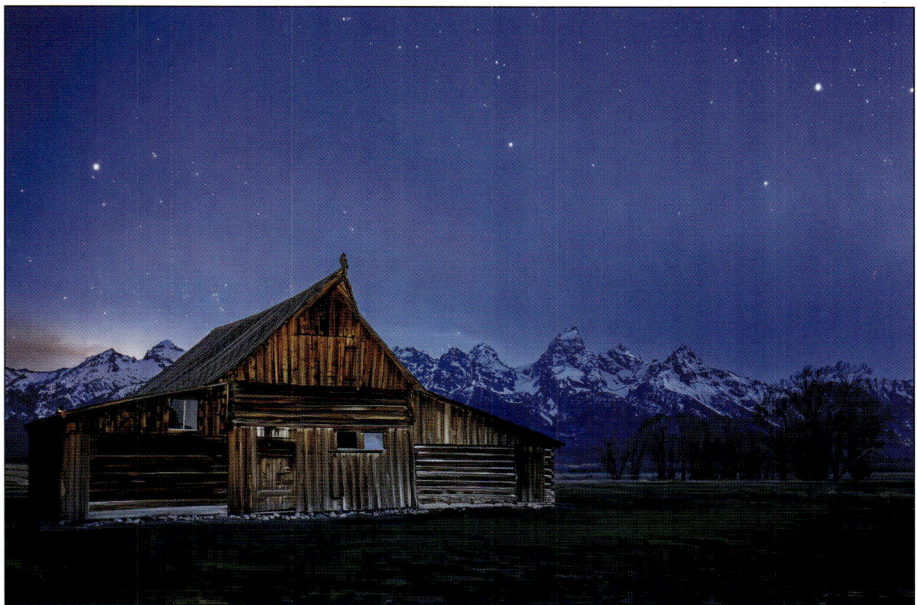

This is a technique that night photographers swear by and for good reason. Blue hour—especially late in blue hour during astronomical twilight—is that fleeting moment about a half hour or more after sunset or just before sunrise that serves up a sky painted with deep blues, setting a dramatic stage for stars and terrestrial elements. Imagine this: You're perched up on a hill, aiming to capture the iconic arch of the Milky Way juxtaposed with a silhouette of rugged mountains. Shooting during the peak of night gets you a brilliant sky, but the land element? It's cloaked in darkness and shadows. Here's where blue hour steps in. By capturing the landscape during this window, you get details and soft light, making your foreground as enchanting as the starry canopy. The technique involves shooting two separate exposures: one during blue hour for the landscape and another when the stars or Milky Way are at their brightest. Then the magic happens in post-processing: Using software like Photoshop, you blend these images, ensuring a seamless transition between the foreground and the night sky. But why not just brighten the foreground in post? Because increasing the exposure of dark regions introduces a bunch of noise. By shooting during blue hour, you get a clean, noise-free image. Camera setup remains crucial, so use a tripod to ensure both shots are from the exact same perspective. If your camera doesn't move, blending the two images will be a piece of cake. If it moves, it's achievable, but it will take longer. A wide-angle lens gives you a broader view of the landscape and sky, and your settings will differ between shots. For the blue hour shot, a lower ISO (maybe 100–800) and longer shutter speed captures the landscape, and for the Milky Way shot, you'll crank up the ISO and open that aperture wide. Remember, blue hour doesn't stick around—plan and be swift.

Moonscapes

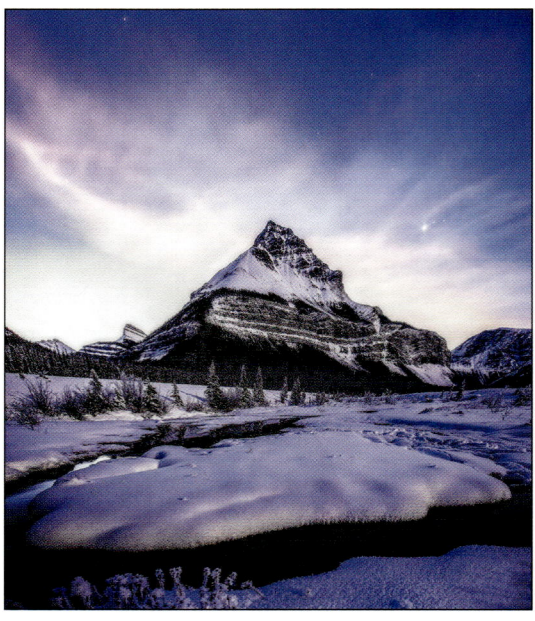

Moonlit landscapes, or moonscapes, bring an almost surreal quality to night photography. Think of it as nature's very own softbox lighting. When the moon pours its gentle luminescence onto the world below, it transforms ordinary scenes into moody, cinematic masterpieces. So, what's the deal with shooting under moonlight? Well, unlike a pitch-black setting where stars are the main illuminators, a moonlit night adds depth, texture, and nuance to your terrestrial elements. Mountains don't merely silhouette; they showcase ridges, valleys, and details. Forests aren't just dark expanses; they're a play of light and shadow, where every tree stands distinct. Getting the shot involves some crafty considerations. First and foremost, the moon's phase and position are pivotal (we looked at them on page 31). A full moon or gibbous moon rises higher, shedding more light onto the landscape below. Yet, sometimes, a crescent moon's subtler glow might be just what you're after for a more mysterious ambiance. Your camera gear is much like what you'd use for other night shoots. I know I will sound like a broken record here, but a sturdy tripod is non-negotiable. A wide-angle lens captures the expanse, while a mid-telephoto can help zoom into specific moonlit details. For settings, the moon's light lets you play with a more forgiving ISO range—somewhere between 400 and 800 is a good starting point. Aim for an aperture of f/4 to f/8, allowing you to capture sharper details across the frame, and your shutter speed can range from 5 to 30 seconds, depending on the moon's brightness and the effect you're after. But here's the kicker: your composition will be elevated when you play with moon positioning. Use it as a back light, sidelight, or even a key light, depending on the light you wish to craft.

Tracked Landscapes

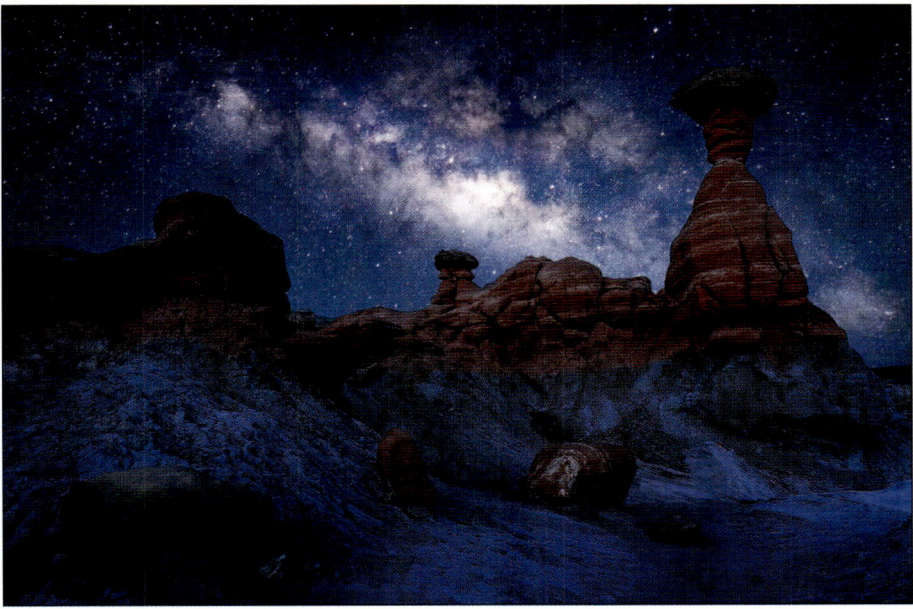

If you've ever looked at a night image and wondered, "How in the world did they capture the Milky Way with such jaw-dropping detail?" there's a good chance tracking was the secret sauce. Here's the basic idea: Our planet is spinning. (No news there, right?) But what this means for astrophotographers is that when capturing the night sky, over time, stars will move in the frame, resulting in star trails. While these can be stunning in their own right, sometimes we want to preserve the pinpoint clarity of each star and the intricate detail of our galaxy. Star trackers are nifty devices that rotate your camera at the exact inverse speed of the Earth's rotation to negate the rotational effect (we looked at this on page 16). While the Earth spins in one direction, your tracker moves your camera in the opposite, making sure the stars appear stationary in the frame, even during a lengthy exposure. This allows longer exposures without star trails, capturing more light and detail from the Milky Way than otherwise possible. "But wait," you're probably thinking, "won't that make the ground all blurry if I'm tracking the stars?" Bingo! This is the thing nobody tells you starting out, which is why we need to become masters at blending if we want to use a tracker with a landscape. First, you'll shoot the sky with the tracker on with a lower ISO, a higher f-stop, and a longer shutter speed, allowing more clarity and detail with the Milky Way. Next, turn the tracker off and capture the landscape as a separate image with the same settings since the star trails are not an issue now. In post-processing, you'll combine these two—the ultra-detailed sky and the crisp, still landscape. The result? A landscape beneath the sky where both the ground and the stars have sharp, stunning detail. Tracked landscapes are an exercise in patience and precision, but the results are nothing short of magical. Just know, Photoshop skills will be a must, but I'll show you how to blend them in Chapters 11 and 12.

Blending & Stacking

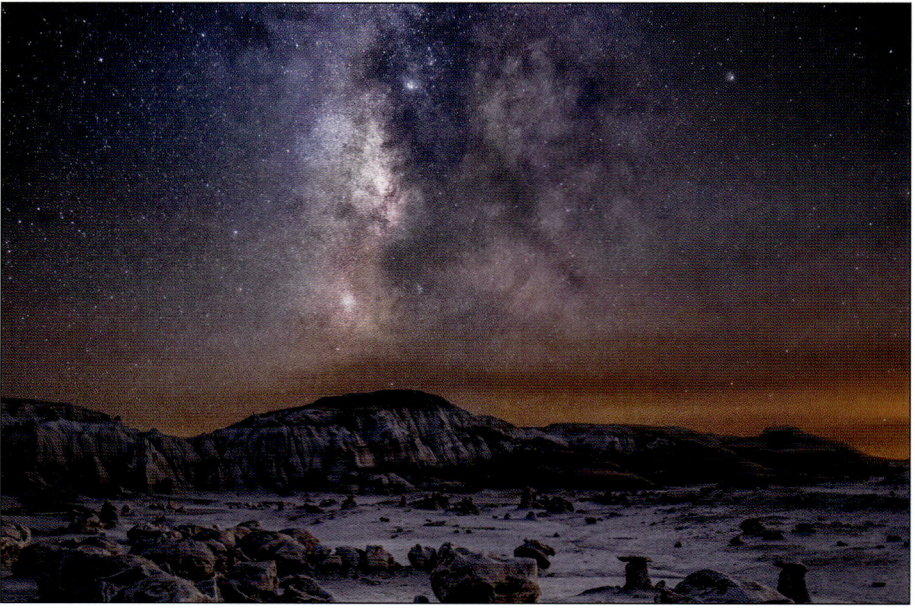

Ever wondered how some night sky photos have that mesmerizing depth, detail, and minimal noise, making the stars pop and the landscape look almost surreal? That magic often comes from another technique called stacking, which when combined with blending (mentioned on the previous page), takes it to the next level. Let's break this down: First, this is primarily about merging two or more images to get the best elements of each. Imagine you took a stellar shot of the Milky Way with your camera's settings optimized for the sky. You've got a fantastic sky, but your foreground is a bit too dark or blurry from using a tracker. Now, imagine a second shot with the settings optimized for the foreground, lighting it perfectly. Blending is about marrying these two in post-processing, merging the detailed Milky Way with that perfectly lit foreground. The result? An image where both the sky and the ground are optimally exposed. Now, what if we could deal with the biggest issue of night photography: noise. Noise arises from using high ISO settings or long exposures, but here's a cool trick: by taking several shots of the same scene with the same settings and then stacking them in post, you can significantly reduce that noise. How? The random noise that appears in one image will likely not appear in the exact same spot in another. When these images are stacked, the post-processing software averages out the pixel values, keeping the consistent details (like stars) and minimizing the random noise. Plus, a bonus is that stacking can also help increase the sharpness and detail of celestial objects. Blending and stacking are the secret ingredients for spicing up your images (again, see Chapters 11 and 12 for more on the post-processing). Together, they elevate night sky photography to an art form, capturing the celestial ballet in all its glory while making earthly landscapes stand out with breathtaking clarity.

Tracking & Stacking

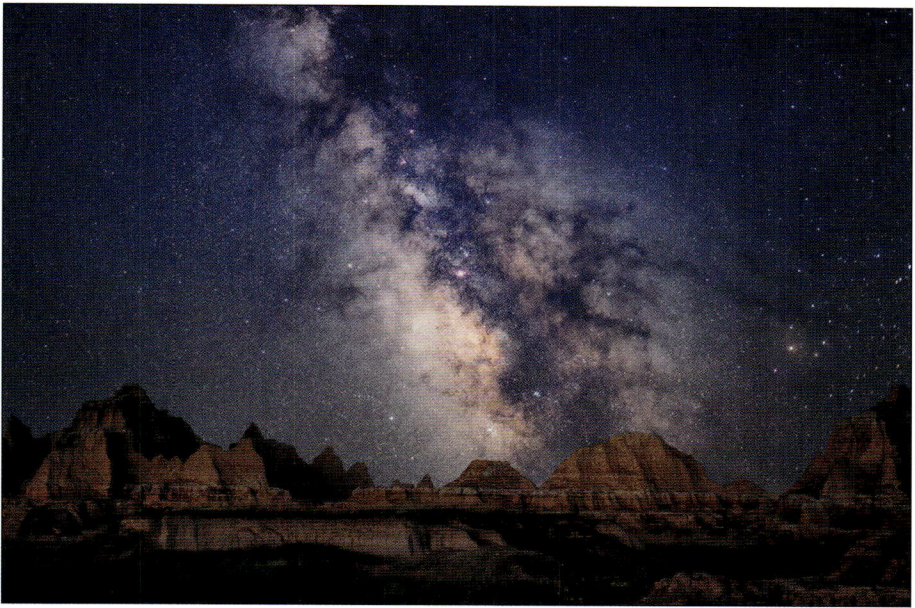

Night sky photography can sometimes feel like you're chasing ghosts—trying to capture faint lights that, to the naked eye, aren't always visible. But with the right techniques, you can unveil the depth and wonder of the universe. If you want to up the game even more, try stacking and tracking. The principle is straightforward: It starts by taking several identical exposures. You're capturing the scene's consistent elements (like the stars) and the random noise differently each time. When you combine or "stack" these images using post-processing software, the constant elements reinforce each other, while the random noise, being inconsistent, gets diluted. The outcome is images with less noise and greater clarity. For those starry landscapes, stacking means sharper stars and a cleaner, more pristine backdrop. But the Earth doesn't stop to let you take photos; it keeps spinning. This means that during long exposures, stars can trail, turning from points into streaks. Enter star trackers (we looked at them on page 71). These are devices that move your camera in opposition to the Earth's rotation. So, instead of getting star streaks in a two-minute exposure, with a tracker, you can get pin-sharp stars. This allows for longer exposures at lower ISOs, resulting in cleaner images with more detail in the Milky Way. But here's where things get interesting: combine stacking with tracking. By using a tracker, you can capture multiple long-exposure shots of the sky with incredible detail and less noise. Then, by stacking these shots, you amplify the clarity and detail even more. The beauty of stacking and tracking here is that they complement each other. Stacking deals with the digital noise inherent in high-ISO shooting, while tracking combats the motion blur of our ever-turning planet. Together, they're a power-duo for the more advanced night photographers. (Once again, see Chapters 11 and 12 for more on the post-processing.)

Telephoto Tracking

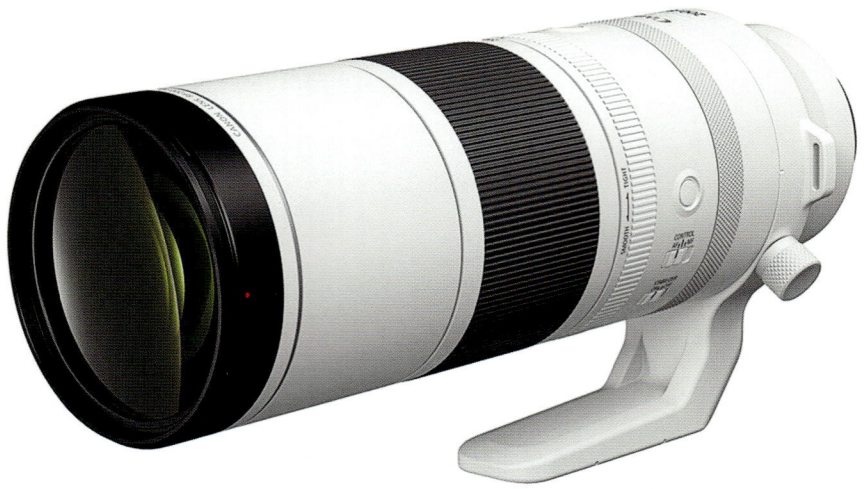

Beyond our Milky Way's shimmering core, there's an expansive universe of wonders to photograph, but capturing these distant spectacles requires more than just a standard setup. Enter the world of deep-sky astrophotography, where telephoto lenses and trackers become your ticket to the cosmos. Fair warning: this is where the budgets increase and astrophotography becomes way more technical. A telephoto lens, especially one with focal lengths above 200mm, brings distant galaxies, nebulae, and star clusters into clear view. These lenses allow for a tighter frame, isolating specific celestial objects and filling the image with them. The vast Orion Nebula, the swirling Andromeda Galaxy, or the dense Pleiades Cluster can be captured in impossible detail with wider lenses. But here's the catch: With greater magnification, any movement becomes more pronounced. Even the Earth's rotation, unnoticed in wide-angle shots, becomes a glaring blur in telephoto images. That's where the tracker comes in. It's essential—or I should say mandatory—for this style of photography (see page 16 for more on them). As we've established, our Earth is a spinning ball, which is great for day-to-day life, but not so much for capturing crisp shots of distant galaxies. As we discussed on the last few pages, a tracker compensates for this rotation resulting in sharp, detailed shots of deep-sky objects, free from star trails, even during long exposures. That's how this all works. The telephoto lens zooms into a distant galaxy while the tracker ensures every star point remains sharp. Putting these two together, it's like having a telescope that can capture images, allowing you to journey deep into space right from your backyard. Deep-sky astrophotography, using telephoto lenses and trackers, is not just about capturing images. It's about capturing the little details in deep space.

Nebulae

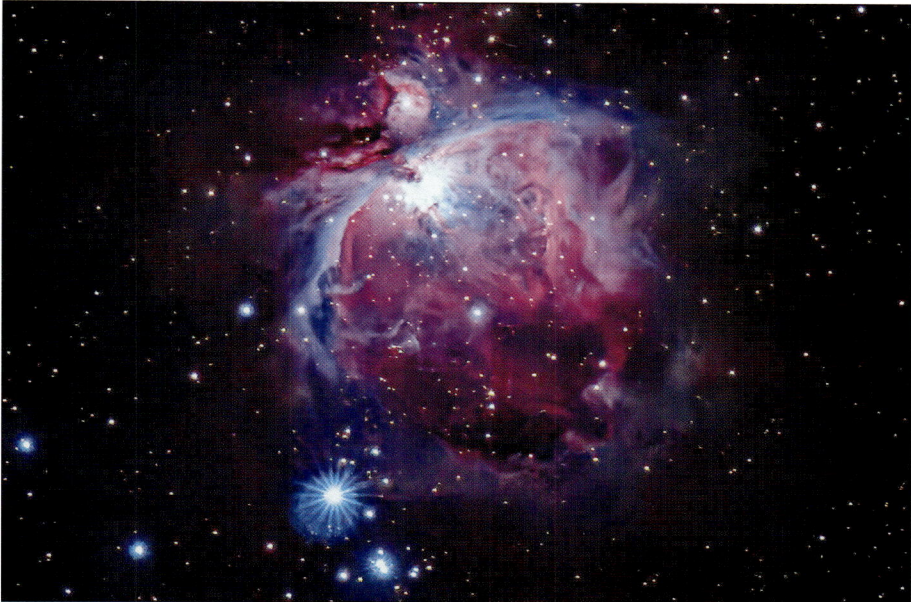

Every night, nebulae hang in our sky (this is a shot of Orion Nebula). These mammoth clouds of gas and dust are celestial nurseries where stars are born and capturing their elegance requires a blend of the right equipment and technique. A mirrorless camera with less mechanical vibration means fewer chances of a shaky image during those critical long exposures. Plus, many mirrorless cameras come with impressive sensors that can capture light effectively, perfect for the faint glow of nebulae. While the universe is vast and nebulae are immense, they can appear as mere smudges to the naked eye. A telephoto lens with a focal length of at least 200mm, preferably 200–800mm, zooms in on these smudges, unveiling their intricate details and structures. Remember, the larger the aperture, the more light the lens can capture, but it's not as sharp. While f/2.8 works here, going to f/4 or even f/8 works wonders. A star tracker compensates for this by rotating your camera to allow for longer exposures at these sharper f-stops (see page 16 for more on them). How to set up and shoot: Stability is key, so mount your mirrorless camera on a sturdy tripod, attach your telephoto lens, then affix the entire setup to your tracker, and ensure your tracker accurately aligns with the Earth's rotational axis (toward Polaris in the Northern Hemisphere). This is probably the most important of the steps. Use Live View on your camera, zoom in on a bright star, and manually adjust your focus until the star is sharp. Opt for a wide-open aperture and start with an ISO between 1600–6400. Your exposure time will depend on the tracker's accuracy and your lens' focal length—a couple of minutes is a good starting point. Now, take your shot, review, adjust settings if necessary, and repeat.

Constellations

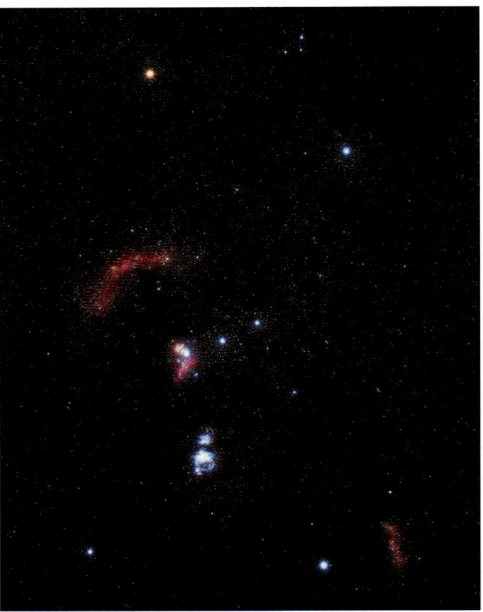

Staring up at the night sky, you'll see patterns formed by stars—these are constellations. For constellations, you want a camera that's adept at low-light situations, like a mirrorless one. The mirrorless camera's electronic viewfinder can also be invaluable, letting you see a digital rendition of your shot before you press the shutter button. While telephoto lenses are great for deep-sky objects, constellations often benefit from a wider field of view. So, a wide-angle lens—anywhere from 24mm to 70mm—will do the trick. And again, a wide aperture like f/2.8 will gather more of that precious starlight, but adding a tracker can help us to increase to a sharper f/4 to f/8 with a longer shutter speed and lower ISO. As always, a tripod is a must. Those stars may twinkle, but you don't want your camera to shake, so be sure your tripod is steady, especially in a windy location. Constellations are faint, so head to a location far from city lights—the darker your surroundings, the brighter the stars will appear. Autofocus can struggle in the dark, so instead, use manual focus. Turn on your camera's Live View, find a bright star, zoom in, and adjust the focus ring until that star is sharp and crisp. With a wide aperture and an ISO between 1600 and 6400, begin with a shutter speed of about 15 seconds to avoid star trails, which can blur the distinct patterns of constellations. Find a constellation—you can even use natural elements, like trees or rocks, to frame and give context—take the shot, review, and tweak the settings if needed. Capturing constellations isn't just about photographing stars; it's about bringing life to the stories that have been told for millennia.

Planets

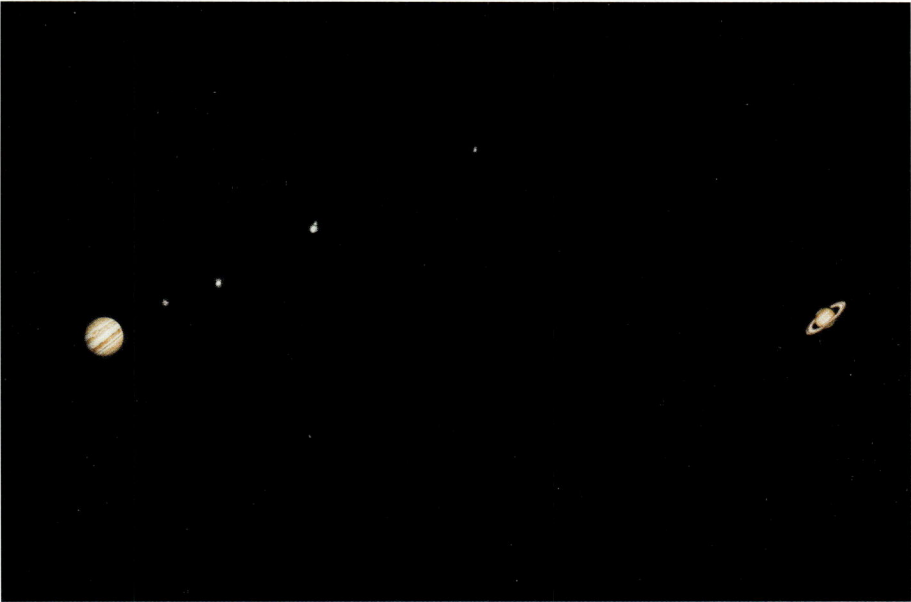

Shooting planets isn't the same as capturing starry skies or even the moon. While bright, they're significantly smaller in the night sky and require finesse (and some serious zoom) to photograph properly. Thanks to their larger sensors and manual settings, both DSLRs and mirrorless cameras are great tools. Their adaptability to various lenses makes them especially suitable, and you can even mount them to most telescopes with adapters. This is also one place a crop-sensor camera is a huge advantage. With its 1.5x to 1.6x crop, it extends your telephoto up to 1.6x the length without a drawback. To bring them into focus and detail, you'll need some serious magnification, so you'll need a telephoto lens—preferably 600mm or longer. I'd prefer to be in the 1000mm+ range for this one. The longer the focal length, the larger the planet will appear in your frame, so this is when a tele-extender or a crop-sensor can be your friend. If you're serious about planetary photography, consider investing in a telescope with a camera adapter—preferably one with a tracker built in, but if not, you'll need to add one. Since your telephoto lens magnifies any movement, even the tiniest shake can blur your shot, so a tripod is a must. Light pollution is your nemesis, so seek out dark areas away from city lights. Due to their size and distance, planets can sometimes appear as star-like points, so zooming in, using Live View, and manually focusing on the planet ensures a sharper image. Start with a fast shutter speed to avoid any movement blur—somewhere around 1/125—and keep your ISO low (100–800) to minimize noise. Depending on the planet's brightness and your lens, your aperture will likely be in the f/5.6 to f/11 range. Due to atmospheric turbulence, shooting planets can be tricky, so consider taking several shots and then stacking them in post to get a clearer image (see Chapters 11 and 12 for more on post-processing).

The Moon

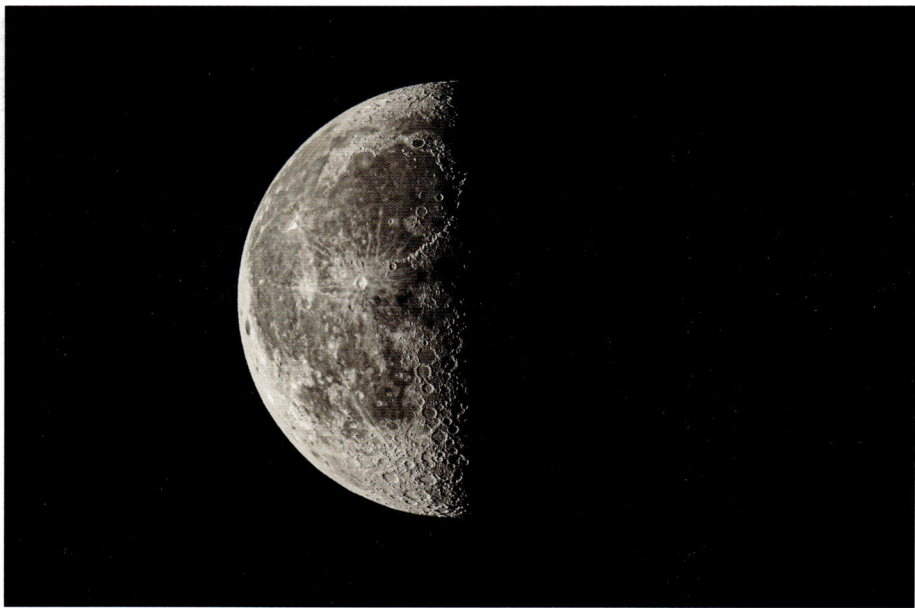

The moon is both a joy and a challenge to photograph. Unlike distant stars and galaxies (see the next page for more on them), the moon is close enough to Earth to showcase detailed craters but also bright enough to easily overexpose in your shots. Your trusty DSLR or mirrorless camera is perfect for this. Pair it with a telephoto lens—think 200mm or longer—to truly capture the moon's details and a sturdy tripod to eliminate shake, given the magnification. If it's a full moon, you can get away with hand-held, but I wouldn't recommend it if you can avoid it. While a full moon is undeniably gorgeous, it's also the brightest, making details harder to capture. A crescent or gibbous phase, where shadows define the craters, can be more visually striking. Given the moon's brightness, it's easy to think you'd treat it like a nighttime subject. Not quite! Treat it like a sunlit subject. Start with the "Looney 11" rule: an aperture of f/11 and shutter speed equivalent to the inverse of your ISO (e.g., ISO 100 with 1/100s shutter speed). Adjust from there based on the moon's phase and brightness. Autofocus can sometimes struggle with the moon, especially if it's not full, so use manual focus, preferably with the assistance of Live View. Zoom in on your LCD to refine that focus and take multiple shots with different settings. Bracket your exposures, capturing some shots slightly underexposed and some slightly overexposed, to ensure you nab the perfect one. The moon's details can be enhanced with a bit of post-processing magic, like sharpening, contrast adjustments, and clarity that can make those craters pop. Remember, photographing the moon is as much an art as it is a science. So, take your time, experiment, and let the moonlight guide your creativity.

Other Galaxies

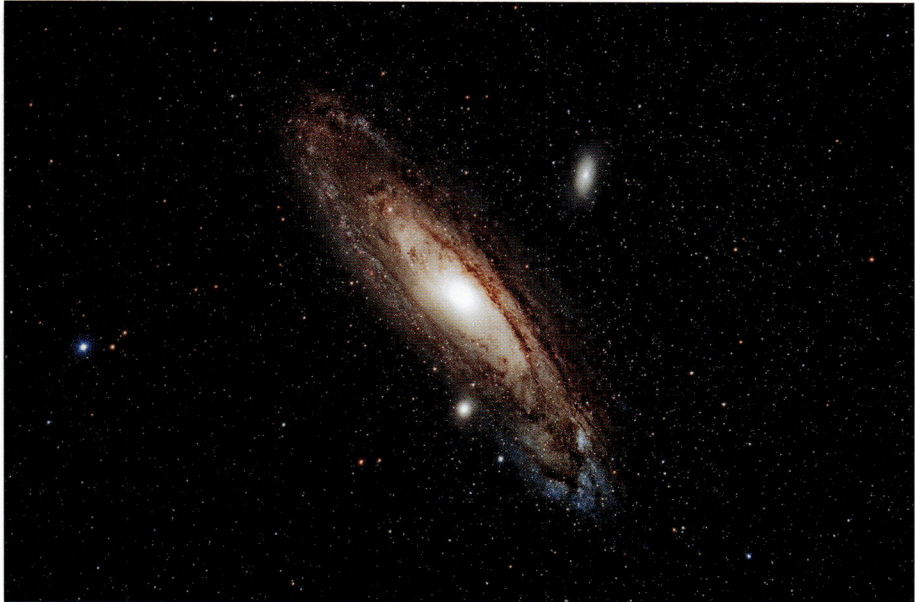

The allure of the Andromeda galaxy (seen here), or M31, has captivated astrono-mers and photographers for years. Not only because of its proximity, but because it's on a collision course with our Milky Way—though that won't happen for another 4 billion years. Until that time, here's how to capture a galaxy: Your mirrorless or DSLR camera can handle this, but a telephoto lens (at least 400mm—as with plan-ets, we need to get close) will get you closer to those galactic details. Stability is paramount, so a robust tripod and a star tracker (to counteract Earth's rotation) are essentials. Light pollution is the nemesis of deep-sky photography, so seek out the darkest skies possible. Check the moon phase—a new moon night or one where the moon sets early is ideal. No clouds? Even better. Manual mode is your friend. Begin with a wide-open aperture and move to a sharper f-stop like f/4, a shutter speed of around 2 to 4 minutes (hence the need for a tracker), and an ISO between 800 and 3200. These settings aren't set in stone—adjust them based on what you see. Auto-focus won't be of much help here, so switch to manual focus, go to infinite, and then use a bright star or planet to get your focus by fine-tuning with Live View. With such faint subjects, capturing multiple exposures and stacking them in post-processing will drastically improve image quality, so consider shooting 20 or more exposures (see page 73 for more on this). Software like DeepSkyStacker can help align and stack your images, reducing noise and bringing out Andromeda's details. Be sure to enhance contrast, sharpness, and color balance to make it pop (see Chapters 11 and 12 for more on post-processing). Lastly, it's crucial to remember patience and practice. Capturing galaxies like Andromeda is a journey, with each session teaching you more about the vast universe and your capabilities as a photographer.

Light Painting in One Exposure

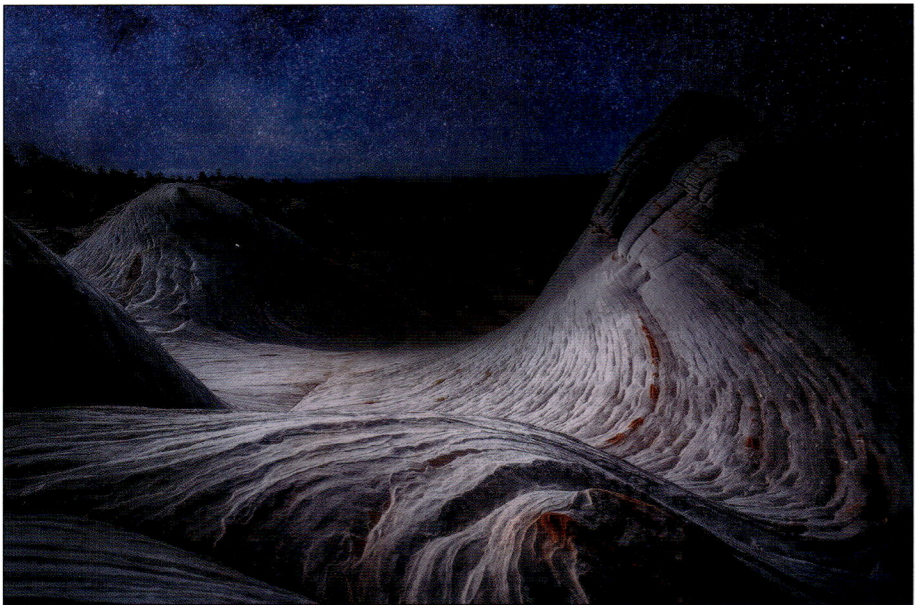

As night photographers, we often face a dilemma: the Milky Way sparkling overhead is adequately exposed, but our foreground lurks in the shadows, almost invisible. Enter low-level light painting—an elegant solution to ensure your foreground doesn't get left in the dark. The key to effective light painting for astrophotography is subtlety—add too much light and you'll overpower the stars. Low-level light painting provides just enough illumination to make the foreground visible without stealing the show from the Milky Way. Think about using continuous LED panels or even your smartphone's screen. They don't need to be high-powered beasts. Just attach a gel or diffuser to soften and warm the light, which ensures it blends naturally with the starlight and turn them down, usually to their lowest settings. For me, a single exposure is the goal, so I start with my camera in manual mode, opting for a wide-open aperture (like f/2.8), a 15- to 25-second shutter speed, and an ISO around 6400, adjusting as needed. Position your light source at an angle to the scene to create depth and texture—I mount mine to light stands outside the scene. Then, I color balance them evenly with the Milky Way, somewhere around 3200K–4200K. If you can't color balance your LEDs, use a gel to change the color toward orange tungsten lights. Rather than shining the light directly at the foreground, skim it across, kind of feathering it up, which enhances texture and avoids hot spots. Experiment with the distance and angle until you get a feel for it. I usually position these dim lights 100–150 feet from my foreground. The power for these lights is usually at the lowest settings and so dim you can barely see them illuminating the scene. Once you've painted your scene with your lights, take a shot and review it on your LCD and look for overly bright areas or harsh shadows. Adjust and try again until it feels just right. Remember, it's all about balance. We'll explore light painting in depth in Chapter 6.

Dealing with Dew

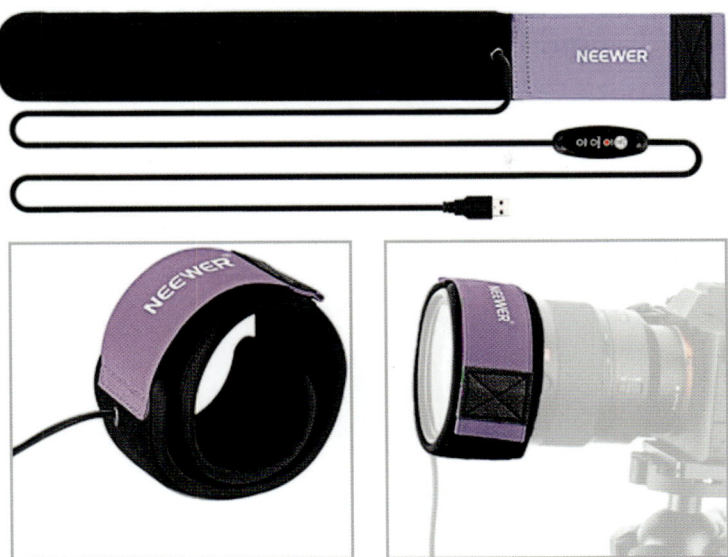

Dew can be both a blessing and a curse for photographers. That early morning dew creates a dreamy atmosphere in landscapes, but becomes a nemesis when you're trying to capture the crisp, clear stars above. It forms when the air cools and can't hold all its moisture, which then condenses on cool surfaces, like your camera lens. Why does that matter? Dew affects clarity. You might have your settings dialed in perfectly, but if a fine mist collects on your lens, your stars will look like blurry blobs. And nothing, I mean nothing, can save a shot once dew sets in. Dew heaters and hand warmers—these are your frontline defense (we looked at these back on page 17). They produce just enough warmth to keep your lens above the dew point, ensuring it stays clear. Looking for a low-fi reliable solution? Strap a couple of hand warmers around your lens using rubber bands. They work similarly to the dew strips, emitting enough warmth to prevent condensation. It's a temporary fix, but it works in a pinch. You can also upgrade to dew strips that are powered by a USB. These provide greater heat and are reuseable since you can recharge the power source. With that said, they take a lot of power and you could run out of power early if you don't have enough. Next, lens hoods aren't just for blocking unwanted light. Lens hoods can also protect against light dew by keeping a little more ambient warmth close to the lens (we talked about this on page 11). Make it a habit to check your lens frequently. If you catch dew forming early, wipe it off gently with a microfiber cloth. When choosing your shooting spot, setting up in places with steady airflow, like hilltops, can reduce the chance of dew formation. Dew is like that uninvited guest at your party. While you can't always prevent it from showing up, you can certainly have measures in place to deal with it promptly. Arm yourself with these tools, and you'll ensure that dew never ruins another stellar astro shot again.

Dealing with Light Pollution

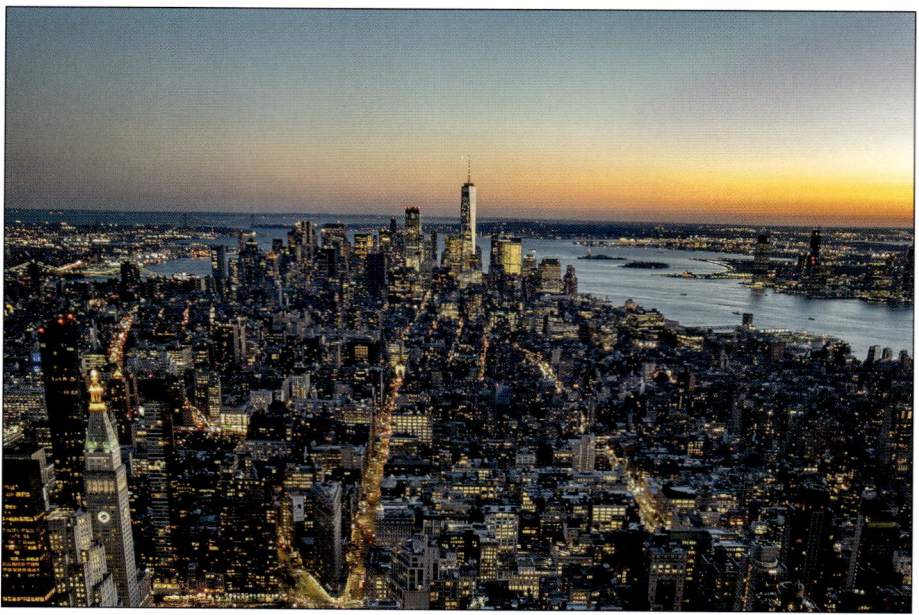

Ah, light pollution, a constant companion and the astrophotographer's frequent foe. It's that pervasive orange or yellowish glow that blankets the horizon in populated areas, drowning out the delicate details of the sky (we talked about it in Chapter 2). If you've ever wondered why you can only see a handful of stars in the city compared to the countryside, this is the culprit. Our cameras, sensitive as they are, amplify this glow, which can overwhelm an image and force us to very low ISO sensitivity. The simplest solution is to get away from it. Light pollution maps are available online and can guide you to dark sky locations. Driving just two hours away from a major city can yield significantly darker skies. What if you can't get that far away? Just as polarizing filters help manage reflections, there are light pollution filters designed to mitigate the effects of certain wavelengths of light pollution (we looked at them on page 15 and will talk about them more on the next page). They can't perform miracles, but in moderately polluted areas, they can give your shots a fighting chance if you just can't get anywhere darker. But, nothing you will filter will be better than just getting to a darker place. Software like Adobe Lightroom or specialized apps like Sequator allow you to reduce light pollution in post-processing, and by adjusting the white balance, reducing highlights, and tweaking color channels, you can reclaim a lot of lost detail. But sometimes, if you can't beat them, you just have to join them and use the ambient light to your advantage. A skyline beneath a starry sky, even with light pollution, can be captivating. It tells a story of nature versus man-made, all in a single frame. The celestial dance of stars and planets has been occurring for eons, and while light pollution may mask its brilliance, it doesn't diminish its beauty.

Do Filters Actually Help?

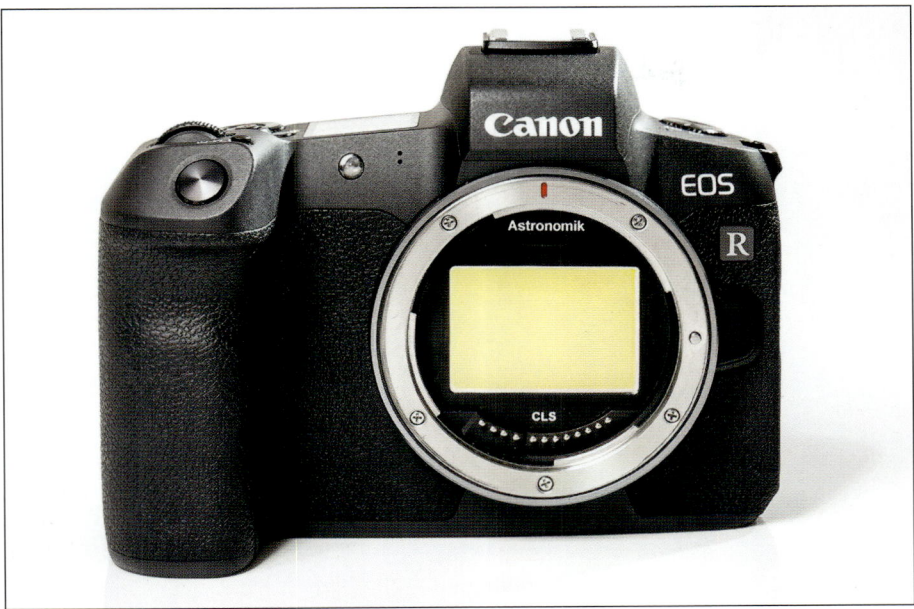

As I mentioned on the previous page, if you've ever tried capturing deep-sky objects or the Milky Way near a city, you know the struggle—light pollution is the enemy. That ugly orange or yellow glow drowns out the stars, kills contrast, and can leave you with a washed-out sky. The good news? Filters can help. The bad news? They're not magic. Light pollution filters cut out certain wavelengths of artificial light, mostly from sodium and mercury vapor streetlights, giving you a darker sky and better contrast. Sounds great, right? Well, yes and no. If you're only a little outside of a city, they can help suppress the glow, but they won't work miracles if you're standing in the middle of downtown. The best solution will always be finding a darker sky. If that's not an option, a good light pollution filter can at least help reduce some of the haze but at the sacrifice of light transmission, which we know is key at night. So, use a light pollution filter only when you absolutely need it. For deep-sky astrophotography, narrowband filters take things to the next level. These filters isolate specific wavelengths of light—Hydrogen-alpha (Ha), Oxygen III (OIII), and Sulfur II (SII)—allowing you to capture nebulae and other deep-sky objects even under moderate light pollution. The catch? You need a modified camera or a dedicated astro camera to really take advantage of them. But if you're serious about deep-sky imaging, these are a game-changer. Then there are neutral density (ND) and polarizing filters. You might be thinking, Wait, those are for daytime shooting! True, but they can be useful for moonscapes and planets, helping to prevent overexposure and bring out details—kind of like sunglasses for your lens. So, do filters make a difference? Yes, but only if used correctly. They won't fix bad conditions, and they're no substitute for proper settings, post-processing, and getting as far from city lights as possible. But in the right situations, they can give your shots a serious edge.

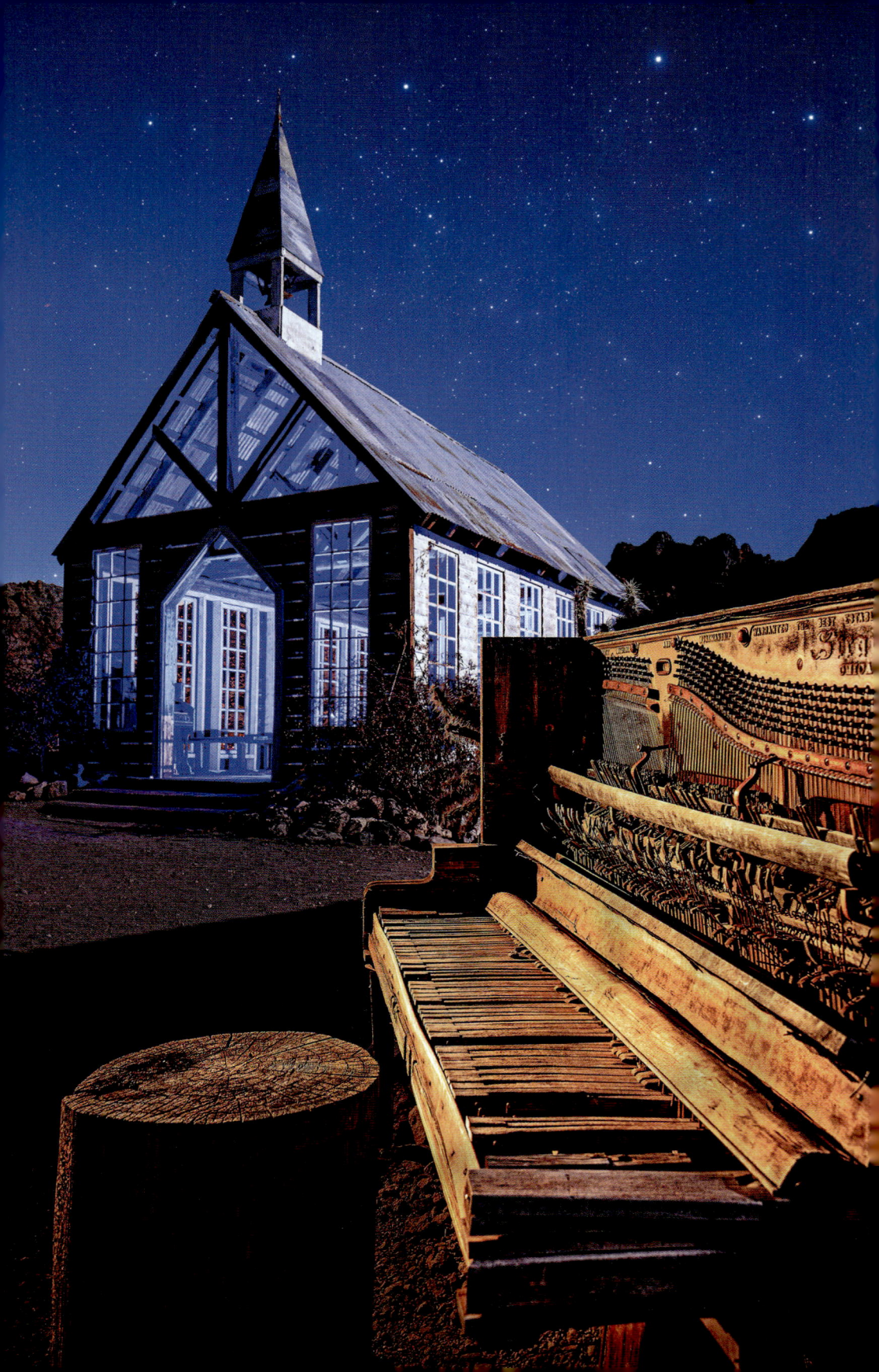

Light Painting

Bringing Your Night Scenes to Life

Night photography is a delicate balance between what's naturally there and what we choose to reveal—the stars, the moon, and the occasional object in the sky. But what about the foreground? What happens when that epic rock formation, twisted tree, or abandoned structure you scouted all day turns into a black void as soon as the sun sets? Light painting is the ultimate cheat code for giving your foreground the attention it deserves without making it look like a crime scene investigation. This chapter is all about using light to sculpt the night, creating depth, texture, and mood without completely overpowering the stars. We'll break down low-level light painting, which is basically the stealth mode of night photography, with no blinding flashes and no random light streaks, just soft, controlled illumination that blends seamlessly into the scene. It's like setting up tiny dim campfires to illuminate your shot, but without the whole "accidentally setting nature on fire" part. But let's be honest—light painting is one of those things that can go very wrong, very fast. Too much light? Your shot looks like it was taken at noon. Too little? Might as well not even try. Wrong color temperature? Congrats, your scene looks like an alien invasion or like it was lit by Soviet-era greenish-blue lighting. We'll go over how to balance light intensity, control color temperature, and use the right angles so your images feel natural and not artificially staged. And because light painting is more art than science, we'll cover different styles and techniques, from soft, ambient glows that gently kiss your foreground to dramatic, high-contrast lighting that makes elements pop. Plus, we'll talk about light wands, bars, and LED panels, so you can go full Jedi master with your illumination game. Light painting isn't about just making something visible; it's about storytelling. It's about using light to guide the viewer's eye through your scene, creating a mood, and enhancing what's already there. When it's done right, it can take your night photography from "pretty cool" to absolutely cinematic. So, let's grab some lights and paint the darkness, without making a mess of it.

Why Light Painting?

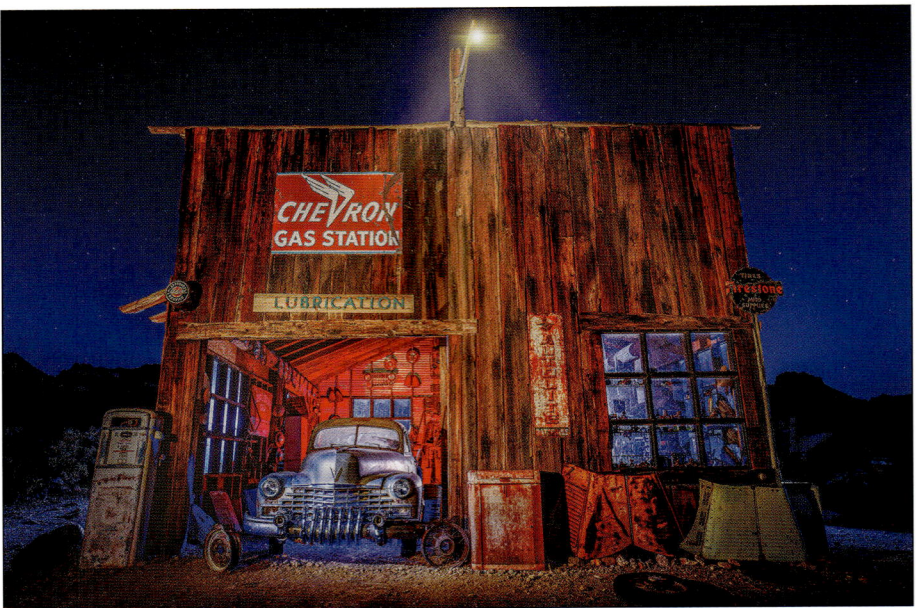

Night photography is akin to painting on a canvas of darkness. While the stars, planets, and occasional meteor provide their own radiant brushstrokes, sometimes the earthly elements of your composition yearn for a touch of light to illuminate their shadows. This is when we use light painting. Imagine standing next to an ancient ruin or beside a twisted, gnarled tree, both barely visible under the night's darkness. With light painting, you can brush light selectively onto these subjects, giving them an illuminated glow that seems to emerge naturally from the darkness. It's about highlighting the depth, texture, and character of subjects that would otherwise remain veiled in shadow. The beauty of light painting is the level of creative control it offers. Unlike stationary lights or flash, your movements can be as fluid or as static as you choose, allowing for dynamic strokes of light that are as unique as your own signature. A slow sweep can provide a gentle, ambient glow, while a quicker pass can produce more defined and dramatic illumination. But why would you want to incorporate this into your shots? First, it allows for a balanced composition where both celestial and terrestrial subjects shine in harmony. Second, it's a fantastic way to guide the viewer's eye through the scene. Our human eyes naturally drift toward light; by painting light onto specific areas, you're determining where you want your viewer to look first and the journey you wish their eyes to take. Light is the language of photography and light painting allows you to write in your own language. And, let's be real, there's an undeniable sense of magic in light painting. It's not just about capturing a scene; it's about interacting with it, merging your own artistic energy with the vastness and depth of the night.

Low-Level Light Painting

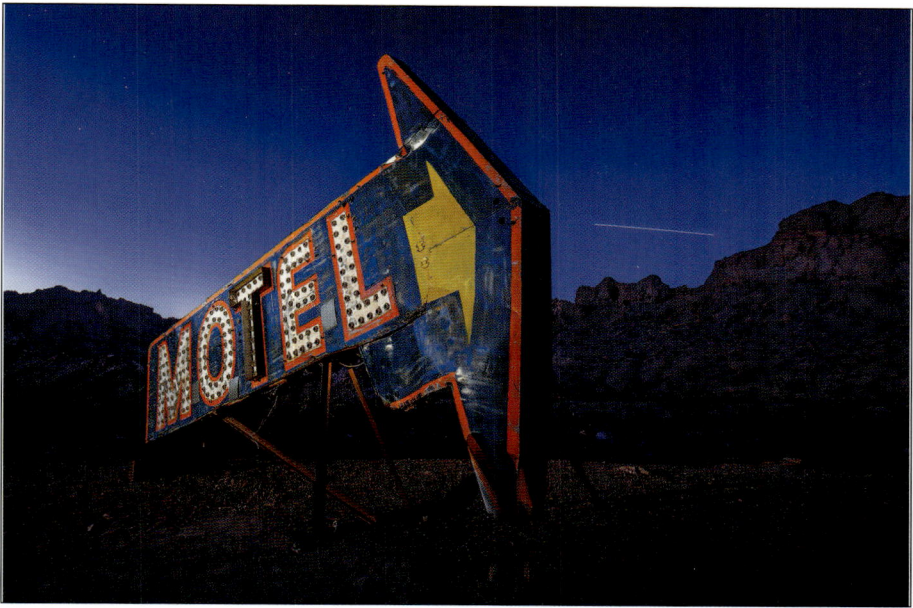

Low-level light painting (LLL) is night photography's answer to studio lighting. This subtle and elegant technique gently lights a scene. Unlike its flamboyant and unreliable cousin, traditional light painting, LLL is all about reliable and repeatable results. The nature of low-level light painting lies in its controlled, continuous lighting. Instead of actively "painting" with bursts from a torch or flashlight, you'll set up dim, consistent light sources (think LED panels, lanterns, or even subtly shielded flashlights), positioned strategically to illuminate your foreground softly. These lights remain on throughout the entire long exposure rather than just for fractions, adding a gentle touch of light to the scene. Why choose LLL over other techniques? Here's where it shines: consistency. Again, LLL provides a steady, predictable light source. You won't find yourself wrestling with varied brush strokes or over-lit sections that traditional light painting can occasionally produce. It's all about achieving balanced lighting. The aim here is not to simulate daylight or brightly light up your foreground. It's about enhancing the night sky, capturing a scene that feels naturally like a night photo but with just enough light to reveal texture, detail, and depth that would otherwise be lost to shadows. There are unintended benefits as it's a more considerate approach, especially in popular night shooting locations, since there's no risk of blinding fellow photographers or disturbing wildlife. Your light setup is unobtrusive, often barely noticeable, yet its impact on the final image is profound. With LLL, you're sculpting with light. The process demands careful placement, adjusting light angles, and choosing the right light intensity to complement the celestial backdrop perfectly. To master LLL is to embrace the philosophy that less is often more. It's a balance of shadows and light, all achieved with a touch so light that it feels like the quarter moon is casting a tender, soft glow on your scene.

Light Painting vs. Low-Level Light Painting

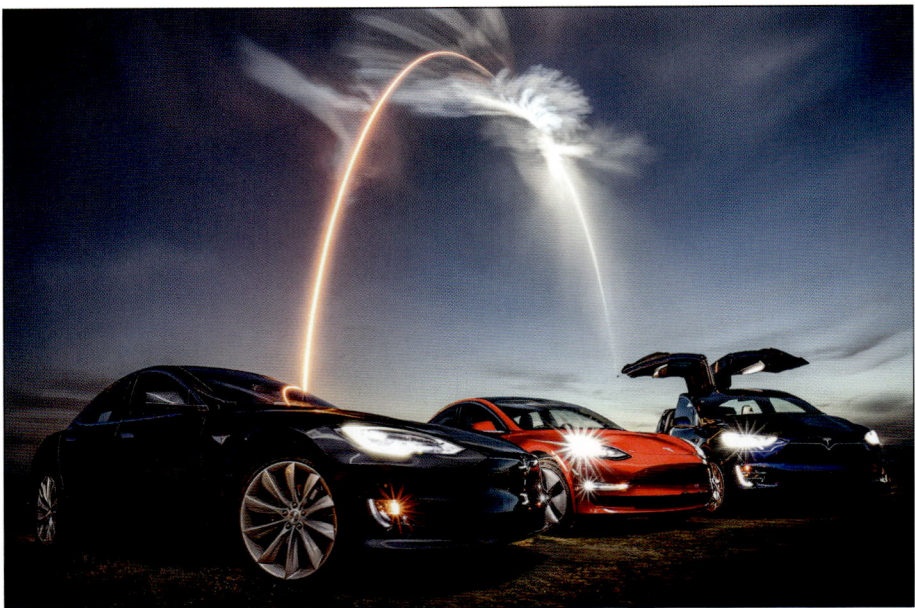

They may seem like siblings of the same family, but dig deeper, and you'll see their distinct personalities. Both serve the ultimate goal: illuminating your nightscapes. However, their methods and impact on the final image differ. Think of light painting as the flamboyant artist of the family, bold and expressive. Using a flashlight or torch, you actively "paint" or "brush" light onto specific subjects during a long exposure. This method requires you to think on your feet, moving and directing light across a scene. The results are dramatic, theatrical compositions where specific elements emerge from the shadows with pronounced emphasis. It's all about timing, direction, and, most importantly, control. Low-level light painting is the more reserved, contemplative sibling. Less "active" than light painting, it uses dim, continuous lighting throughout an exposure. Often using LED panels or lanterns set at minimal brightness, the goal is to gently light the landscape without overpowering the stars or other celestial features. It is less about dynamic movement and more about strategic placement, balancing ambient light with the sky's natural glow. Its outcome is a softer, more ambient feel, maintaining the scene's nighttime essence but with added depth and clarity. Which is right for you? If you love being part of the scene, playing with light and shadow, traditional light painting might be your thing. It offers more direct control and can lead to striking, unique images where the act of creation is as enjoyable as the result. However, if subtlety is your jam, and you'd rather capture a scene that retains a more natural, undisturbed feel, low-level light painting might be the way to go. It's especially useful in locations with other photographers, ensuring you don't disrupt their shots with abrupt flashes. Or, like me, just embrace both. Whichever you choose, remember: both methods are just tools in your ever-expanding night photography toolbox. Experiment with both.

Blending Color Temperatures

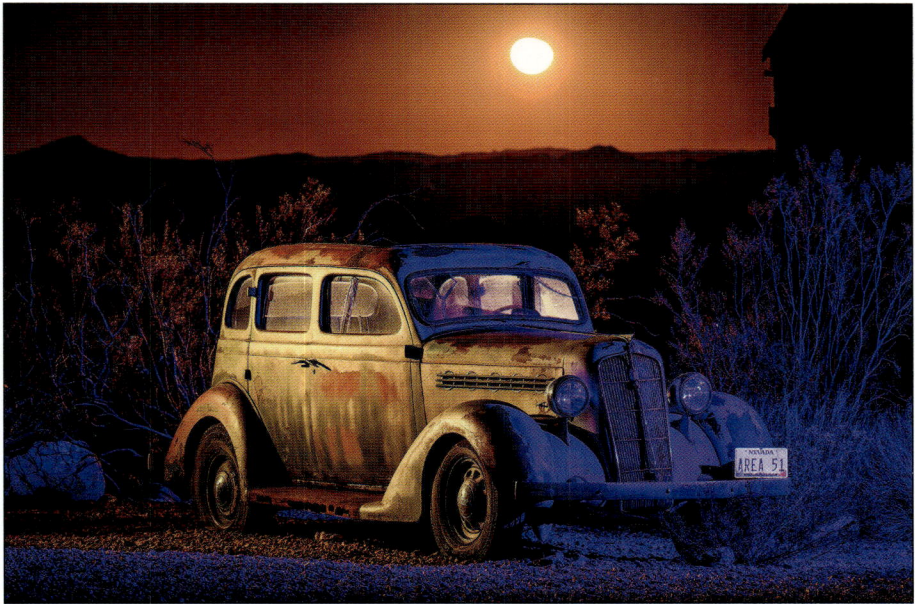

Light painting feels like magic, but when you introduce different color temperatures, the results can be downright enchanting. It's like painting with both light and color, adding new depths and dynamics to your nightscapes. A quick refresher: Color temperature refers to the hue of light sources and is measured in kelvins (K). Warm light (like candlelight) can sit around 2700K, while daylight can hover around 5500K, and cooler, blue-toned light can surpass 6500K. With light painting at night, you'll probably want to start out by using warm LEDs or gels to accentuate specific elements, like rocks or trees, giving them a warm, inviting feel. Contrast this with cooler lights for other parts of the scene, and you introduce a dynamic play between the two, making key elements in your scene pop. But we have to remember to mimic natural sources of light, so we use color temperatures to replicate them. A subtle orange LED can evoke the warmth of a campfire, while a cooler tone might hint at moonlight. It's about crafting a story with light where the illumination has a purpose. A night sky usually has a warmer temperature. Warm low-level light painting can provide a beautiful complement to this, creating a dynamic balance in your composition. Conversely, cooler lights can give the scene a more harmonious feel. For example, if you're shooting near urban areas, there might be ambient light pollution. So, use color temperatures in your light painting that complement or counterbalance this ambient glow. You can neutralize an orange streetlight glow with cooler-toned light painting of the same brightness. Shooting RAW? (You should be!) You can fine-tune color temperatures in post, giving you leeway to experiment in the field and refine later. However, when mixing color temperatures in light painting, it's like introducing a new element to your scene. Each hue and shade brings its own mood, emotion, and drama to your night photos. Don't go too far—it should be subtle.

Lights for Light Painting

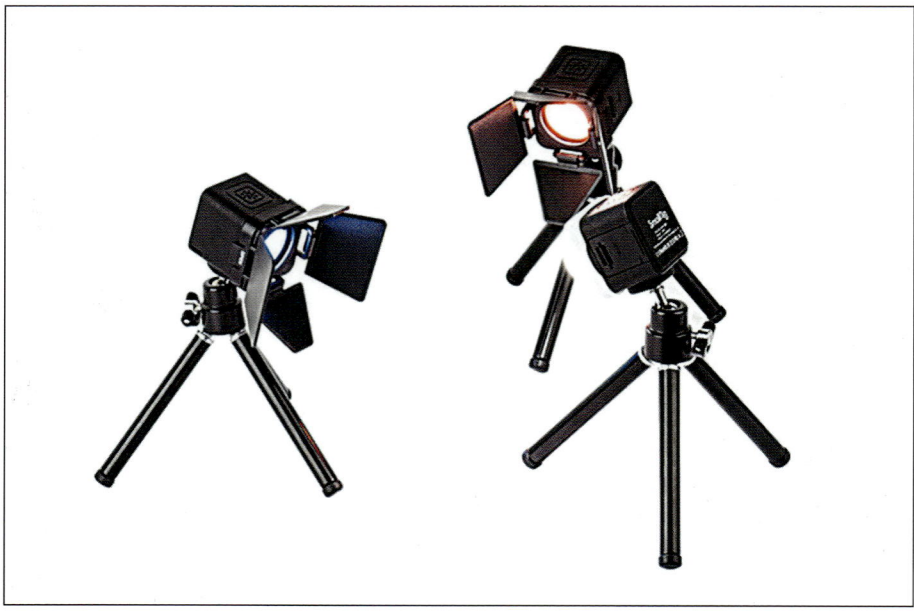

The idea with light painting is not to flood your scene with light, but to gently brush it with light, enhancing texture and detail, making the terrestrial elements pop against the Milky Way or starry backdrop. So, I suggest that you ditch the intensely bright flashlights. Not that they don't have a place, but for a more controlled spread, opt for adjustable LED panels, hopefully with diffusion. They're versatile, offer a consistent light source, and many even come with color temperature control. Just be sure they can be dimmed to tweak the intensity to your liking. Most lights that I use have a wireless remote, which lets you adjust the brightness from a distance. You can place your light source, go to your camera, and dial in the amount of light you need without dashing back and forth. Next, modify that light! Adding gels can introduce color to craft a mood, while adding more and more diffusion to soften the light, eliminating harsh shadows. Remember, you're going for subtle light, and it's not just about the tool, but how you use it. Think of light as liquid—the closer you are, the more concentrated it is. Pulling your light source farther away and angling it can create a softer, broader light spread. Some scenes might benefit from a continuous light source, while others only need a brief light stroke. Try both. And, if you're out in the field for a while, having an external power bank can keep your light sources powered. If like me, you like to use low-level light painting, you're going to need portable light stands. I prefer ones that pack down small and fit in my backpack, however any stand will do. The key here is having something that will allow you to adjust the angle of the light. Low-level light painting in astro-landscapes is all about nuance. It's not about creating a daylight scene; it's about gently revealing what's there, allowing stars and landscape to share the stage harmoniously.

Settings for Low-Level Light Painting

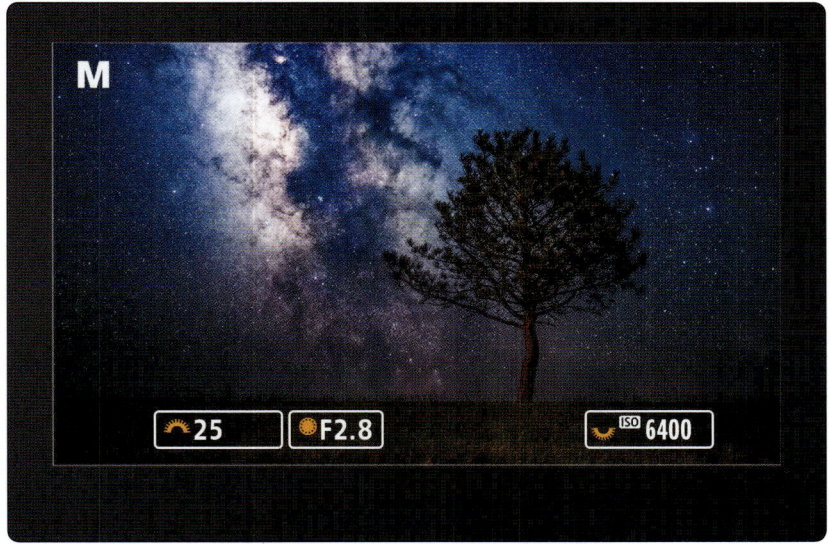

Astrophotography's first rule is to let the stars shine. But ensuring your foreground isn't left in the shadows can be just as hard of a task. Low-level light painting requires subtlety, and getting your settings right is crucial. First, stick with a wide aperture, typically f/2.8. This allows your camera to gather light efficiently both for the stars and the low-level light you introduce. Next, your shutter speed primarily focuses on capturing the stars without trailing—somewhere between 15–25 seconds, depending on the focal length of your lens—and the wider the lens, the longer the exposure before the stars trail. During this exposure time, you have a window to apply your light. Whether you shine your light source for the entire duration or for just a part of it will determine the intensity of the light painting. Start with an ISO setting of 6400. Remember, raising ISO increases sensitivity but also introduces noise. But here's the thing: since you're introducing external light (even if it's just a little bit), you might find that you can occasionally drop the ISO a tad for cleaner shots. Begin with the dimmest setting on your light source and aim for the least amount of light that reveals the desired details. If your light source allows for adjusting color temperature, warm tones (around 3200K) can often complement the night sky. However, this is subjective and can be adjusted based on the mood you're aiming for. The bottom line is that your settings won't change too much when you introduce a little bit of light, and that's the goal. We put just enough light into the scene to balance it.

Light Painting Techniques

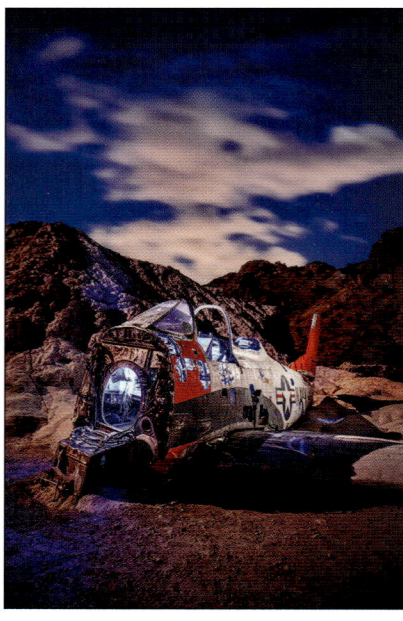

Venturing into the realm of night photography, you're not just battling the darkness; you're seeking to master it. With several techniques at your disposal, you can craft scenes that astound and mystify. Let's go through a few of them that I use all the time: Instead of directly shining a light onto the subject, cast it from the side. This technique brings out texture, especially in rugged landscapes, creating a dramatic interplay of light and shadow. Next, use a reflective surface (like a white board or even a rock) to bounce your light source onto the subject. It diffuses the light, softening it, and provides a gentle glow rather than a direct shine. Try placing the light source behind objects to create silhouettes or to emphasize translucent subjects, like leaves or tent fabric. This can add depth and layers to your composition. Concentrate light on a particular subject or area, leaving the rest in relative darkness. This directs the viewer's attention and can emphasize a focal point, whether it's a lone tree or a rock formation. Like I mentioned earlier, colored gels can be placed over your light source to introduce different hues—blue can mimic moonlight, while warmer colors can add an ethereal touch to specific parts of your landscape. Some photographers use "light brushes", moving the light source during the exposure to either evenly light a larger area or give a hint of motion. Many modern torches and lamps allow you to adjust the intensity—this is invaluable. Being able to dim your light source helps to prevent overpowering the scene. Try slowly panning a beam of light across the scene during the exposure. This technique, when mastered, can give an even coverage, especially over larger areas. Just remember: light painting isn't about flooding the darkness with light; it's about revealing the details from the shadows, complementing the stars above. Practice each technique, and in time, you'll develop an intuition and a sense of how to light up your scene.

Low-Level Light Painting Styles

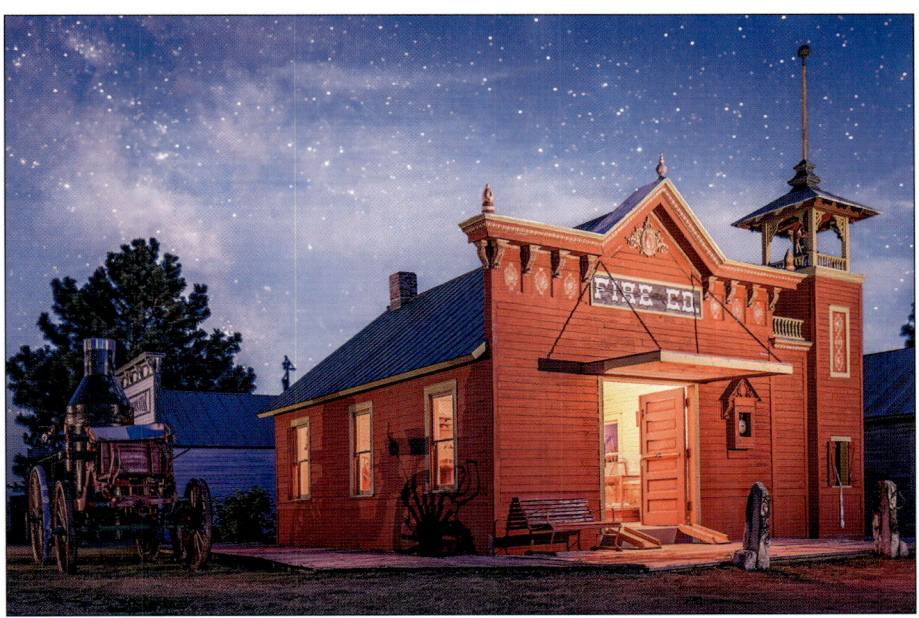

There are a bunch of styles I apply to my low-level light painting, a technique that, when mastered, can really make an impact, and each style has its own allure:

Soft ambiance: The intention is subtlety. Using soft, diffused lighting, gently reveal the foreground's contours and textures without overpowering the night sky.

Dramatic contrasts: By applying intense light from sharp angles, sculpt the landscape with bold contrasts, which brings out striking shadows and might lean into a more surreal or theatrical vibe.

Monochromatic moods: Using colored filters or gels, bathe the scene in a single hue. Whether it's a cool blue that whispers of moonlit nights or a fiery red that speaks of alien terrains, this style can transport viewers to realms beyond our own.

Layered illumination: By lighting various elements in the frame separately and then blending them in post, you can achieve a layered, multidimensional effect, crafting a narrative within the image.

Backlit silhouettes: Placing the light source behind a subject creates an ethereal silhouette that glows as if they're backlit by the sky. This style paints a contrast of shadows and form, highlighting the interplay between light and darkness.

Interactive elements: Add human subjects or props interacting with the light source, holding lanterns, tracing patterns with light sticks, or casting light beams skyward.

Lighting a sculpture: Treat the landscape as a sculpture, and use light to chisel, define, and mold it, revealing facets and depths hidden with harsh or flat illumination.

Using Light Bars and Light Wands

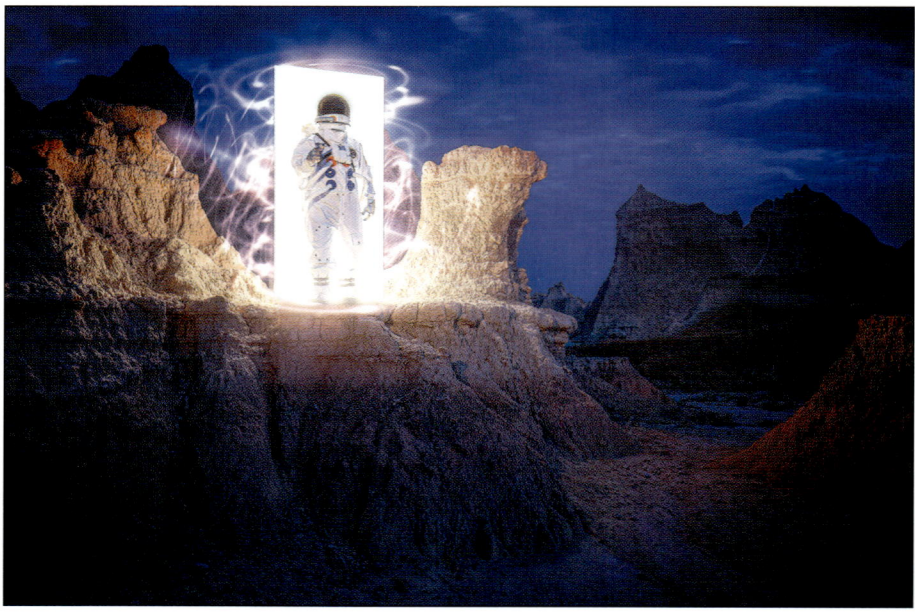

Two of the most magical things in my light painting toolbox are light bars and light wands. Light bars are elongated light sources, often resembling fluorescent tubes, which emit a continuous and uniform glow. Their primary charm lies in their ability to cast broad and even light, perfect for creating an ambient mood in larger spaces or when showcasing vast terrains. Imagine a dark, rugged canyon softly unveiled by the gentle sweep of a light bar, or an old ruin coming alive under its glow. Light wands are more versatile and often more dynamic and come with an array of features that can be tailored to your whims. Some are color-adjustable, others have variable brightness settings, and a few even boast strobing or patterned effects. With their slender form, they're perfect for intricate designs and more deliberate, controlled strokes. A light wand might be your tool of choice for sketching ethereal glyphs in the air or highlighting intricate details of a statue or monument. Both tools, due to their form factor, can be used for creating mesmerizing streaks or trails of light in long-exposure shots, adding movement and dynamism to the frame. Whether you intend to have a ghostly apparition or a fiery trail, these tools deliver.

Adding Light Streaks

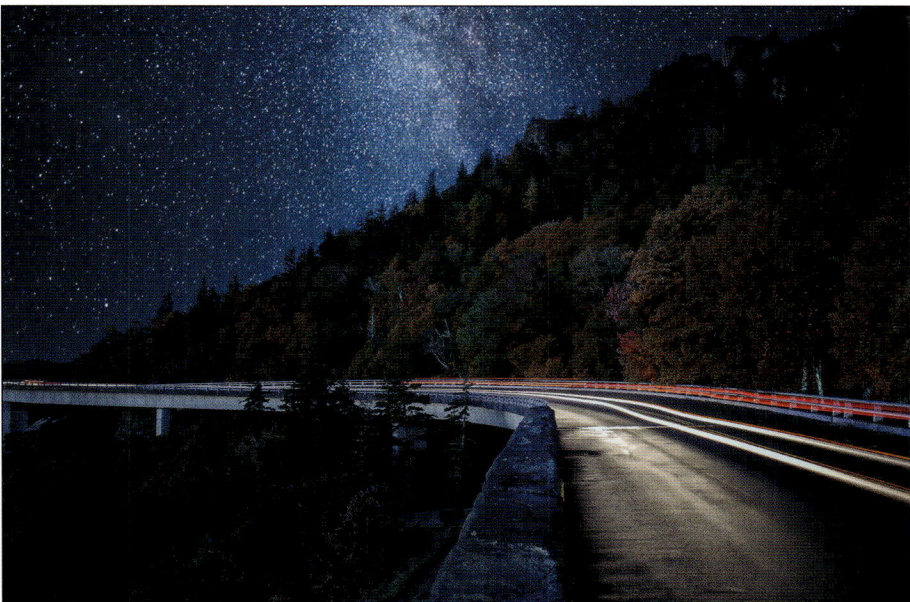

Light streaks are bright light sources that rapidly move through your frame, like car headlights or a passing jet. They're dynamic lines and patterns formed by the deliberate movement of light sources during a long exposure, and they transform the frame from a static capture to a dynamic scene. I love these because it's an elegant ballet, where beams become ballerinas and darkness their stage, and we can position the dancers in a frame to lead the viewer's eye into the scene. You could summon a celestial scene where streaks mimic falling stars, or create an urban narrative, giving the illusion of neon traffic in a desolate landscape. The beauty of light streaks lies in their unpredictability and uniqueness—no two streaks are ever truly identical. To achieve compelling light streaks, you must visualize their intended path and motion. Steady, deliberate movements yield uniform streaks, while quicker, erratic motions produce jagged, energetic trails. The choice of light tool, its color, and its brightness, add layers to this radiant tale. Yet, it's not just about the streaks. It's about the harmony they achieve with the environment. How a streak echoes the curve of a river, or how it highlights the arch of a natural doorway, adds depth and context to the frame. Light streaks in light painting aren't just a technique; they're a form of storytelling.

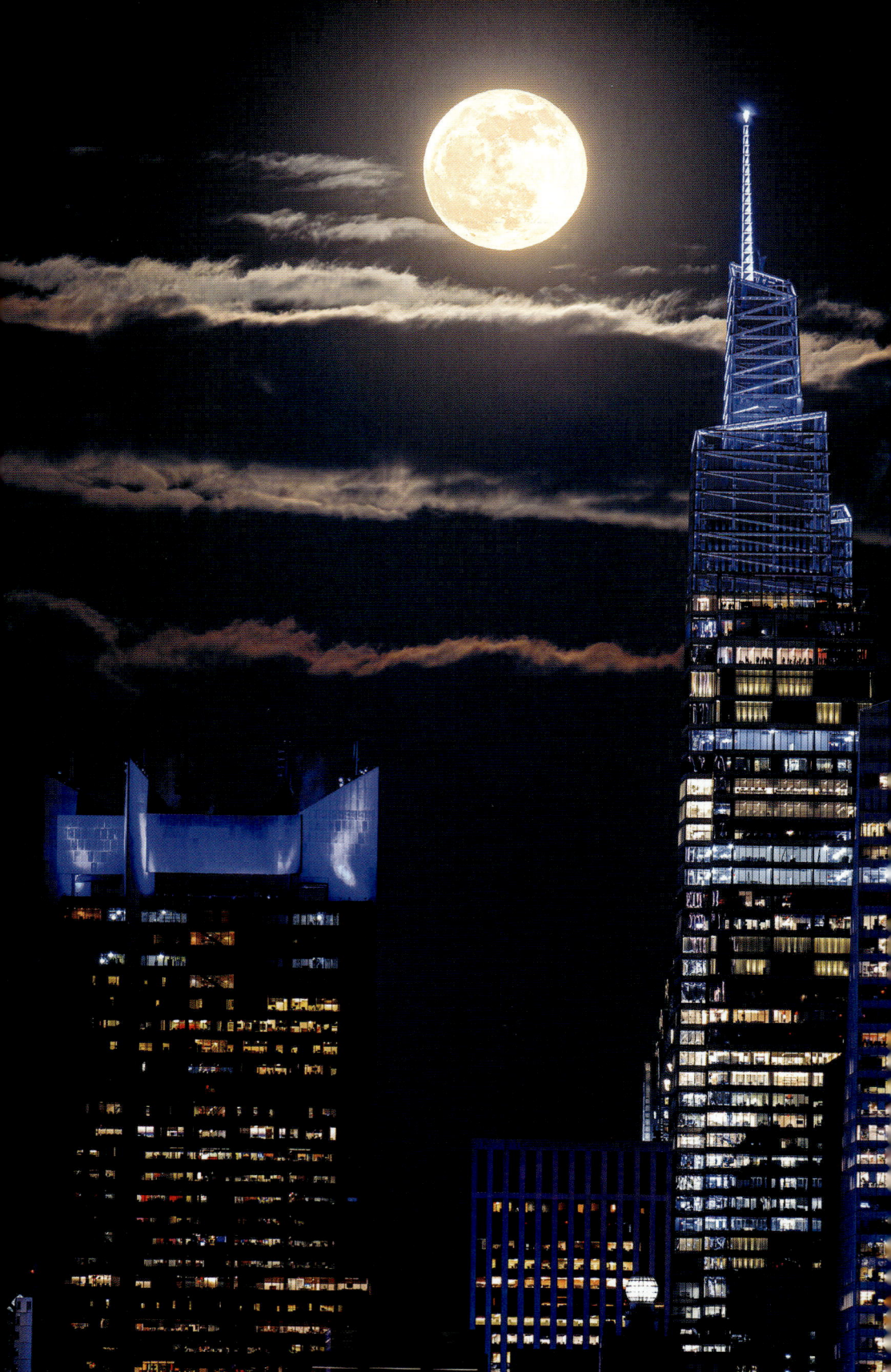

7

Nighttime Cityscapes

Capturing the Pulse of the City After Dark

Shooting cityscapes at night is like trying to conduct an orchestra where half the musicians are neon billboards, the other half are blinding streetlights, and somewhere in the background, a car's headlights completely wreck your exposure. Welcome to the challenge (and thrill) of nighttime city photography, where chaos meets composition, and light is both your best friend and worst enemy. This chapter is all about finding order in the madness and using the city's glow to your advantage. We'll talk about how to balance bright highlights and deep shadows so your shots don't look like an overexposed mess. You'll learn how to embrace reflections, using wet streets, glass buildings, and even puddles to double the drama of your frame. And of course, we'll cover how to use long exposures to turn the city's energy into art, whether that means capturing car light trails, smoothing out water reflections, or blurring the movement of busy streets into a dreamlike scene. Timing is everything with cityscapes. And, twilight, a.k.a. blue hour, is your golden ticket. It's when the city lights turn on but the sky still holds just enough natural light to balance your exposure. It's like nature and urban life decided to work together for once and the result? Absolute photographic gold. And yes, we have to talk about tripods and the infamous tripod police. If you've ever been setting up for a shot only to have security wave you away like you're planning a heist, you know the struggle. But, don't worry, I've got solutions, from using a Platypod for low-profile stability to finding ledges that double as makeshift tripods. Shooting cityscapes is about more than just getting the exposure right. It's about capturing the vibe of the city—the movement, the colors, the way artificial light breathes life into concrete and glass. Let's step into the glow and master the art of shooting cities after dark.

Chasing Twilight

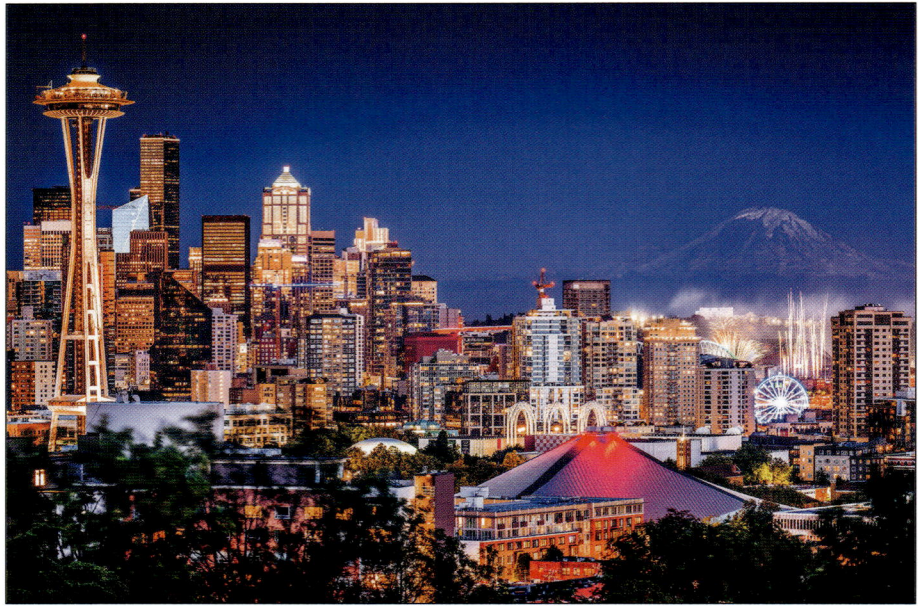

Twilight is the moment that lingers after the sun sets and arrives just before sunrise, sometimes called blue hour. For cityscape photographers, this is the best time to capture dramatic cityscapes. During twilight, the ambient light hangs in a delicate balance, not overwhelmingly drowning out the night's lights. It melds seamlessly with the city's own artificial luminance, ensuring neither steals the show. And oh, the skies at twilight! Hues of deep blue and purple with a warm glow from the setting sun, offer a rich backdrop that amplifies the glint of city lights, making sky-scrapers gleam and streets sparkle. Yet, it's not just about the lights. Twilight retains just the right amount of natural glow to accentuate the intricate architectural details of buildings that might otherwise disappear. Plus, Earth's atmosphere acts like a huge reflector, reflecting the light from the play of light and shadow—so unique to this time—bringing out the vibrancy of colors in a way that's starkly different from the harsh contrasts of full-blown nighttime. Neon signs shimmer with a soft intensity, and streetlights cast a gentle glow rather than glaring beams. Twilight also offers a chance to show the dance of time. Longer exposures during this period blur the bustling city movement—cars turn into streaks of light and pedestrians merge into a fluid motion. This dynamic activity contrasts beautifully with the stillness of towering buildings, creating a photo that is alive with energy yet sharp with detail. And above all, there's an undeniable mood that twilight brings—one of transitions, of change, and of anticipation. As day transitions to night, twilight captures our cit-ies in their best light.

Capturing City Lights

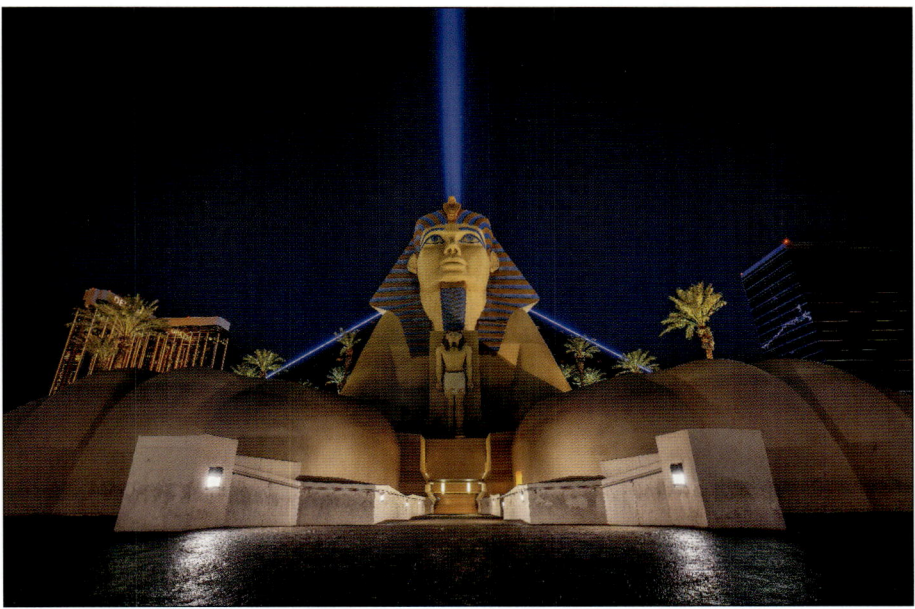

City lights—from towering skyscrapers to a streetlamp at the corner café—are both a blessing and a challenge in nighttime photography. They paint the city in light, but mastering them requires a balancing act. As evening falls, and the city begins to illuminate, the first lights are often the gentlest. The cobalt blue of the night's sky offers a muted backdrop against which the initial flickers of neon, LED, and tungsten glow, making their presence known. It's a time of soft contrasts and emerging patterns. But as darkness descends, these lights multiply and intensify—bright billboards, streaming car headlights, window glows, and shimmering reflections off tranquil waters. These light sources, each with its own color temperature and intensity, can be overwhelming, but they're not insurmountable. Underexposure usually helps here. Another thing we can do is embrace the reflections. Water bodies, like a calm river or a recent rain's puddle, transform city lights into mesmerizing mirror images, doubling the drama and depth of your frame (see page 105 for more on this). But be careful as those bright spots can lead to distracting lens flares. The key is balance—not every light deserves the spotlight. Metering is your compass here, as it measures light from a small area to get the right exposure for your subject. Spot metering can help isolate and prioritize, ensuring that your subject—either a historic building or a bustling street—is perfectly illuminated while background lights accentuate rather than dominate. Yet, amidst this bright glow, never lose sight of the shadows because they possess the contrast that brings a cityscape alive. Capturing city lights is like conducting a symphony. Each light has its own rhythm, and the trick is bringing them together to create a photo that really nails the city's nighttime vibe.

White Balance & Warmth

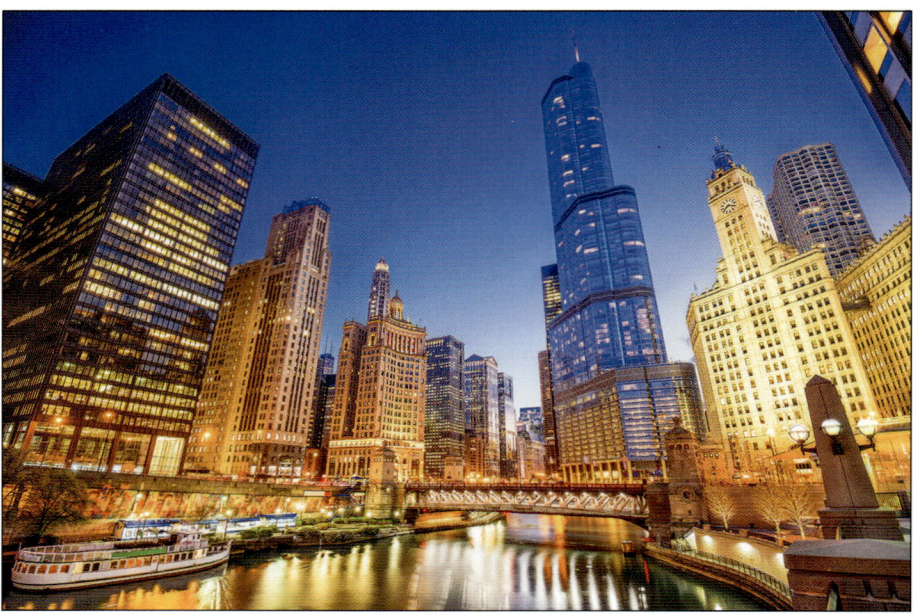

Imagine the city as a grand theater: the lights, its actors; the buildings, its set; and the shadows, its backdrop. As a photographer, your role isn't just to capture the play; it's to be the director, deciding on the mood and tone of your scene. This is where white balance comes in, where warmth and coolness balance, and your image's tone is sculpted. At the heart of the city's pulse is its warmth. Those glowing street-lights, the amber tint of a café's window, or the golden hue of a distant building, they all give life to the city's heartbeat. But, set your white balance too warm, and your city might appear as if it's submerged in a sea of reddish orange. Too cool, and you risk draining its vibrancy, rendering it in sterile and lifeless greeny blues. This is where luminosity masking in post becomes your friend. With it, you can selectively add warmth to those city lights, making them pop, drawing your viewer's eye right where you want it (see Chapter 12 for more on post-processing). But, don't forget about the city's mysterious alleys and its silent streets, bathed in the gentle embrace of moonlight or the distant glow of a neon sign. These shadows, often leaning toward cooler hues, provide depth and contrast to your warm lights. Using luminosity masking, again, cool down these shadow details. It's like adding a gentle blue filter, creating a more pleasing and visually coherent tone to the scene. Mastering the delicate balance between warmth and coolness, especially in a scene as dynamic as a city at night, sets a great nighttime cityscape apart. It's about recognizing the city's dual nature, its bustling warmth and night coolness, and using white balance to weave these elements into a photo that's both vibrant and harmonious. (*Note:* See page 44 for more on white balance settings.)

The Art of Under-the-Radar Cityscape Shooting

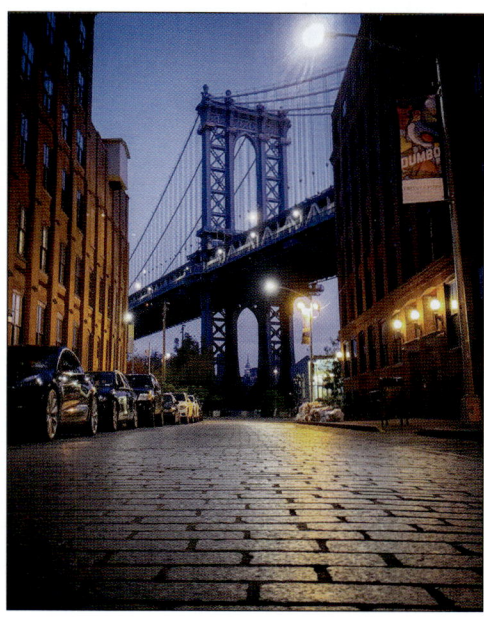

Navigating the city at night, camera in hand, is much like being a secret agent on a covert mission. Your objective? Capture the city's essence without drawing unwanted attention, especially from the ever-watchful tripod police. Why? Because as I'm sure you've noticed by now, a tripod is essential in night photography. But, they tend to be frowned upon in certain locations by security since they can be a liability and a safety hazard. How do you avoid the tripod police? By using a small, inconspicuous tripod, or even better, a Platypod (we looked at it on page 6). While a small tripod can be a lifesaver, offering portability and quick setup, a Platypod takes stealth shooting to a whole new level. Think of it as your photography secret agent. Sleek, flat, and incredibly versatile, it lets you set up shots from unique low angles, or on surfaces where a traditional tripod might not work. A Platypod can be placed on a ledge, a bench, or even on the ground. But, its inconspicuous nature doesn't mean a compromise on stability as it offers a rock-solid base for your camera, ensuring you get those tack-sharp shots, even with longer exposures. By keeping a low profile, you not only evade the prying eyes of the tripod police, but also immerse yourself deeper into the city's narrative. There's freedom in being unobtrusive, allowing you to truly observe, connect, and capture the city's heartbeats without disruption. In the world of nighttime cityscape photography, sometimes the best gear isn't the biggest or most obvious. It's the tools that allow you to blend in, to be part of the scene, and to shoot with both confidence and discretion.

The Magic of Long Exposures

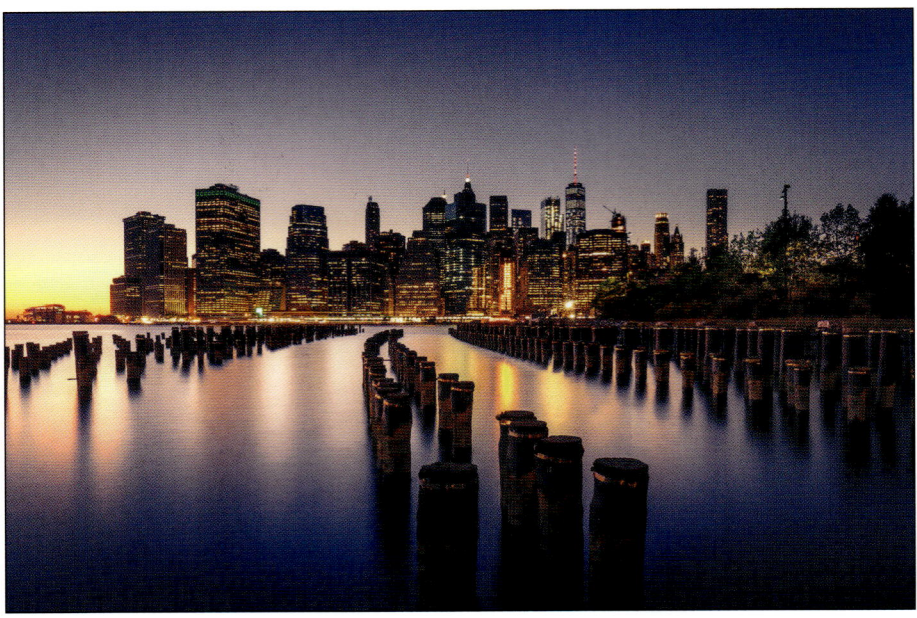

Imagine the city at night as a bustling, living organism. Cars race by, and as we learned when talking about light streaks (on page 95), they leave streaks of light in their wake. With longer exposure times, pedestrians blur into ghost-like apparitions. Skyscrapers stand tall, their windows twinkling like stars. Now, what if you could capture all that dynamic energy in one frame, freezing time while letting the city move? Enter the art of long exposure. Nighttime cityscapes can be about light and motion, and long exposure is your tool to weave them together. By keeping your camera's shutter open for extended periods, you allow light to pour into your sensor, even at a lower ISO. But it's not just about the lights. Long exposures can also reveal the subtle textures hidden in the shadows, creating a rich contrast that makes your images pop. The glistening wet roads after a light drizzle, the gentle ripples on a placid river, or the sweep of clouds across the moonlit sky—all these nuances come alive with this technique. Now, you might wonder about the challenge of shooting long exposures amid city hustle. What about camera shake or unwanted elements entering your frame? This is where stability meets preparation. A solid tripod or a reliable support like the Platypod is crucial. And remember to scout your location in advance, considering angles that showcase the city's movement yet provide a semblance of stillness. One crucial tip: embrace patience. Long exposure is as much a meditative process as it is a technical one. It's about projecting the city in slow motion in your frame, appreciating every nuanced shift and every fleeting moment. So, the next time you're in the heart of the city after dusk, don't just snap and go. Set up, slow down, and let the city motion reveal its nighttime tale on your sensor.

Crafting Time-Lapses

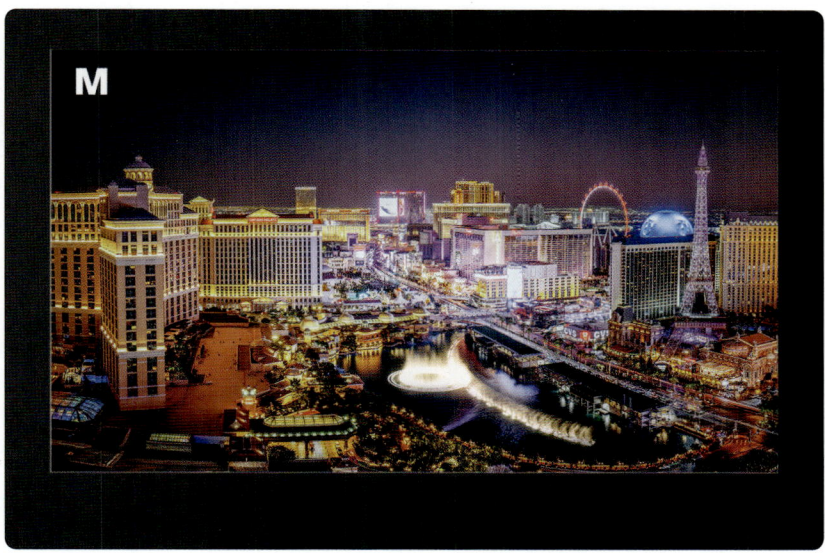

Time-lapses allow you to capture the world in a unique way. A bustling intersection, with its never-ending stream of traffic, turns into a vibrant dance of lights. Skyscrapers, often static in our everyday observation, appear as living entities as clouds drift by in their windows and the light reflections flicker. And the gradual transition from twilight's blue hour to the deep darkness of night becomes a mesmerizing visual journey. Nighttime cityscapes present their challenges for time-lapse photography, though, because light conditions change dramatically. One moment, you're balancing the last golden rays of sunset, and the next, you're adjusting for neon signs and streetlights. So, mastery here requires understanding of your camera's manual settings. Adjusting your exposure settings to account for the decreasing ambient light is essential, ensuring you capture the city's glow without underexposing or overexposing your sequence. And let's not forget interval settings. Decide on the duration of your time-lapse and the playback speed, and based on that, set an interval that captures the movement smoothly. For busy streets, shorter intervals like 2–3 seconds might work, while for slower transitions, like cloud movements or fading twilight, 10–15 seconds could be ideal. And, as I've repeated many, many times, stability is key. Any shake or movement can disrupt the sequence, so a sturdy tripod is your best ally, and using tools like an intervalometer can make the process seamless. Lastly, embrace the movement. Time-lapses are more than just sped-up videos; they're stories in the motion of the city. Your job is to tell the tale of the city as it transitions from evening into night, capturing its essence, its soul, in still frames sequenced together in a video. (*Note:* See Chapter 9 for more on time-lapses.)

Capturing Silhouettes

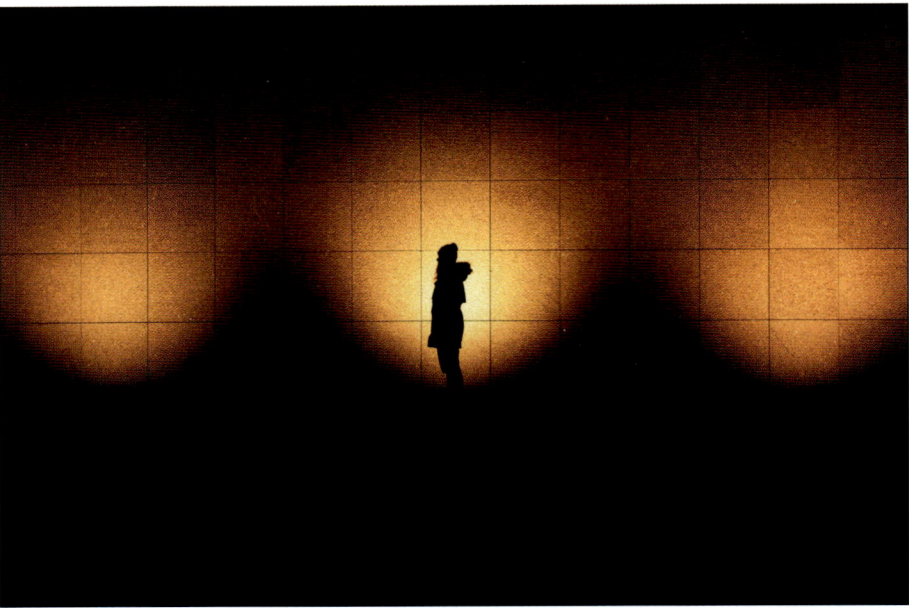

The bright lights of the city might, at first, seem like a night photographer's arch-nemesis. But, they can be your most unexpected allies. City lights are diverse. From the warm tungsten glow of streetlamps to the cold blue LED hues, and the vibrant neons of signboards, they paint the cityscape with an eclectic mix of tones. This spectrum of colors can add depth, contrast, and intrigue to your images. When you position yourself to shoot with lights—instead of against them—you'll find they can add a dramatic backdrop or even serve as a leading line guiding viewers through your composition. Plus, you can use these lights as key lights or main lights to light up a subject or a model you want to position into a cityscape. Silhouettes and shadows are integral to night photography. Strong city lights, especially from behind your main subjects, can cast intriguing shadows, creating mystery and depth. Whether it's the silhouette of a person waiting at a lit bus stop or long, stretching shadows of trees against a building's illuminated facade, these moments capture the essence of night-time urban life. However, with great power comes great responsibility. It's easy to get overwhelmed by the brightness and end up with overexposed images. Regularly check your camera's histogram and adjust your settings accordingly (see Chapter 3 for more on settings). A slightly underexposed shot can always be corrected in post, but blown-out highlights from bright lights are often lost forever.

Adding Movement with Reflections

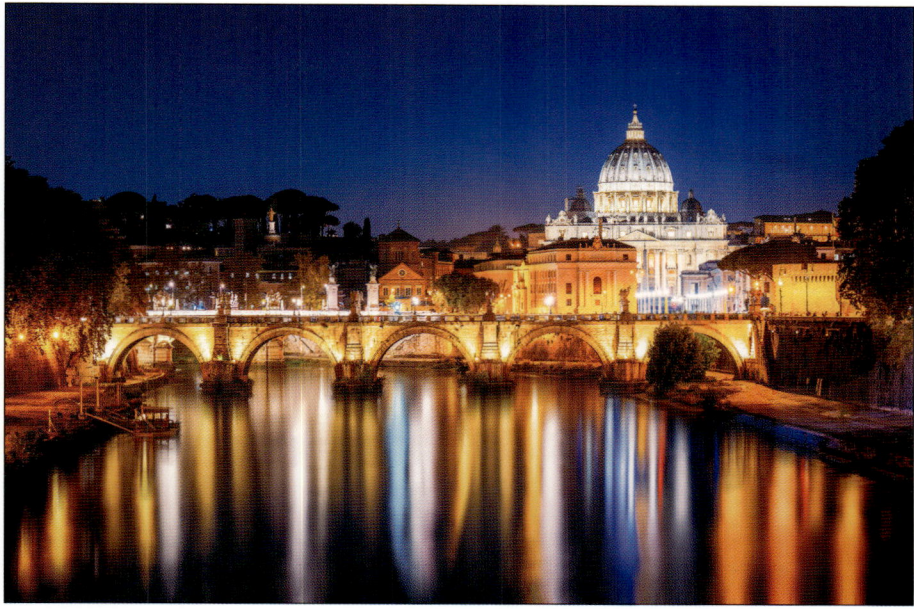

City lights don't just illuminate buildings—they reflect, bounce, and shimmer off every surface they touch. If you're not using reflections in your nighttime cityscape shots, you're leaving a ton of creative potential on the table. The most obvious place to find reflections? Water. After a fresh rain, city streets transform into mirrors, doubling the drama of neon signs, streetlights, and car headlights. A puddle can become a portal to another world, turning an ordinary crosswalk into something cinematic. And if you're near a body of water, a river, or even a fountain in a city park, you can use those reflections to frame your scene in a way that makes your shot feel larger than life. But reflections don't stop at water. Glass buildings, wet sidewalks, polished cars, and even the surface of a phone screen can be used to add depth and layers to your shot. Position yourself so that your foreground catches a reflection of the skyline, or shoot through a reflective surface to create symmetry. Want to get really creative? Use long exposures to turn moving reflections—like taillights skimming across wet pavement—into glowing streaks of color. If you want even more control over reflections, a polarizing filter can help. It lets you reduce or enhance reflections depending on the effect you want. Need to cut glare from a glass building? Twist the filter. Want to make those streetlight reflections pop even more? Adjust accordingly. Just keep in mind that polarizers reduce light, so you may need to compensate with a longer exposure or higher ISO. Nighttime cityscapes are already full of movement, color, and energy, so using reflections adds another dimension, pulling viewers deeper into the frame and giving your shot a dynamic, immersive feel.

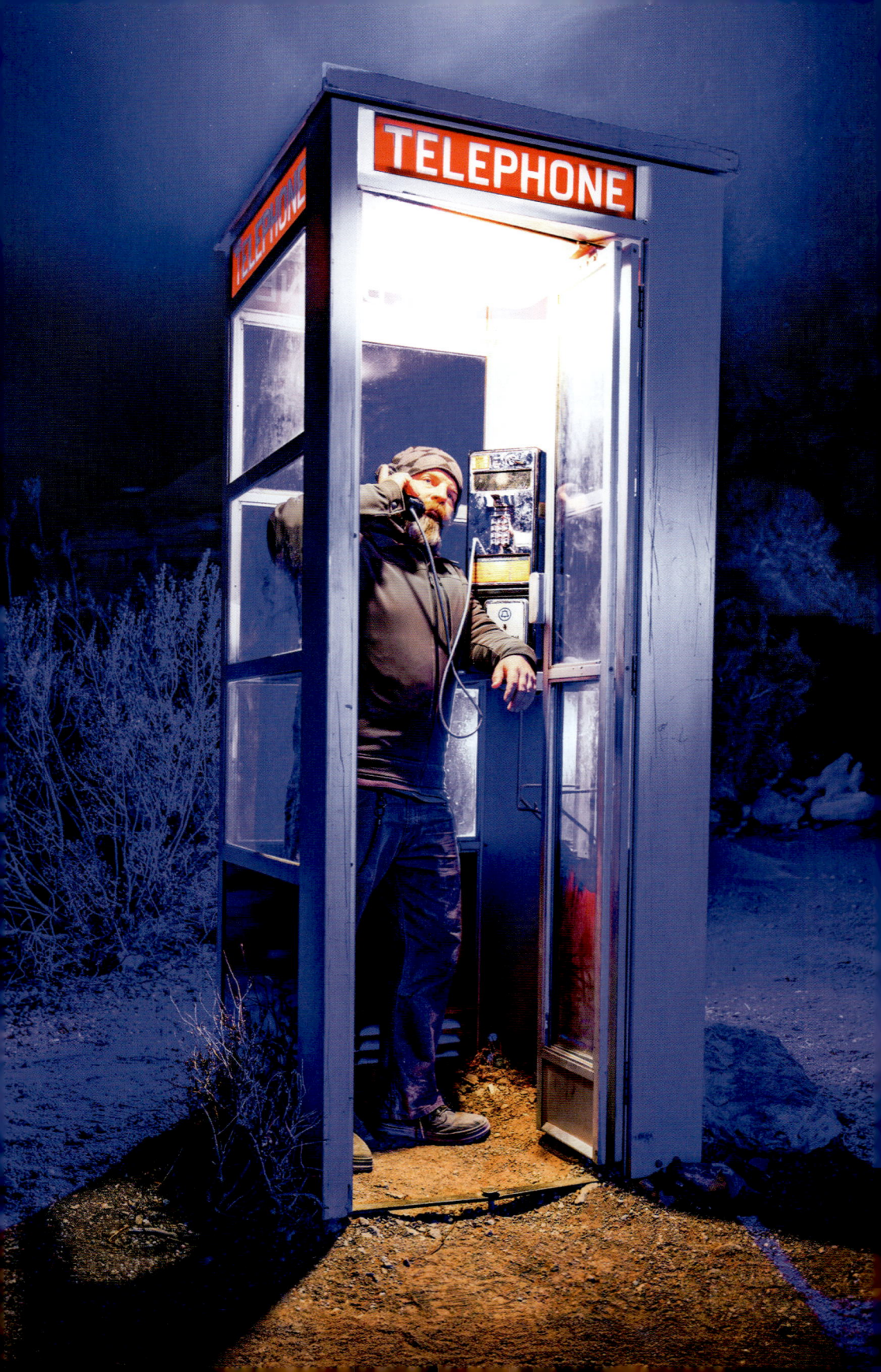

Nighttime Portraits

Bringing Faces to Life After Dark

Taking portraits at night is like trying to have a deep conversation at a loud concert—you've got to work around the chaos and find your moments of clarity. Everything that makes daytime portraits easier—abundant light, fast autofocus, and predictable exposure—pretty much disappears the second the sun sets. But here's the thing: night portraits have a magic that daytime just can't match. The glow of city lights, the mystery of deep shadows, the cinematic mood that comes from working with just the right amount of light—it all adds up to something special. In this chapter, we'll look at how to work with the light you have, create the light you need, and balance your settings to get sharp, stunning portraits in low light. We'll talk about why shooting wide open (think f/1.4, f/1.8, or f/2.8) is your best friend, how to use high ISO without turning your image into a grainy mess, and why shutter speed is the secret weapon for keeping your subject sharp while still embracing the ambient glow of the night. And let's not forget about bokeh—those dreamy, glowing orbs of background light that can take a simple portrait and turn it into a cinematic masterpiece. The good news? At night, bokeh comes naturally. The bad news? Nailing focus at f/1.4 is like trying to thread a needle in the dark. We'll go over how to lock in sharp focus, manage depth of field, and use creative lighting setups to enhance your shots without making them feel overproduced. Speaking of lighting, continuous light sources, LED panels, streetlights, and even car headlights can all become part of your creative toolkit. We'll break down how to mix artificial and natural light, how to use motion to create dynamic portraits, and why environmental portraits at night tell a richer story than a standard headshot ever could. Great portrait photography isn't just about perfect lighting; it's about capturing a mood, an energy, and a feeling. And when you learn how to work with the night instead of fighting against it, you'll create portraits that feel alive, cinematic, and unforgettable.

Capturing Portraits at Night

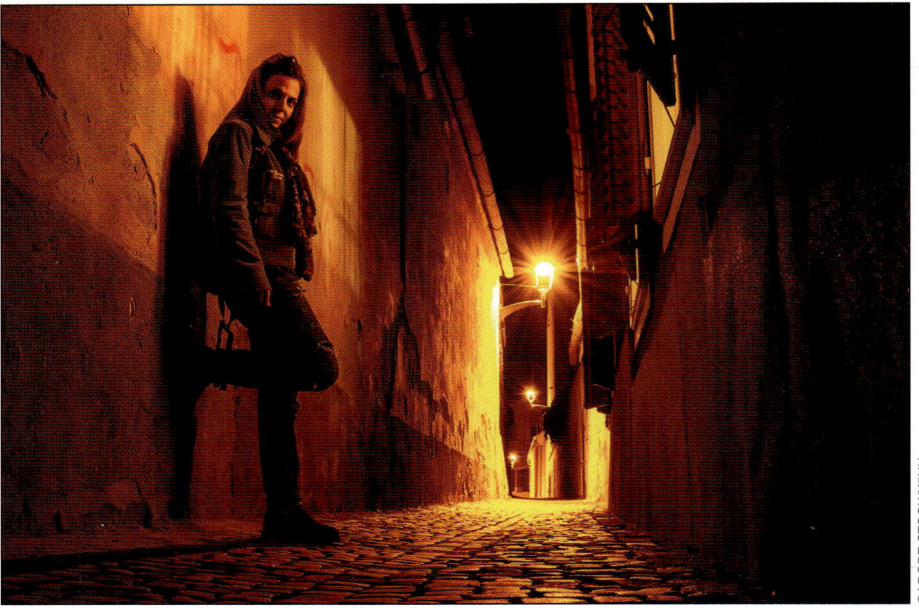

©ADOBE STOCK/KSHU

Nighttime offers a different perspective for portrait photography. The intensity of the day is replaced by the subtlety of the night's hues and the shimmering lights of the city. But, the same rules apply. The facial expressions, light, and color still rule, but the night allows for more control. At night, the interplay of light and shadow becomes key. Unlike during the day, where light is abundant, nighttime light can be sparse. Here, light isn't just about exposure; it's a brush, painting character and emotion onto your subject. Whether it's the soft glow of city neon, the warm tone of a streetlamp (as seen here), or the cool luminescence of LED panels, each light source can become your key light. Nighttime portraits also open the door to dynamic backdrops. The inky silhouettes of cityscapes, the shimmering reflections of urban lights on rain-slicked streets, or the beauty of a moonlit landscape can elevate a portrait from a mere capture to storytelling with the ease of sculpting light at night. This all sounds great, right? But, there's a challenge: it's called darkness. Here, your techniques are tested. Focusing becomes a challenge in the dark, and stabilization, often a necessity, becomes an issue. High ISOs might be called for, but with them comes the noise. It's a balancing act. We must select a shutter speed high enough to get a sharp portrait, but low enough to let in light so we don't have to run up the ISO. It's this very challenge that makes nighttime portraits so rewarding. When done right, and using the tips in this chapter, we're able to balance the settings to create the images we envision.

Shoot Wide Open

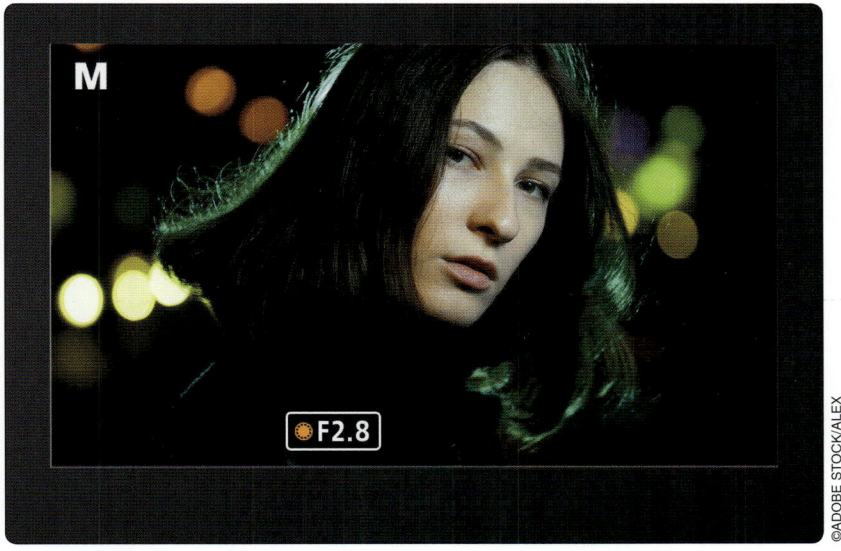

©ADOBE STOCK/ALEX

Aperture is key for nighttime portraits for letting in light without running your ISO too high. Shooting wide open—using a large aperture like f/2.8, or even better, f/1.4 or f/1.8—will help to keep those shutter speeds high to freeze the movement of your subject while keeping your ISO low. No matter how much we try, people will move and shutter speed will do more than anything to keep your images sharp. In the dim evening glow, every photon of light becomes valuable, and a wide-open aperture is like flinging open the doors, inviting in all the light possible. This is crucial, not just to expose our subject properly, but to keep our ISO settings in check, preventing noise from tarnishing our portrait and also to keep that shutter high enough to freeze the motion. But it's not just about the light. Nighttime is a realm of mystery and allure, and a wide aperture unfurls the perfect stage setting: a creamy, dream-like bokeh. This shallow depth of field makes our subject pop, setting them center stage while relegating distractions to a blurred oblivion. Street lights, passing cars, or the distant glimmer of stars become soft orbs of color, adding depth and dimension without stealing the limelight (see the next page for more on bokeh). There's also an intimacy invoked by shooting wide open. In the subdued ambiance of night, a portrait can capture the emotions and mood often drowned out by the intensity of daylight. The soft focus envelops our subject, drawing the viewer closer, making them feel like there's more of a mystery with the photo. Yet, focusing must be precise—even a slight miss with a wide-open aperture can throw crucial details out of focus. But for those willing to embrace the challenges, shooting wide open at night isn't just a technical choice; it's an artistic one.

The Magic of Bokeh

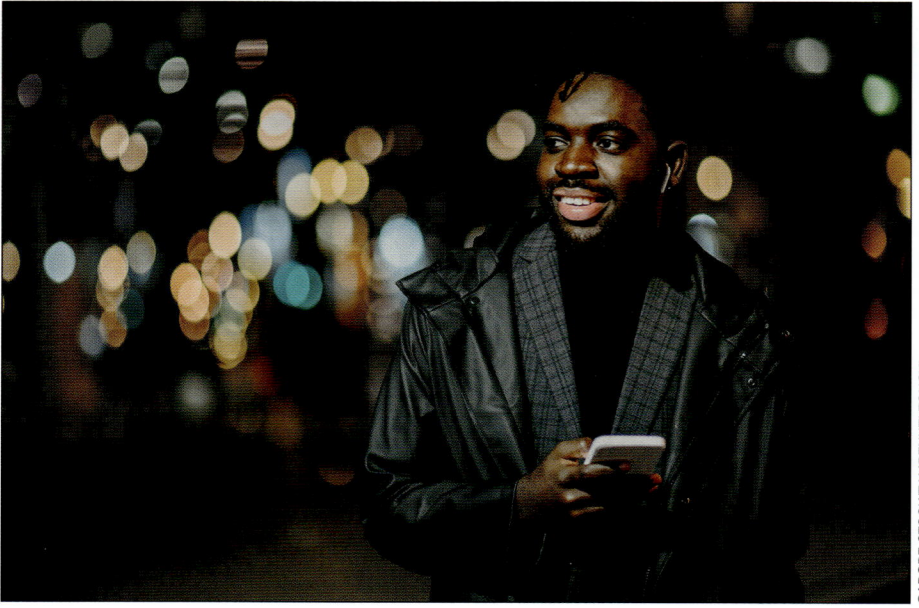

©ADOBE STOCK/ZAMRZNUTI TONOVI

In nighttime portraiture, few effects capture the moment quite like bokeh. It's that enchanting blend of defocused lights and colors that seem to blur whimsically in the background—a glowing background against which our main subject stands out in sharp detail. By night, our world is speckled with pinpricks of light. Streetlamps, neon signs, distant stars—each is a potential player in the bokeh behind your subject. Like I mentioned on the previous page, shooting with a wide aperture—think f/1.4, f/1.8, or even f/2.8—transforms these mundane sources of light into dream-like colorful orbs, sometimes soft and creamy, other times radiant and dazzling. They merge and meld to create an ethereal backdrop—one that lends depth and atmosphere to our nighttime portraits. But the magic of bokeh isn't just its visual charm; it's the potential it holds to focus your viewer's attention. A portrait shouldn't be merely a visual record; it should tell a story. Bokeh can set that mood, whether it's the romance of string lights, the gritty neon pulse of a city at midnight, or the serenity of a starlit night. With bokeh, we aren't just capturing a person; we're capturing a moment, a feeling. What's the challenge? Precision. When dealing with a shallow depth of field, the tiniest shift can mean the difference between a subject's eyes being tack sharp or lost in softness. It's an exercise in millimeters. We always want our subject's eye sharp, but at f/1.4 that could be a matter of just the slightest adjustment in focus or distance. For those willing to embrace this challenge, the rewards are portraits that don't just show a face, but that tell tales of the night and isolate the subject from the background with that bokeh.

Use a High ISO to Freeze Motion

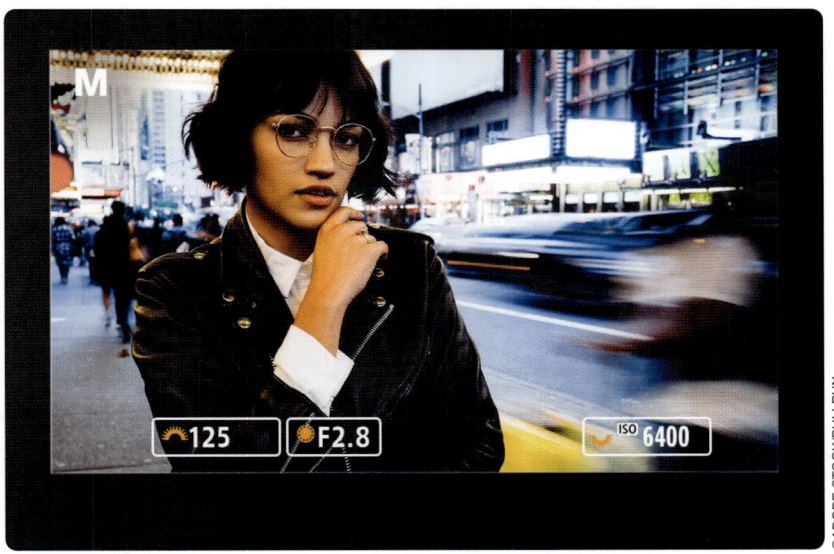

While the night is alluring, it's elusive, particularly when your subject is a living, breathing, moving human being. Here's where the magic of high ISO enters the frame. In the world of photography, light is the essence, and at nighttime, by definition, it's sparse. People, unlike statues, are dynamic. We move, breathe, and have a hard time remaining still. We have this innate rhythm—a blink, a subtle turn of the head, a fleeting smile. To capture these raw, candid moments amidst the low light, we often reach for a higher ISO. Now, I know what some of you are thinking: "High ISO? Noise? Grain?" But remember, with today's advanced camera sensors, we can push the ISO further than ever before without significant degradation in image quality. By boosting the ISO, we're amplifying the camera sensor's sensitivity to light. This, in turn, allows us to use faster shutter speeds, which are crucial for freezing those spontaneous moments and minute movements. Imagine trying to capture a candid laugh or a twirling dance in a dimly lit city night or under the starlit sky. With a low ISO, you risk blurring the essence of that action. But with a higher ISO, you're able to seize the motion, frame the emotion, and encapsulate a split-second of genuine human expression. Yes, there's a balance to strike. Too high an ISO might introduce noise. But in portraiture, especially at night, a sprinkle of grain can sometimes add to the rawness and the authenticity of the moment. What's crucial is that blink, that smirk, that unspoken emotion—the very heartbeats of our subjects. By embracing higher ISOs, we're not just taking a picture; we're capturing a fragment of life under the canopy of the night. For a guide, keeping your ISO where you can reach 1/125th of a second or higher tends to work best.

Add Motion to Your Portraits

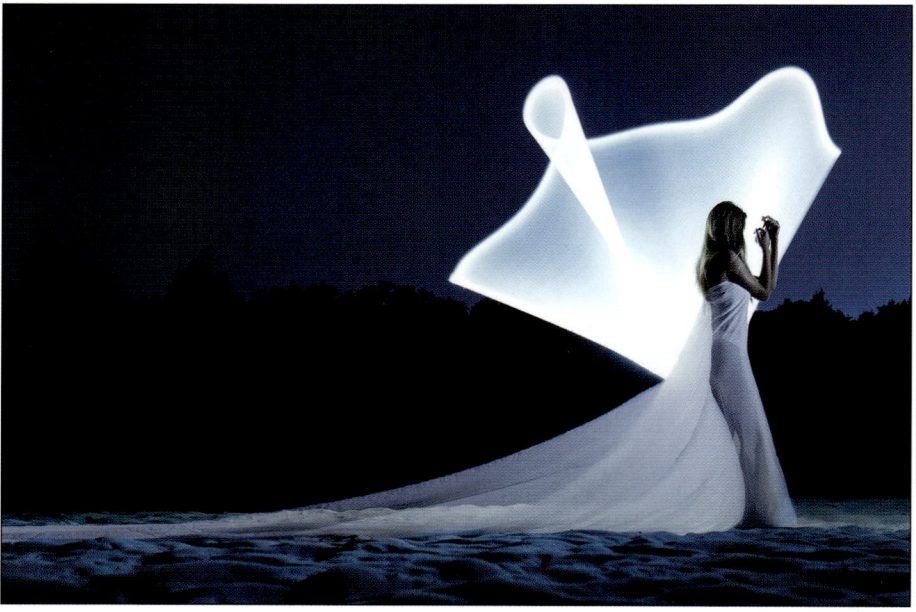

©ADOBE STOCK/MIHAIL_PUSTOVIT

As we've discussed, nighttime is filled with shadows and highlights, so when it comes to portraits, adding motion creates breathtaking photos. Whether it's a dancer's pirouette, a cyclist in motion, or a lovers' embrace, capturing movement at night is about balance and creativity. In this game of darkness and motion, your shutter speed becomes a tool. Slow it down below, say, 1/30 of a second to as high as a few seconds, and you can create ethereal trails, such as a flowing dress turning into a ghostly river or the mesmerizing path of a twirling object in hand. It's about embracing the blur and using it to narrate a story. But, control is key. You may want the motion blur, but also need a portion of the image sharp to anchor the viewer's eye. This is where flash can freeze a part of the frame while the rest melts into motion. Pairing a slower shutter with a burst of flash creates that dichotomy between stillness and motion. So, consider experimenting with a flash setting called rear curtain sync. While settings will vary based on the effect desired, a shutter speed of 1/15 might render beautiful streaks of light around a sharply focused face. Play around and experiment and sync your settings with your vision. But, remember, night adds complexity. You're dealing with less light, often unpredictable, and color temperatures that can shift dramatically. Your ISO and aperture help that shutter speed, keeping the image exposed correctly without losing the essence of the night. Utilize the surroundings—streetlights, car headlights, or even the soft glow of a mobile phone can become part of the scene. Compose with care, for in the world of night motion portraiture, every light and shadow can either be a character in your frame or an unwelcome intruder. It's an intricate balance of settings, timing, and vision, but when done right, it translates into something timeless and beautiful.

Use Continuous Lighting

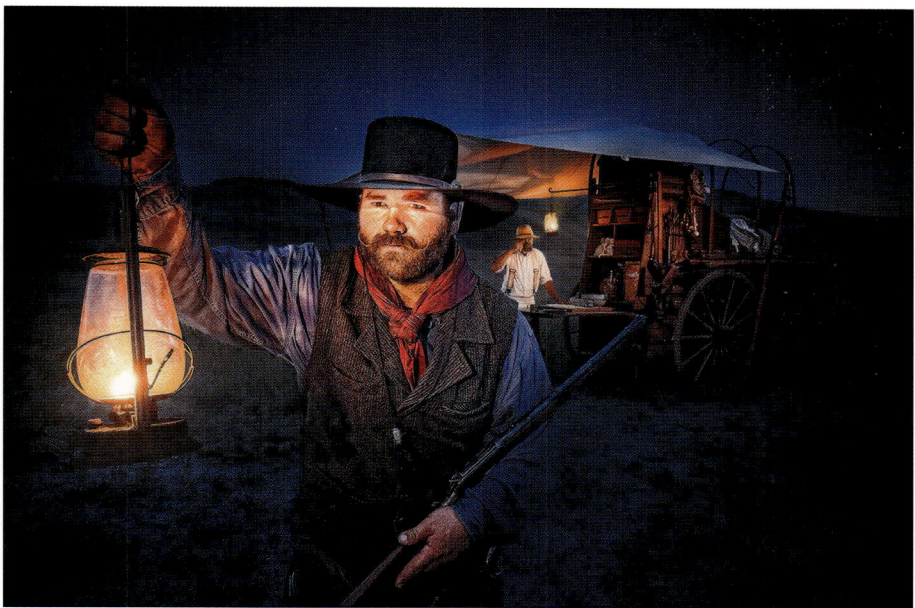

Continuous lighting has opened up a realm of possibilities for nighttime portraits. By using them, you can sculpt, paint, and play with light in a way that was previously confined to studio settings. With these small light sources, the world becomes your studio. Continuous lighting is like holding a brush that's constantly painting with light. Unlike flash, you can see in real time how the light falls, shapes the face, creates shadows, and dances in the eyes. It's an immediate, intuitive way of working that fosters creativity and collaboration between you and your subject. Battery-powered LEDs and other portable lights are fantastic tools for this task (see Chapter 1 for more on these). They're lightweight, often adjustable in color temperature, and can be easily positioned to create the perfect angle of light. Some can even mimic firelight or other natural sources, giving you a creative edge in telling your story. Wide-open apertures work beautifully here, allowing that continuous light to glow softly, creating an ethereal quality. You can emphasize the bokeh, turning background lights into dreamy spheres, giving the image depth and character (see page 110 for more on bokeh). Since they're portable, you can move them around to easily create different effects. You can backlight, sidelight, or even create dramatic top lighting. Your subject can even hold the light, making them an active participant in the creation of the image. Continuous lighting also helps freeze motion since you're not relying on a flash and retaining the ambient light. With the right balance of shutter speed and ISO, you can capture sharp images without losing the ambient feel of the night. And while these lights provide beautiful control, they also honor the night. You're not washing away the dark; you're merely sculpting within it. Using continuous light for night portraits can be tactile, responsive, and full of potential.

Use Off-Camera Flash

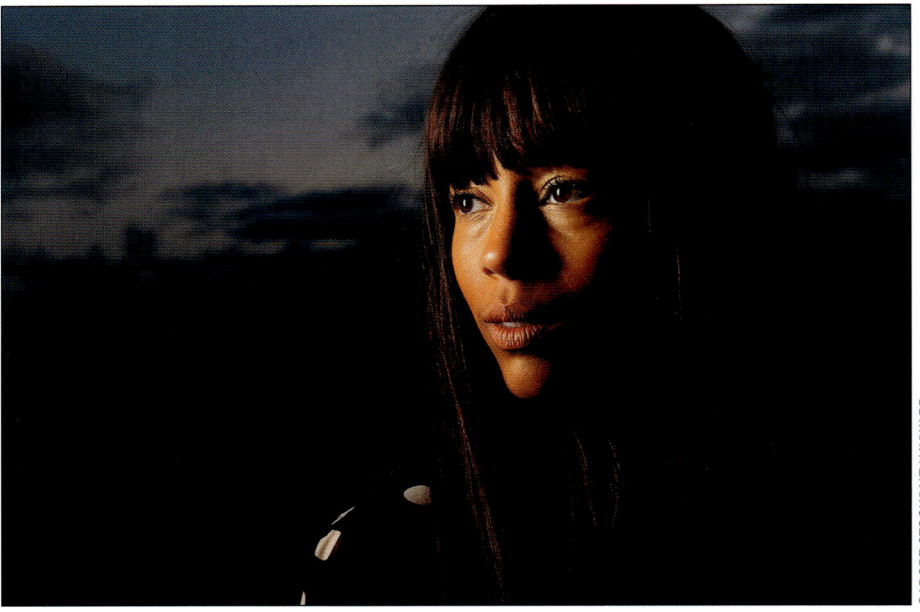

©ADOBE STOCK/MAT HAYWARD

Shooting portraits at night is already a challenge, but trying to do it without control-ling your light is like cooking in the dark—things might turn out okay, but you're mostly guessing. That's where off-camera flash comes in. You'll notice that I said "off-camera flash." Don't miss that part or this tip will be worthless since on-camera flash shouldn't even exist. A good off-camera flash setup gives you full control over your light, allowing you to separate your subject from the background, freeze move-ment, and add drama that ambient light alone just can't achieve. Unlike continuous lighting (which can work great but often lacks power at night), a well-placed flash burst can illuminate your subject without losing the mood of the scene. The trick? Balancing flash with ambient light so your subject doesn't look like they were pasted onto a different background. You want your flash to be a complement, not the only light source. Keep your shutter speed slow enough to retain the ambient glow of city lights, while using the flash to subtly highlight your subject. The rear curtain sync flash setting is a game-changer here, letting you freeze motion while keeping natural light trails in the background. And forget about pointing your flash straight at your subject—it's all about direction and diffusion. Using a softbox, an umbrella, or even bouncing the light off a nearby surface can create a much more flattering and natural look. Bare flash can be harsh, but modified flash? That's where the magic happens. For those who love motion in portraits, mixing flash with a slower shutter speed can add creative blur while keeping your subject sharp. Think city lights streaking behind them as they walk through a neon-lit street, or a dancer with a frozen pose while the rest of the scene melts into motion. Using off-camera flash isn't about overpowering the darkness, it's about sculpting light to work with the shadows, creating portraits that feel dynamic, cinematic, and full of energy.

Environmental Portraits

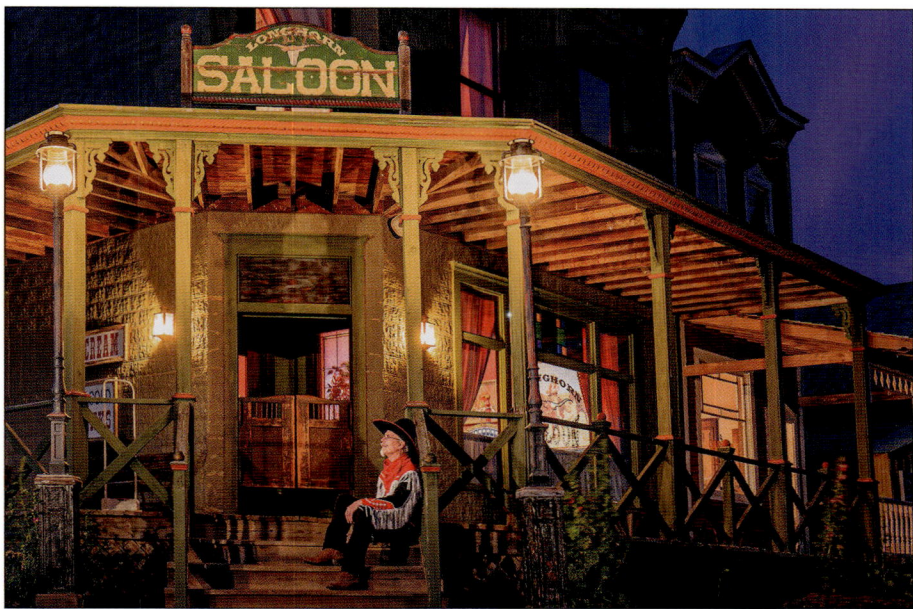

This is about capturing people in their surroundings and painting a complete picture of who they are by including elements of their world. When applied to night photography, it opens the door to storytelling that's rich, nuanced, and visually compelling. Just like Joe McNally, who made a name for himself by mastering this art, you can also create powerful imagery with the allure of the night. When working with environmental portraits at night, you must understand how to balance your subject with their surroundings. Wide apertures can be used to ensure the subject is the focus, allowing the environment to softly fall into the background while still remaining a vital part of the story. However, you may also want to narrow the aperture to keep more of the scene in focus, depending on the story you want to tell. This is also where flash and portable lights, like LEDs, can be used to illuminate the subject. But, be careful not to overpower the natural ambiance of your subject's environment. The goal is to complement the existing light, not replace it. This could mean using a gentle fill light to add a catchlight to the eyes or a subtle rim light to separate them from the background. Higher ISO settings can be used to keep the shutter speed fast enough to freeze any motion, ensuring that the ambient light is captured. Remember, the environment is a crucial part of the image, and you want it to be seen, felt, and experienced. A well-crafted environmental portrait is a dialogue between the person and their space. At night, the shadows deepen, the contrasts are more pronounced, and the evening's quiet adds an emotive layer to the image. These portraits are about seeing the unseen, feeling the night's pulse, and translating that into an image that resonates. Like Joe McNally does, your task is to find the balance, the harmony between person and place, and to tell a story that's as complex and beautiful as the night itself.

Group Portraits

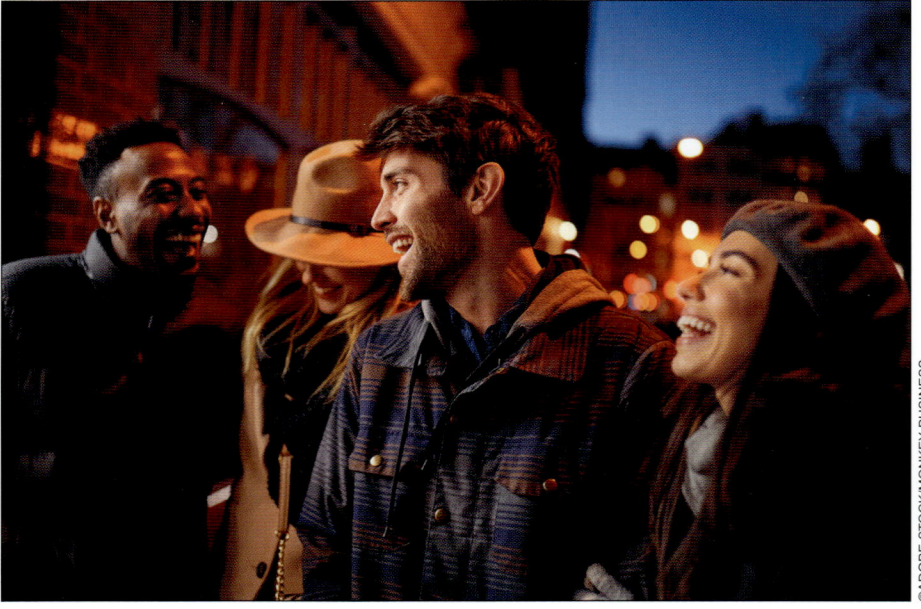

©ADOBE STOCK/MONKEY BUSINESS

Photographing groups at night presents a unique set of challenges and opportunities that can yield some striking results. It requires careful attention to lighting, composition, and exposure settings, but with some insights, you can create memorable group portraits. It's important to recognize that you have multiple subjects to consider, and each person must be well-lit and sharply focused. Yet the overall composition needs to be balanced, and the scene should still convey the intrigue and ambiance of the night. Lighting becomes a pivotal factor, and whether you're using streetlamps, flash, or portable LEDs, you need to ensure even illumination across all faces. This might mean employing multiple light sources or carefully positioning a single light to avoid casting shadows on some group members. Soft diffusers can be handy to prevent harsh shadows and highlights. Aperture settings may require careful consideration because while shooting wide open may create beautiful bokeh and isolate subjects from the background, it might also narrow the depth of field too much, leaving some group members out of focus. A slightly smaller aperture (like f/4 or f/5.6) can give you a broader focus range to ensure everyone is sharp, and higher ISO settings can be used to allow for faster shutter speeds, which are essential to freeze the motion in groups where people are naturally more animated. Be mindful of noise, but remember, capturing the moment is vital. Composition plays a crucial role, so positioning people at varying distances from the camera can create a dynamic depth, but it also requires diligent focusing. It's often beneficial to arrange the group in a way that everyone can be seen and the surrounding environment can still play a role in the story. The dynamics of group interaction can add energy and life to the photo, so encourage interaction and look for those spontaneous moments with real emotions. This can all lead to powerful images that resonate with viewers.

Capturing Portraits with Your Phone

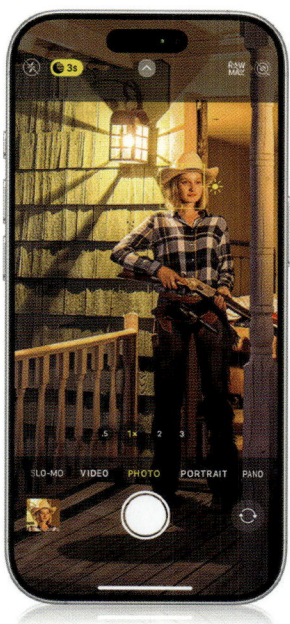

This is entirely achievable with modern smartphone technology. Understanding your phone's capabilities is key, so familiarize yourself with features like manual controls, night mode, and dedicated night portrait modes. Utilizing night mode can be particularly effective for portraits in minimal lighting, as this mode often takes a series of exposures and blends them into one image. Stability is crucial for clear images in night photography, so consider using a tripod or stable surface to minimize camera shake. Finding the right light is essential and soft and diffused light sources, like streetlamps or gentle artificial lights, can provide a pleasing glow without harsh shadows. Focusing carefully is also paramount because autofocus might struggle in low light. So, if possible, manually focus on the subject's eyes or ensure the focus point is precise. Composition also plays a crucial role, with the darkness often providing a minimalist backdrop that lets your subject shine, so experiment with different angles and adhere to the rule of thirds to create a visually pleasing scene. Once you've captured the image, don't be afraid to enhance it with the powerful editing tools available on many smartphones—fine-tuning exposure, contrast, and color balance can turn a good shot into a great one. Embrace the night and its unique conditions. The dark surroundings add a dramatic and mysterious atmosphere to portraits, allowing for creative experimentation with shadows and highlights. Capturing portraits at night with your phone's camera is about leveraging your device's features, applying the principles of good photography, and having the creativity to make the most of the nighttime environment. With a bit of practice, your smartphone can become a versatile tool for creating stunning night portraits. We'll dive deeper into using your phone for night photography in Chapter 10.

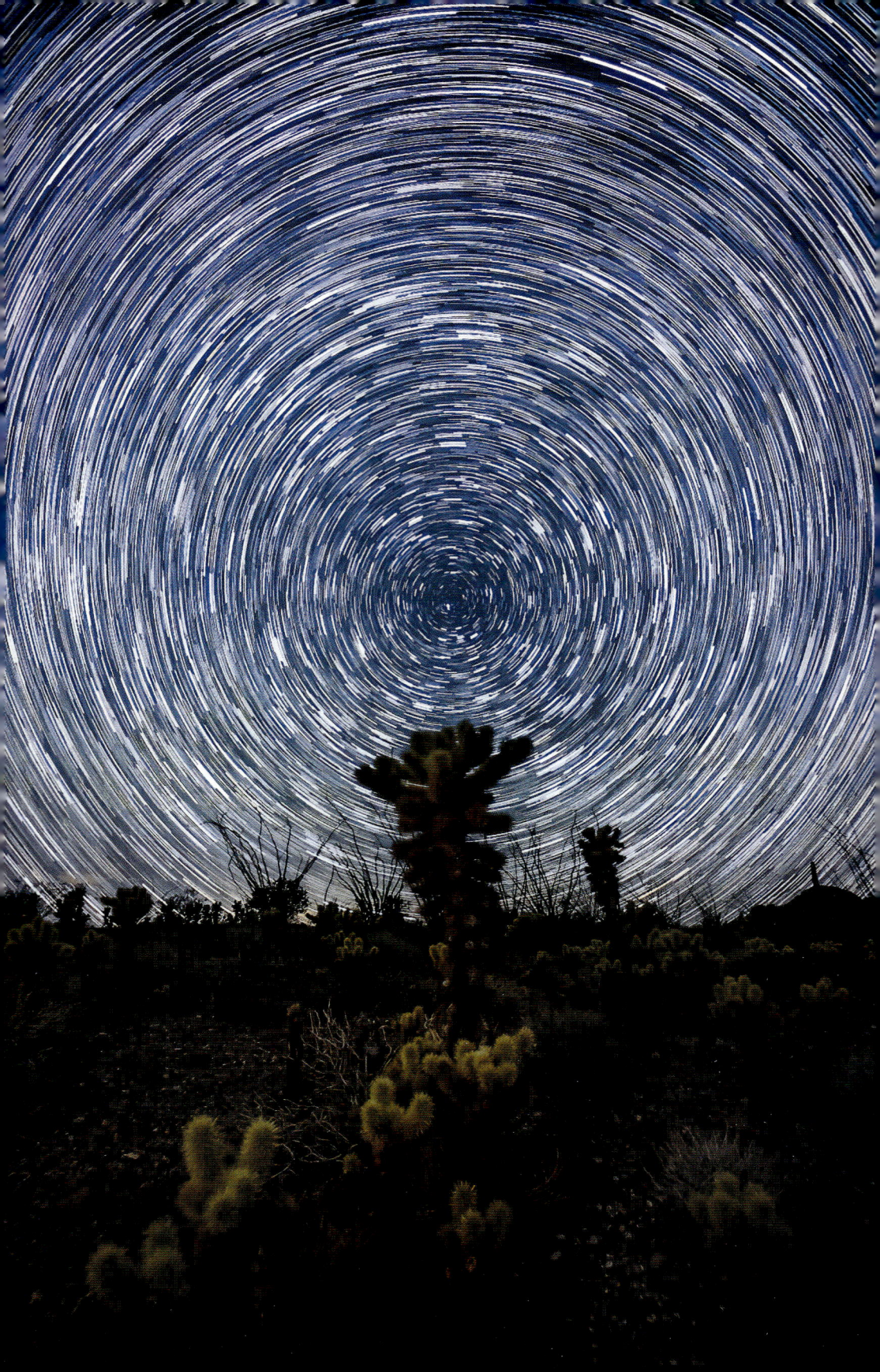

)))) ● ◐ ⑨ ◑ ● (((((

Star Trails,
Time-Lapses & More
Capturing the Movement of the Night

Night photography is usually about freezing a moment in time, but sometimes, the real magic happens when you let time run wild. This chapter is all about those long-exposure techniques that turn the night sky into swirling trails, moving light into dynamic streaks, and entire hours into mesmerizing sequences of change. Whether you're capturing star trails, time-lapses, meteor showers, or even rocket launches, this is where night photography transforms into something cinematic. Where instead of capturing just one frame, you're telling an entire story. We'll start with star trails—one of the most breathtaking ways to show the Earth's rotation in a single image. If you've ever looked at a long-exposure shot of the night sky and seen those perfect circular streaks around the North Star, you've seen this in action. You don't need a fancy tracking mount or telescope, just patience, a sturdy tripod, and a method that doesn't result in your camera battery dying at the worst possible moment (trust me, I've been there). Then there are time-lapses. Instead of one long exposure, you're shooting hundreds (sometimes thousands) of images and stitching them together into a short video that condenses hours into seconds. It's a mix of planning, endurance, and accepting that you're about to spend a lot of time standing in the cold. But we're not stopping at the stars. We'll also dive into light streaks, and meteor showers, and even photographing the International Space Station as it passes overhead. And for the ultimate night photographer's challenge? Rocket launches. Few things are as exhilarating as capturing a launch streak arcing across the sky, turning science and engineering into pure visual poetry. So, whether you're stacking images for star trails, setting up interval shooting for a time-lapse, or waiting for that perfect meteor to streak across your frame, these techniques let you bend time to your will. Master them and you'll never look at a static night photo the same way again.

Star Trails

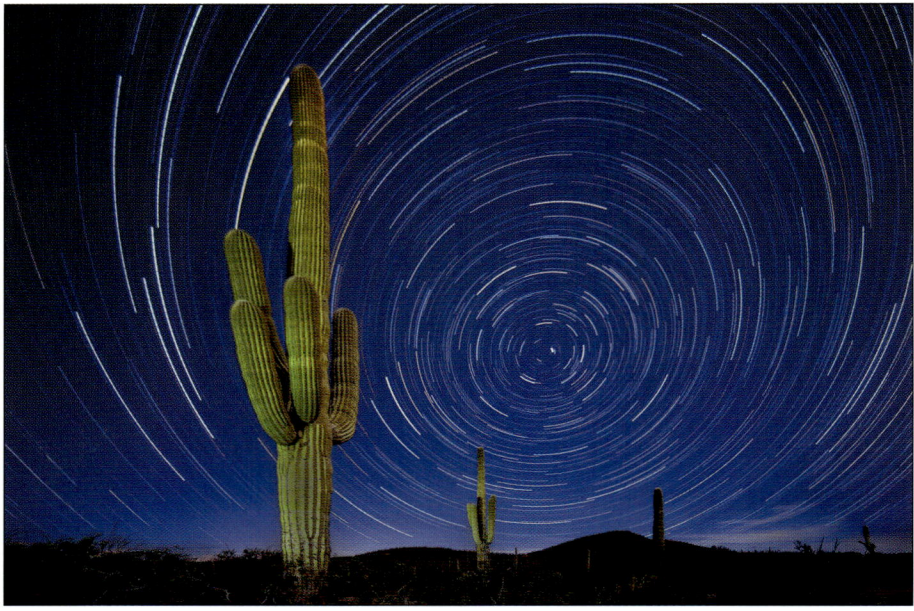

To photograph star trails, you must first understand the concept of star trails. As the Earth spins on its axis, the stars appear to move across the sky. By using a long exposure, their motion creates beautiful streaks or trails that paint a unique picture of time and space. Here are some keys to shooting star trails: First, find a place with minimal light pollution, as dark skies allow the stars to shine brightly. However, one thing to remember is that star trails can be acceptable even with high light pollution. All you really need is clear skies and the ability to see bright star points with your own eyes. Including an interesting foreground, such as a tree or mountain, can add depth and context to your image. Like everything else you've read about so far, sturdy equipment is key. A robust tripod is essential for minimizing vibration and ensuring sharp, clear trails. A wide-angle lens allows you to capture a large portion of the sky, and a cable release helps avoid camera shaking during the exposure. Experiment with compositions and exposures. A north-facing view with Polaris, the North Star, will create circular trails, while other orientations will create different patterns. Finally, post-processing should be considered to enhance the image—adjusting contrast, sharpness, and color can emphasize the trails and improve the overall impact (see Chapter 12 for more on post-processing). Star trail photography is an exciting way to connect with the universe and create compelling images that tell a story of time and movement.

Star Trail Settings

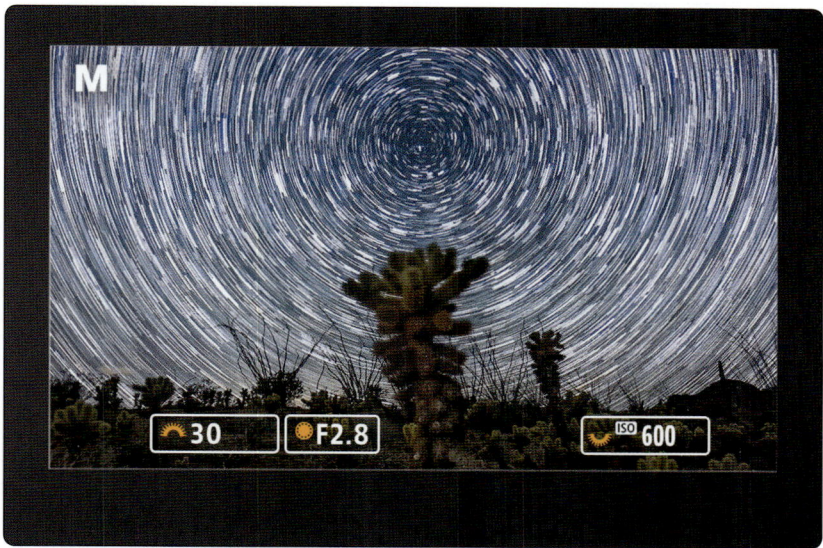

Settings are crucial when shooting star trails. A wide-open aperture, around f/2.8 or f/4, will let in more light. But, you might want to raise that even higher to f/5.6 or f/8 if you only want to keep the brightest stars in the sky, so as not to over-whelm the scene with every little pinpoint of light. Something else that can help is to keep the ISO relatively low to minimize noise—around 400–800—since we don't care about freezing the stars. Exposure times can vary. A single long exposure of 30 seconds to 30 minutes creates shorter trails, and stacking shorter exposures like 30 seconds can create segmented trails with a different aesthetic. This also allows for what I like to call a 3-for-1-star trail. If you were to take a sequence of images at 30 seconds wide open at a higher ISO—something like f/4, 30 seconds, and ISO 6400—you can get a single exposure that can pass for little to no star trails, a time-lapse of the scene, plus a stacked exposure of the star trails. Hence, 3-for-1. In contrast, you can set a higher f-stop and much lower ISO and leave the exposure open for over an hour. The main drawback to these star trails is that someone could mess up your shot with a bright light. To achieve this effect, you might shoot as low as ISO 100 and f/11 in a dark spot for over an hour. Just make sure to have a fully charged battery and nobody around to ruin your shot. I prefer to hedge my bets and stack shorter exposures in case anything goes wrong. Plus, this method allows me to create time-lapses of the star trails building or moving throughout the sequence I take in one session. Finally, if you're looking for fine points of light, focus on infinity, then manually focus on a bright star to ensure sharpness. However, if you want the trails of light to bloat and add more color to the stars, consider leaving the stars just a tad out of focus. This will allow the stars to be pronounced in your scene.

Keeping Star Trails from Becoming a Mess

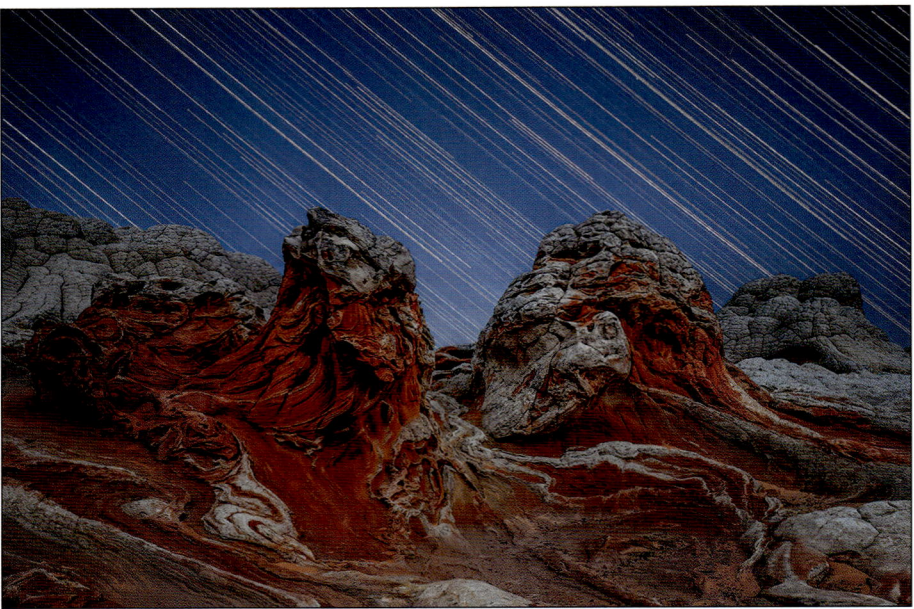

Star trails are one of the most dramatic ways to capture the passage of time at night, but if you've ever tried shooting them and ended up with an overexposed, washed-out sky, you know they can be frustratingly tricky. The key isn't just keeping the shutter open long enough to show movement, but knowing how to balance light, color, and contrast so your trails look stunning instead of like blown-out streaks of light pollution. The most common mistake? Too much brightness. If your trails are too thick and overpower the stars behind them, it's likely because your ISO is cranked too high or your aperture is too wide. Unlike other types of night photography, star trails don't require high ISOs. Instead, dropping down to ISO 800 keeps the noise in check while still capturing enough detail. If you're shooting a single long exposure, try f/5.6 or f/8 instead of wide open. This helps keep only the brightest stars visible, making for cleaner, more distinct trails. If you're stacking multiple exposures, the risk of overexposure is even greater. Each frame adds up, and if your base shots are already too bright, stacking them will just make the trails too thick and unnatural. To fix this, reducing your individual exposure time, somewhere around 20–30 seconds per shot at a lower ISO works well. Then, when stacking, use the Lighten blending mode in post, which keeps the brightest parts of each image while discarding unnecessary light buildup. And don't forget color. If your sky looks too orange or yellow, blame it on light pollution. Shooting from darker locations helps, but using a custom Kelvin white balance (3400K–4200K) can correct unwanted color shifts. In post, you can further refine the look by adjusting the contrast and highlights to make the trails stand out without overpowering the background. The secret to perfect star trails? Patience, balance, and a little bit of finesse. Get those settings dialed in, and you'll have trails that look clean, smooth, and perfectly exposed every time.

Light Streaks

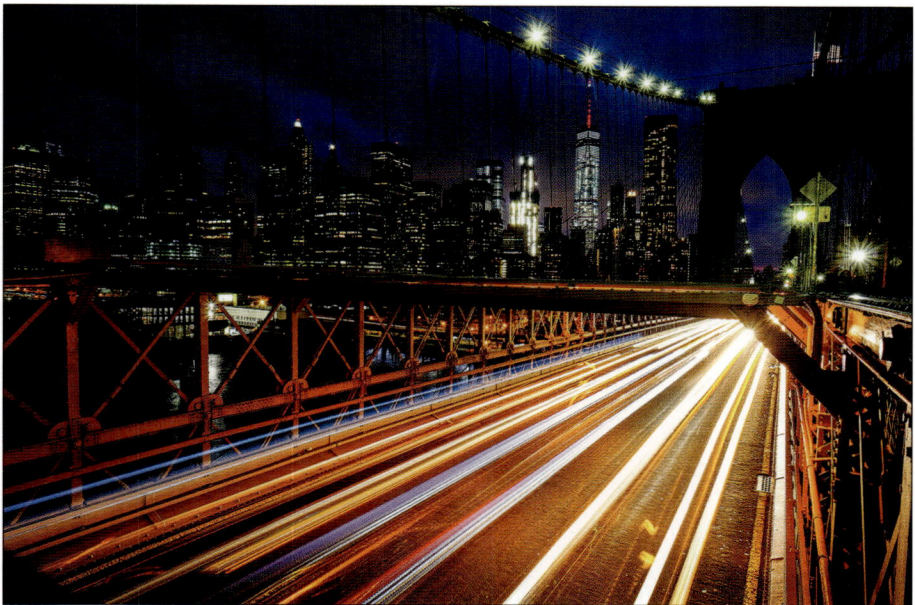

Light streak photography often uses car headlights and taillights or even stars and streetlights (we talked about this a bit in Chapter 6). The essential principle is capturing the movement of light over time through a long exposure. A busy street with moving cars, a bustling cityscape with moving lights and motion, or a landscape with hikers with headlamps can all be good locations. If you're shooting car lights, an overpass or a road with curves can add an appealing twist to your streaks. Not to sound like a broken record, but a sturdy tripod is crucial as you'll be using slow shutter speeds, and a remote shutter release can be helpful to minimize camera shake. A slow shutter speed is key to capturing light movement, and depending on the speed of the light, you might set it anywhere from a few seconds to several minutes. Aperture and ISO can be adjusted to balance the exposure. Generally, a mid-range aperture like f/8 to f/11 and a lower ISO around 100–400 work well. Consider the direction and flow of the lights and position yourself to capture that movement in a visually compelling way. Foreground elements or leading lines can enhance the composition and timing can be critical, especially with fast-moving subjects like cars. It might take a few attempts to get the perfect exposure and alignment. Often, some adjustment in post-processing will help bring out the best in your light streaks, so contrast, saturation, and sharpness can all be tweaked to emphasize the streaks (see Chapter 12 for more on post-processing). Light streak photography is about more than just technique; it's about capturing a feeling of movement and speed. It's a way to bring energy and dynamism to what might otherwise be a static scene. Like painting with light, it's an opportunity to use your camera to create something imaginative and lively.

International Space Station Passes

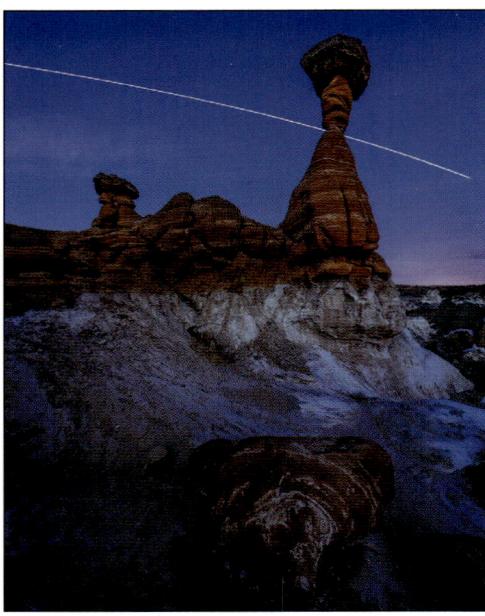

Capturing twilight passes of the International Space Station (ISS) when it's lit up by the sun below the horizon is an exhilarating endeavor that requires precise planning, timing, and execution. Start by tracking the ISS through specialized apps or websites to find the exact times and directions for twilight passes in your area (just Google "Spot the ISS"). Unlike a regular night photo, twilight offers a stunning backdrop where the sky is dark enough to view the ISS, yet there's some ambient light to enhance your composition. Selecting a location with minimal light pollution that offers a clear and unobstructed view of the sky is essential. Also, consider including an interesting landscape or foreground. Of course, you'll need a sturdy tripod to provide the stabilization needed for a long exposure and a wide-angle lens (14–35mm) is preferable, allowing you to capture more of the sky. Manual focus set to infinity typically works well, and an aperture of around f/4 to f/5.6 can allow enough light in, or more like f/8 to f/11 if there's too much ambient light and you need to dial down the exposure. Depending on the twilight conditions, your ISO might range from 100 to 1600, and the shutter speed can vary from a few seconds to a few minutes given the ISS's speed across the sky. When it comes to composition, carefully frame your shot, considering the ISS's predicted path. You can take a series of images as the ISS moves or one extended exposure to capture its entire trail. Timing and patience are paramount here. Use a remote shutter release or your camera's self-timer to avoid any shake, and start shooting a bit before the scheduled pass time, continuing until it disappears. Lastly, don't overlook post-processing. If you've opted for multiple shots, you might need to stack them in Photoshop to create one continuous trail and fill in the gaps between exposures. The result? A breathtaking capture of humanity's technological achievements set against the natural beauty of the twilight sky.

Meteor Showers

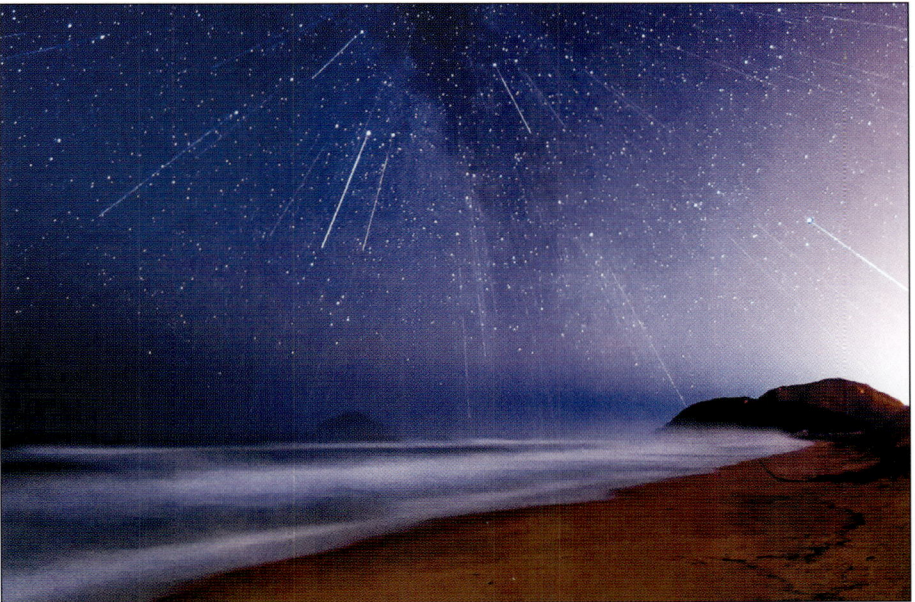

Photographing meteor showers is an exciting and rewarding challenge that combines patience, skill, and a bit of luck. These celestial events occur when Earth passes through the debris left by a comet, causing meteors to streak across the sky. Capturing these brief, brilliant flashes requires preparation and an understanding of the fundamentals. First, plan your shoot by identifying the date and peak time of the meteor shower you want to capture. There are websites and apps dedicated to astronomical events that can provide this information. Next, find a location away from city lights where the sky is clear and dark, preferably with an interesting foreground to complement the celestial spectacle. A wide-angle lens, often between 14mm and 24mm, will allow you to cover a large part of the sky, increasing your chances of capturing a meteor. Set your camera on a sturdy tripod and use a cable release or remote control to minimize camera shake. Manual focus set to infinity will typically yield the sharpest stars. The aperture should be as wide as possible, like f/2.8 or f/4, to let in enough light, and an ISO setting between 800 and 6400 will generally be sufficient. Shutter speed is crucial here; setting it between 15 and 30 seconds allows you to capture the meteor's trail without overexposing the stars. Experimenting with different exposures might be necessary based on the ambient light and desired effect. Compose your shot with the meteor shower's radiant point in mind, which is where the meteors appear to originate. Including a striking landscape element or an intriguing subject can add depth and interest to your image. Remember, patience is key. Meteor showers can be unpredictable, so take continuous shots throughout the night using a time-lapse technique (see page 127). The meteors' quick and sporadic nature means you'll need to shoot many frames to capture those elusive meteoric streaks.

Rocket Launches

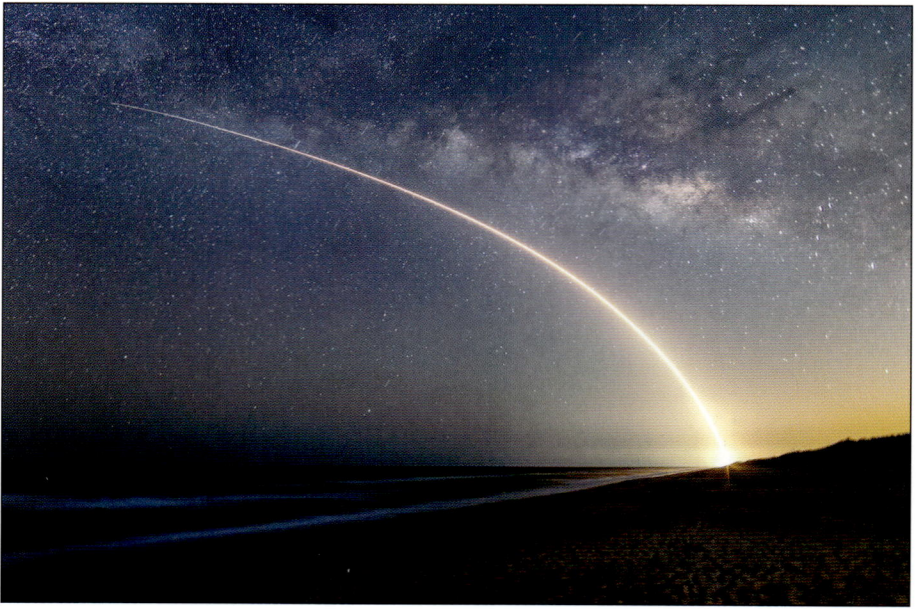

Speaking of streaks, photographing rocket launch streaks is an awe-inspiring experience that combines the thrill of a launch with the artistry of night photography. Capturing that perfect streak as the rocket arcs into the sky requires planning, precision, and the right techniques. The first step in photographing a rocket launch is to know when and where it will take place. Websites dedicated to space launches provide schedules (a great one is FlightClub.io), and a bit of research will help you determine the best vantage point for your shot. Next, scout your location ahead of time. Position your frame in the expected path of the rocket, and include any foreground elements that can add depth or context to your image. The great thing here is that 8–25 miles away from a launch pad tends to be the best vantage point and I've even been up to 250 miles away from a pad for a streak. Since launch pads are secure, this really helps to get great rocket streak photos. Equipment-wise, a sturdy tripod is essential, a wide-angle-to-moderate telephoto lens will typically provide the flexibility you need, and a remote shutter release can help prevent camera shake during the long exposure. Manual focus set to infinity is usually ideal, and an aperture of f/8 to f/11 will give you a good depth of field. Start with a low ISO, like 400–800, since the rocket's intense brightness can cause overexposure—the closer to the pad, the lower the number may need to go. As for shutter speed, you'll use a long exposure, often several minutes, to capture the entire launch sequence. Compose your shot with the rocket's trajectory in mind and set up your camera to take continuous exposures if you're uncertain about the exact time needed. You can merge these exposures later in post-processing to create the full streak. When the launch is imminent, start your exposure just before ignition or wait until you see the glow on the horizon.

Time-Lapses

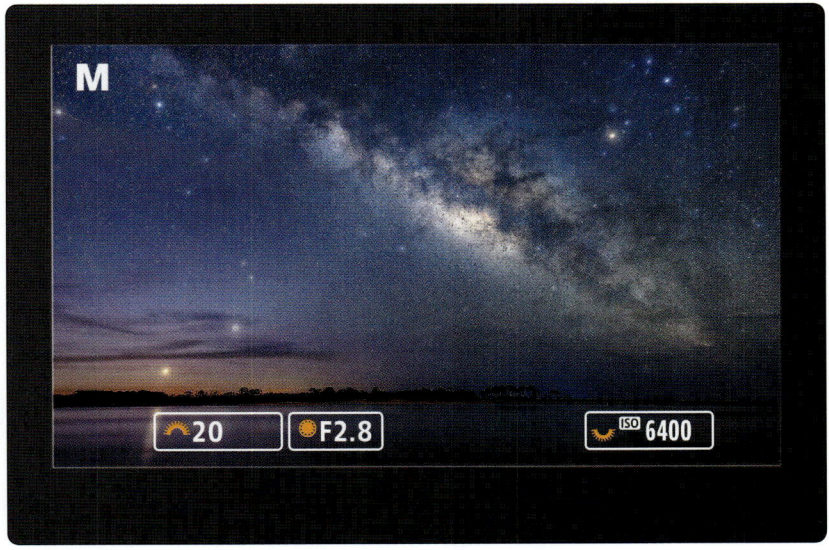

Creating a night time-lapse is a beautiful way to showcase the dynamic and often unseen movements of the night sky. It's more than just a series of photographs; it's about capturing a motion played out by stars, planets, and sometimes even meteor showers rotating above the earth. The key? Location, location, location! Finding the perfect spot is your first step. Whether you're aiming to capture the Milky Way's graceful arc or a cityscape with stars, you'll need an area with minimal light pollution and a fascinating foreground to add scale. You'll want a sturdy tripod to keep your camera stable, a fast wide-angle lens to gather as much light as possible, and an intervalometer to control the timing of your shots (we looked at this on page 7). For the settings, start by focusing your lens to infinity and dial into the stars. Set your aperture to its widest setting, like f/2.8, and adjust your shutter speed to around 20 seconds. ISO typically ranges from 1600 to 6400, but adjust this based on your test shots. You'll determine the interval between shots. A shorter interval (like 20 seconds) creates a smooth motion, while a longer one (like 60 seconds) will make things move quickly but stars and cars will trail more. Remember, the entire sequence might take hours to shoot, so plan accordingly. You'll want hundreds of shots to create a decent-length video, so patience is vital here. Just think, if you want a 30-second video using a 30-frame-per-second format, that's 30x30 or 900 still frames just to make that 30-second clip. Post is where your time-lapse comes alive. Using software like Adobe Photoshop or Premiere Pro, you'll import your images as a sequence of those 900 frames. Adjusting color, exposure, and adding music will bring your time-lapse to life. But, be prepared for weather changes, dew on the lens, or any interruptions from curious wildlife or other people. Like any art form, mastering night time-lapse takes practice, experimentation, and learning from mistakes.

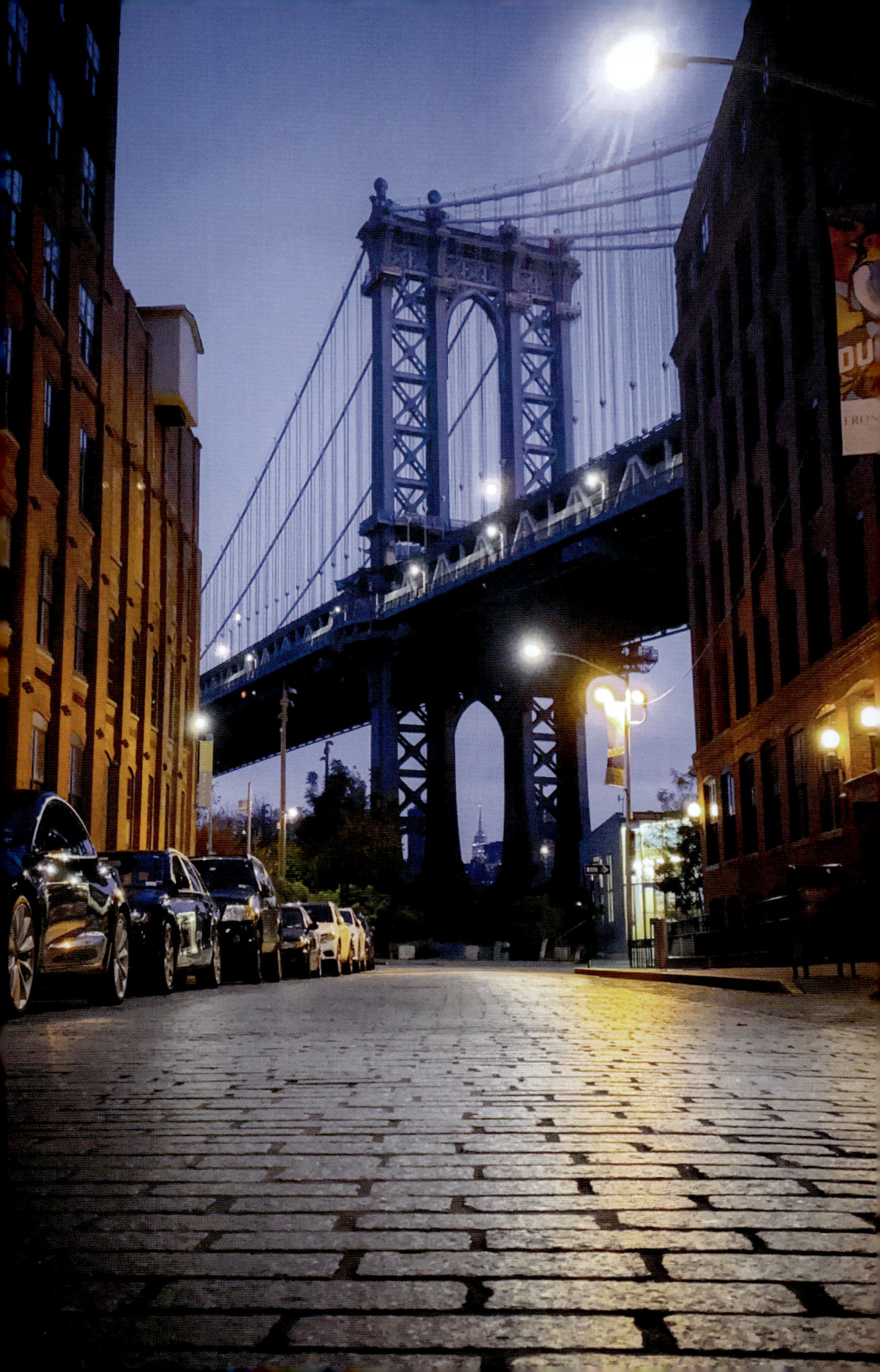

10

Using Your Phone

Turning Your Pocket Camera into a Night Photography Powerhouse

Once upon a time, if you wanted to take a decent nighttime photo, you needed a big, expensive camera, a heavy tripod, and enough technical know-how to make a rocket scientist jealous. Now? You've got a powerful night photography tool sitting in your pocket. Smartphones have gotten so good at low-light photography that it's no longer a question of "Can I shoot the night with my phone?" it's "How far can I push it?" This chapter is all about maximizing your phone's potential to capture stunning night photos. Whether you're using an iPhone, an Android, or some other device with a halfway decent camera, you already have everything you need to shoot stars, cityscapes, light trails, and even astrophotography, without carrying a full camera bag. We'll cover how to use Night mode (because let's be honest, it's basically magic), why a small tripod makes a world of difference, and how to tweak settings like shutter speed, ISO, and focus to get even better results. You'll learn how to use third-party apps that unlock pro-level controls, how to stabilize your shots without a tripod (hello, creative hacks), and even how to capture star trails and the Milky Way with just your phone's camera. And let's not forget the power of computational photography—the secret sauce that blends multiple images, reduces noise, and enhances details in ways that even some dedicated cameras struggle with. Your phone isn't just taking one picture; it's processing an entire sequence of shots, stacking them together, and delivering a final image that looks way better than what your eyes saw. So whether you're out on a spontaneous night adventure, capturing a stunning city skyline, or lying on your back trying to get a shot of the stars, this chapter will show you how to make the most of the camera that's always with you. Because in the end, the best night photo is the one you actually take, not the one you miss because your camera was sitting at home.

Night Modes

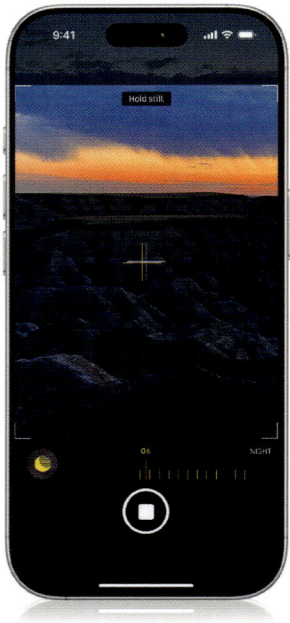

In today's world, capturing the essence of night with just a smartphone isn't just a possibility—it's a reality. Thanks to the leaps in computational photography, smartphones now have night modes that enhance the darkness, bringing out vibrant details and colors that were once lost in shadows. These sophisticated systems harness the power of AI to stitch together multiple images taken at different exposures and higher ISOs and automatically blend those frames into a single photo that's bright, sharply detailed, and deeply colored, all without the need for complex post-processing or, in some cases, an expensive tracker. Computational photography isn't just about brightening up a night photo; complex algorithms enhance texture, reduce noise, and balance the contrasts, making each night shot look great. This means that even in the most challenging low-light conditions, from the dimly lit corners of a city to the sprawling, starlit skies, your smartphone's camera becomes a powerful tool that captures the night's magic with surprising clarity and depth. Moreover, these advancements democratize photography, putting the power to create stunning nightscapes into the hands of anyone with a smartphone. It encourages exploration and creativity, urging photographers to experiment with compositions and perspectives that were once challenging without specialized gear. The night mode on your phone is not just a feature; it's your ticket to use your camera that is always with you, inviting you to capture the stories of the night. So, the next time you're out at night and don't have your DSLR or mirrorless camera, don't hesitate to reach for your phone. With just a few taps, you're ready to seize the night, proving that in photography, the best camera is the one you have with you—especially if it's smart enough to see in the dark with computational photography.

Astrophotography with an iPhone

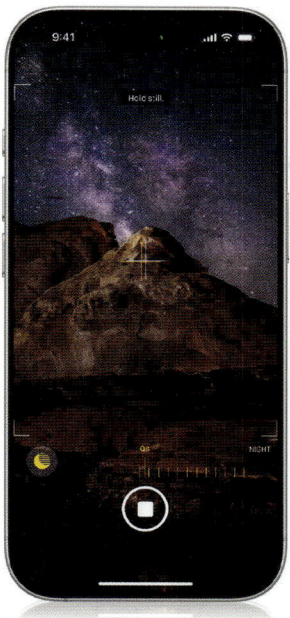

With your iPhone, particularly the Pro models, you can leverage its advanced Night mode capabilities. Here's a step-by-step to unlocking your iPhone's astrophotography potential:

- **Choose a Dark Location:** Find a spot far from city lights for the clearest view of the stars. It's doesn't have to be super-dark, though. Your iPhone works better with some ambient light.

- **Mount Your iPhone on a Tripod:** Stability is key for long-exposure shots.

- **Switch to Night Mode:** Available on recent iPhone models, your Camera app's Night mode automatically activates in low-light conditions (or you can download a third-party app that allows manual control over settings). For manual control, tap on the Night mode icon and swipe to increase exposure time.

- **Use the 1x Wide-Angle Lens:** If your iPhone has multiple lenses, select the 1x wide-angle option since it has the best low-light performance.

- **Focus Manually:** Tap-and-hold on the screen where you want to set focus, ideally on a bright star or distant light, to lock focus.

- **Adjust Exposure:** Use the Night mode slider to maximize exposure time, enhancing star visibility. Adjust exposure times to as much as 30 seconds to let in enough light for capturing the stars, but experiment with different exposure times.

- **Delay the Shot:** Use your Camera app's timer feature to avoid shaking the camera when tapping the shutter button.

Astrophotography with an Android

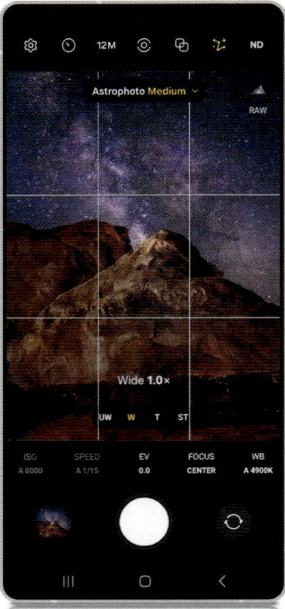

With an Android smartphone, especially high-end models, you can utilize the Astrophotography features available in the camera's Pro RAW mode. Samsung Galaxy Ultras and Google Pixel Pros have specific astrophotography modes that utilize built-in features to enhance nighttime photography. Especially in flagship models, like the S25 Ultra or the Pixel 9 Pro, their cameras are equipped with sensors and software optimized for low-light photography. Here's a step-by-step:

- **Choose a Dark Location:** Look for spots away from city lights for clearer star views. Some ambient light is okay, as these camera sensors handle low-light conditions well.

- **Mount Your Phone on a Tripod:** Ensuring it remains steady is crucial for long-exposure shots.

- **Switch to Pro Mode:** Found in the Pro RAW Camera app, Pro mode allows for select Astrophotography modes, crucial for astrophotography.

- **Use the 1x Wide-Angle Lens:** If your Android has multiple lenses, select the 1x wide-angle option since it has the best low-light performance.

- **Focus Manually:** Manually set focus to infinity to keep stars sharp and experiment with various compositions.

- **Adjust Exposure:** Set a longer exposure time—4 to 10 minutes—to capture more starlight. The camera will track the sky and automatically stack the images.

- **Delay the Shot:** Use your camera's timer feature to avoid any shaking when tapping the shutter button.

Capturing Star Trails

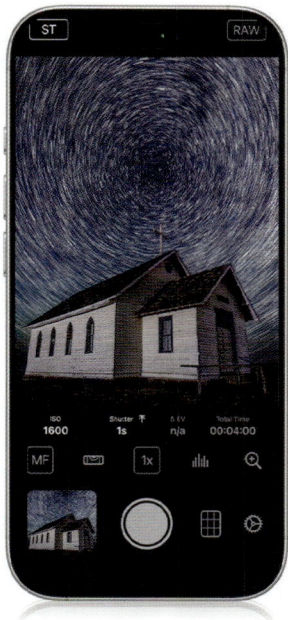

Star trail photography captures the apparent motion of stars across the sky due to Earth's rotation, creating mesmerizing circular patterns. Apps like Even Longer enable you to take long-exposure shots, significantly simplifying the process. By allowing for extended exposure times, these apps help record the continuous path of stars, resulting in stunning star trail images that highlight the beauty and dynamism of the night sky. Capturing star trails involves setting up for a long exposure to allow the camera to record the stars' movement across the sky. You'd typically need to find a dark location, mount your phone on a tripod for stability, and use an app that allows extended exposure times to capture the trails created by stars due to Earth's rotation. Setting up these apps to capture star trails is easier than using a DSLR or mirrorless camera because all we have to do is set the total exposure time and start recording the image. We can even use features like Even Longer's Save Interim Results that saves the star trails as it builds the long exposure. This is great since sometimes a 30-minute star trail might look better than say a 45-minute exposure. With traditional star trails, we might have to start all over again if we don't like the overall exposure time. Bottom line, advanced photography apps offer features for extended exposures, making it easier to capture the trails as Earth rotates. With the right setup and conditions, your phone can produce impressive star trail images. (*Note:* See page 136 for more on using third-party apps.)

Triggering Your Phone's Camera

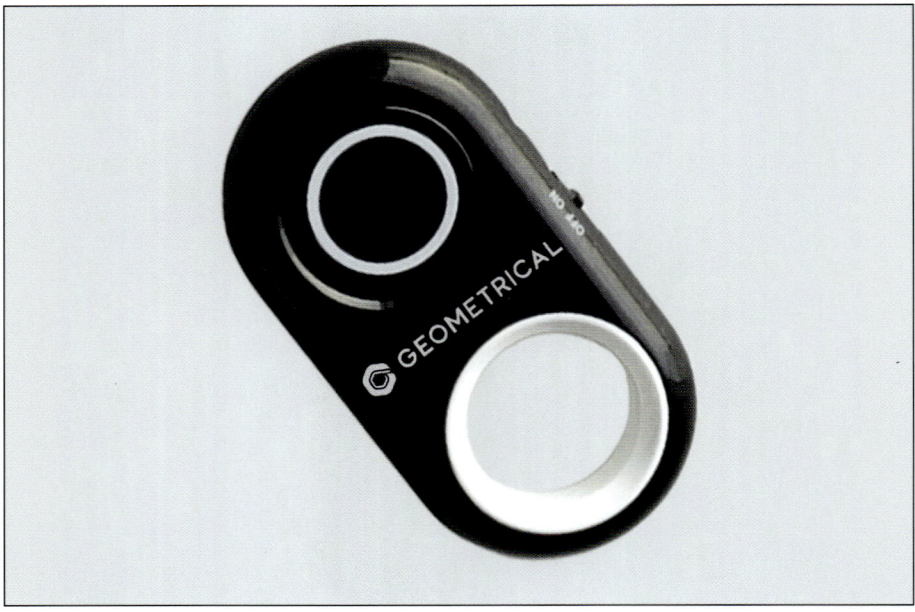

Capturing night photos with your phone's camera can be revolutionized by various remote triggering methods. Bluetooth triggers allow you to snap photos without physical contact, maintaining stability. Watch apps, compatible with smartwatches, offer convenience by triggering your phone's camera right from your wrist. Timer delays are built into most smartphone camera apps, providing a hands-free option to avoid camera shake. Wired triggers, though less common, offer a direct connection for reliability. And, wireless triggers, including IR remotes or smartphone apps, offer flexibility and distance from the camera, perfect for astrophotography or group shots. Each method ensures sharp, clear photos by minimizing camera movement. My two favorite methods are using either a simple Bluetooth trigger or using my watch as a shutter. To set up a Bluetooth trigger, first, be sure both the trigger and your phone's Bluetooth are turned on, then pair the devices via your phone's Bluetooth settings. Once connected, mount your phone on a tripod and position it toward your subject. Open your camera app and use the Bluetooth trigger to take photos remotely. To use your smartwatch as a camera trigger, be sure it's compatible with your smartphone, often through a specific app designed for remote camera control. After installing the required app on both devices and making sure they are paired (usually via Bluetooth), set up your phone on a tripod, and then use the watch app to trigger your camera remotely. Both of these methods are particularly useful for reducing camera shake, allowing for clearer shots. (*Note:* For more detailed instructions, check your devices' user manuals and your phone's user guide, as the process may vary slightly between different models and brands.)

Use a Small Tripod (That Fits in Your Pocket)

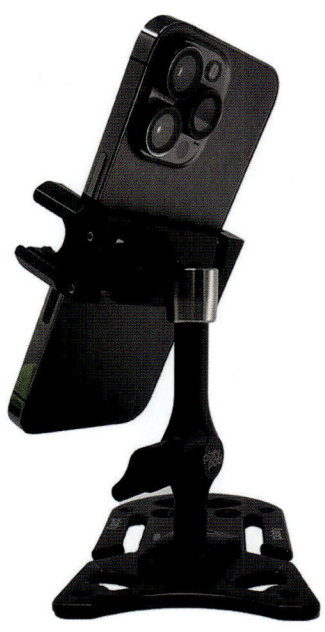

Using a small portable tripod with your phone's camera for night photography offers a blend of stability and convenience. These lightweight tripods are easy to carry, set up quickly, and can be adjusted to various heights and angles, ensuring your phone remains steady for those long-exposure shots without adding bulk to your gear. This setup is ideal for capturing crisp, clear night photos, whether you're shooting the starry sky or cityscapes, without the hassle of carrying cumbersome equipment. One of my favorite setups for mobile nighttime photography is combining the PlatyPod Ultra with the PlatyPod Grip. The Ultra serves as a versatile and stable base, perfect for uneven surfaces or tight spots where traditional tripods won't fit. Paired with the Grip, which securely holds your smartphone, this setup allows for precise positioning and stability for long-exposure shots without the bulkiness of traditional gear. It's ideal for capturing the night sky or city lights with ease and portability. You can find more details about these at PlatyPod.com. The Pocket Tripod Pro is another excellent setup for mobile photography, especially for those prioritizing portability. While it may not offer the same level of stability as the Platypod, its compact design, which allows it to fit easily in your wallet or pocket, makes it an incredibly convenient option for night photography on the go. It's an innovative solution for those looking for a lightweight, easy-to-carry support for their phone. You can find more about this one at pocket-tripod.com. Having a tripod for phone-based night photography is critical because it provides the stability required for long-exposure shots. Without a tripod, even the slightest movement can blur the stars or celestial bodies you're trying to photograph, compromising the quality of your images.

Use Third-Party Apps

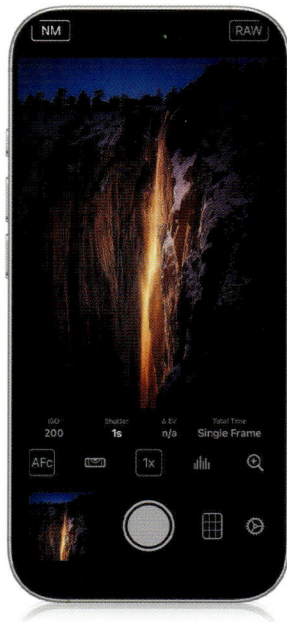

Third-party phone apps significantly enhance night photography capabilities, offering features beyond your smartphone camera's scope. These apps allow for expanded night modes, including light trails, and star trails by providing manual control over camera settings such as exposure, ISO, and shutter speed. This control allows you to capture the night sky and its wonders with greater detail and creativity, pushing the boundaries of what's possible with night photography using your phone. One of my favorite apps is Even Longer for iOS, which is great for capturing light trails and enhancing night mode photos. It offers advanced features that allow you to take long-exposure photos, perfect for creating dynamic images of moving lights at night. These types of third-party apps typically let you experiment with exposure settings to capture the beauty of night scenes vividly, making them invaluable tools. Light trail modes in these apps allow you to capture images of moving light sources at night, such as car headlights, creating continuous streaks of light across the image. This mode utilizes long-exposure techniques, keeping your camera's shutter open longer to record the light's path. It's a popular feature for creative night photography and offers a way to turn ordinary scenes into dazzling displays of light and motion. Another use for these apps is capturing the International Space Station (ISS) and satellite passes, which can add a fascinating dimension to night sky photos. Since they often include features that allow for long exposures, they allow you to track the movement of satellites and the ISS across the sky, resulting in striking light trails that record their path. This type of night photography requires precise timing and location information to align the camera with the satellite's trajectory and offers a unique blend of scientific observation and artistic expression. (*Note:* We looked at capturing the ISS back on page 124.)

Get Creative

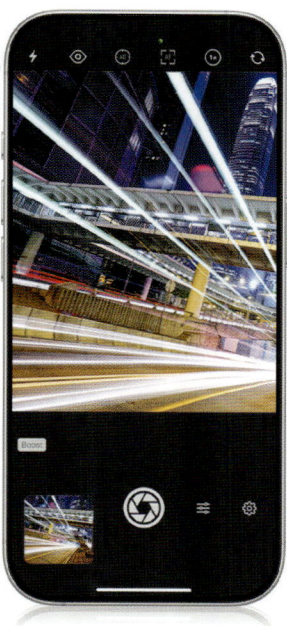

Smartphones are getting ridiculously good at nighttime photography, but most people stop at just snapping brighter shots of dark scenes. If you really want to push your phone camera's limits, there's an entire world of creative night photography techniques you can pull off, if you know how to work with what you've got. One big opportunity is intentional motion blur and light trails. Most smartphone night modes are designed to eliminate blur, but what if you want it? Apps like Even Longer (for iOS) or Slow Shutter Cam (for iOS and Android) let you override your phone's default settings and turn moving lights—like cars, city lights, or even hand-held LEDs—into streaks of color and motion. A busy street? Now it's a river of light. Fireworks? A swirling, glowing masterpiece. And if you want to get really creative, try spinning a flashlight or waving another phone's screen in front of the lens while shooting a long exposure—instant DIY light painting. Then, as you learned earlier (on page 133), there are star trails. While not as powerful as a DSLR or mirrorless, by using stacking apps (or a manual long-exposure mode), you can create trails that show the motion of the stars over time. Another cool trick is blending photos. Some apps allow you to take two images—one in twilight and another at night—and merge them. This technique lets you create surreal shots where a city's skyline is glowing with neon, but the foreground is still well-lit with detail. The point is your phone is capable of way more than just "good" night photos. With the right apps, settings, and a little creativity, you can turn your mobile shots into art. No heavy gear is required and it fits in your pocket.

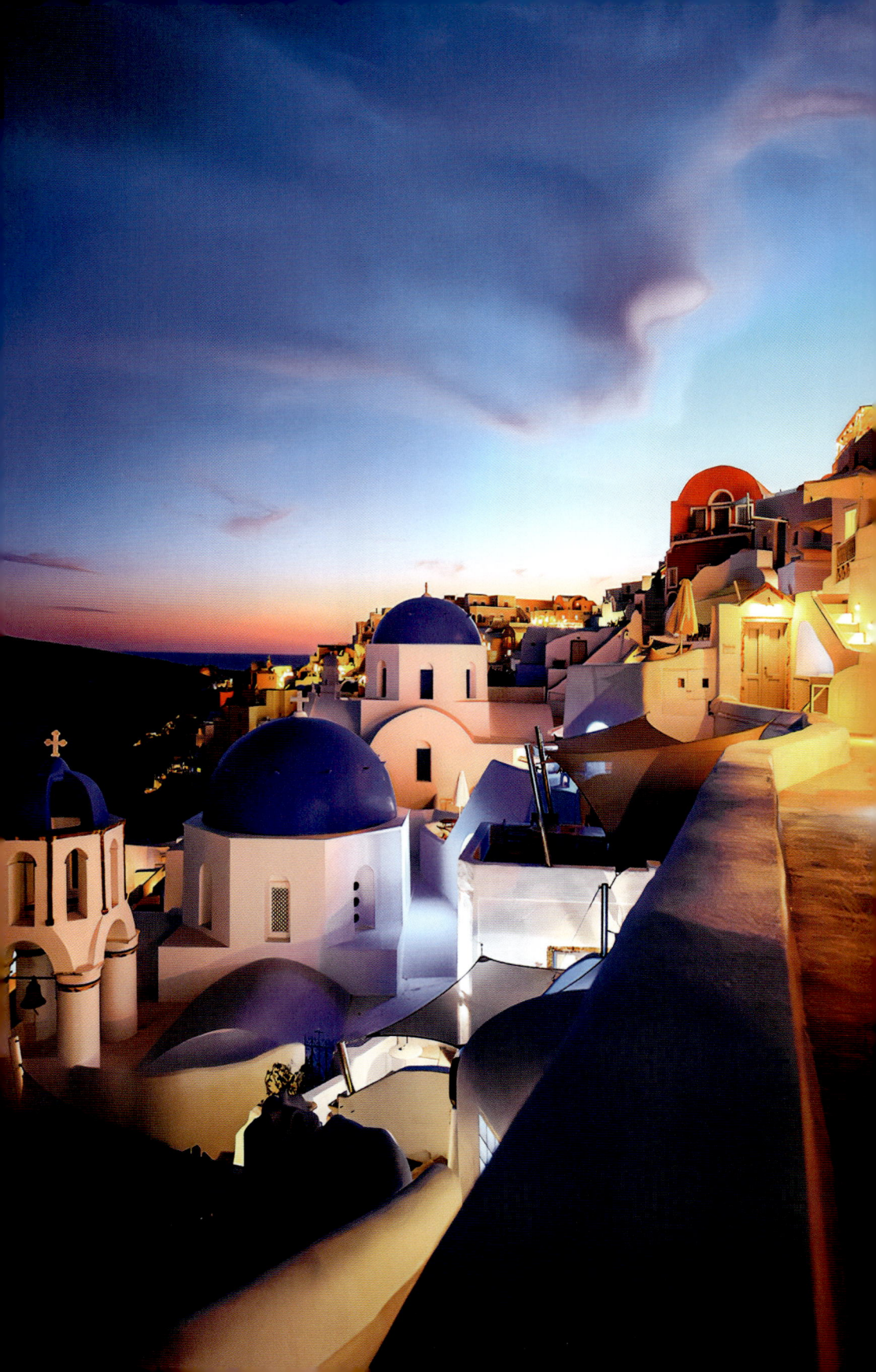

Shooting for Post

Setting Yourself Up for Success

Let's be honest, nobody gets their best night shots straight out of the camera. If they say they do, they're either lying or haven't zoomed in yet. Post-processing is where night photos truly come to life, but great editing starts with how you shoot. It's not about fixing bad shots in Photoshop; it's about capturing images with post in mind, so you have all the data you need to work with later. This chapter is all about shooting smart so your edits are easier, cleaner, and way more effective. We'll cover things like bracketing to save shadow details, how to avoid overblown highlights that can't be recovered, and why RAW is non-negotiable if you want full creative control. You'll also learn how to blend multiple exposures, whether you're stacking star trails, merging foregrounds and skies, or doing that magic trick where you shoot the foreground at blue hour and blend it with a night sky for insane detail. And let's talk about tracking and stacking. If you want razor-sharp stars, but don't feel like hauling a star tracker, stacking multiple short exposures is your secret weapon. We'll break down how to shoot for clean Milky Way images, time-lapses, and even deep-sky astrophotography without drowning in noise. Plus, we'll go over moonlight blending, day-to-night conversions, and why sometimes the best way to shoot the night is to start before it even gets dark. Our goal? Less frustration in post, and more time creating stunning images (to help out, I created some post-processing videos showing you how to do these edits. You'll find them on the book's companion webpage mentioned on page 185). The best edits don't start in Photoshop—they start in the field with a smart approach that makes everything easier later.

Single-Exposure Milky Way Image

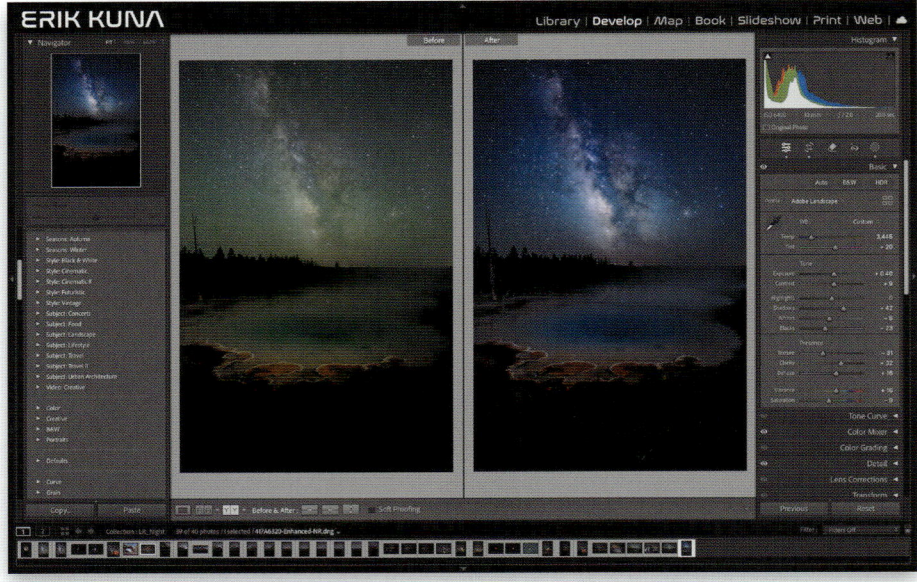

Crafting the Milky Way in your RAW photos involves a few essential post-processing steps to bring out the beauty of the galaxy's full splendor. But, the key here is your settings before you start. If your ISO is too low or your f-stop is too narrow or your shutter speed is too short, there is nothing you can do in post to fix it. That's why we spend so much time on settings and techniques before post (see page 68 for these). However, once we set up our camera correctly and get those settings right, making the photo come alive in post is easy. Start by adjusting the white balance to neutral-ize the color in your sky and foreground. If you used a proper Kelvin temperature (as we talked about on page 45), this should be easy. Then, we tone the image by adjust-ing exposure, vibrancy, and saturation to light up the galaxy's core without washing out its delicate structures. One way of further enhancing is to add clarity, reduce texture in the sky, and dehaze the sky. By reducing texture and adding clarity, the specks of stars will be deemphasized, and the core will pop. Next, tweak the contrast to deepen the sky's darkness and make the stars pop. From here, we can fine-tune the white balance to enhance the Milky Way's natural colors, leaning slightly toward cooler tones to mimic the night's ambiance. Sharpening is your friend, but apply it wisely, and utilizing noise reduction on your RAW file to keep the image clean while preserving the stars' integrity is key with a single exposure. Try using tools like On1 NoNoise or Topaz Denoise to help eliminate the noise. Finally, enhance the image's vibrancy and saturation to bring the cosmic colors to life, but remember, subtlety is key here, too. You're aiming to reflect the night sky's true beauty, not overshadow it with heavy-handed editing. Through careful adjustments and patience, you can transform a RAW file of the Milky Way into a breathtaking astrophotography shot.

The Blue Hour Blend

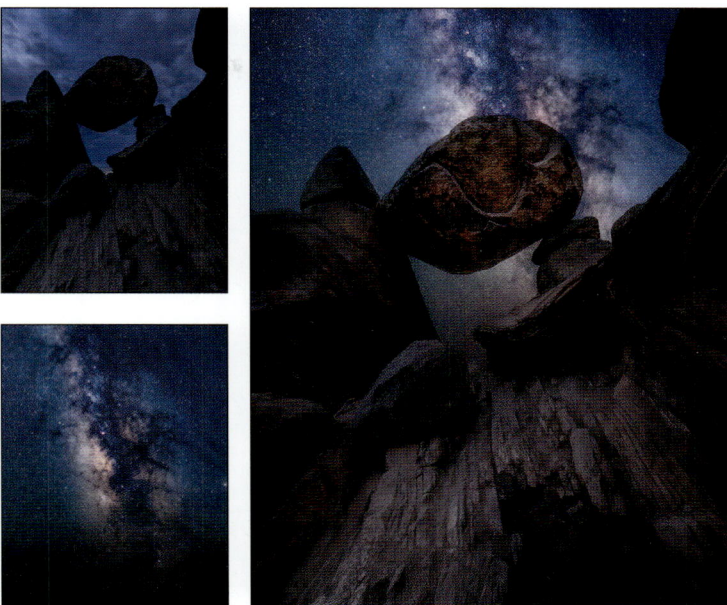

Let's look at a sneaky little trick that can take your night photos from "meh" to "How did you *do* that?" The Blue Hour Blend is the secret sauce to getting those beautifully detailed foregrounds while still capturing a stunning night sky (we looked at this on page 69). Here's how it's done: (1) Shoot your foreground at blue hour. That magical window just after sunset or before sunrise is your best friend because the landscape still has just enough light to reveal all the details without the harsh contrast of a flashlight or artificial lighting. Expose your foreground while there's still some ambient light, but it's dark enough to match the mood of a night shot. Your settings: Keep your ISO low (100-800) for clean, noise-free detail; aperture at f/8 to f/11 for deep depth of field (you want that landscape looking sharp); and shutter speed at whatever it takes to get a proper exposure—usually a couple of seconds with a tripod. (2) Shoot your night sky. Once the stars are out and the sky is looking epic, shoot this separate exposure. Since you no longer care about the foreground (you've already nailed that part), your settings will change: ISO 6400–12800 (to capture faint stars); aperture wide open (f/2.8 or faster); and shutter speed at 10–20 seconds (long enough for light, short enough to avoid star trails). (3) Now, the Photoshop magic (the fun part) where we combine the two shots. Open both images, placing the starry night sky shot on the top layer, and then use a layer mask to hide the blue hour sky, revealing your crisp night sky underneath. *Pro Tip:* Use Select Sky (see page 154) to make this process even faster. If the blend looks unnatural, feather your mask or use a slight color grade to match tones. And just like that, you've got the best of both worlds: a perfectly lit foreground and a stunning night sky, all in one seamless, mind-blowing shot. Give it a try, and don't tell anyone how easy it actually is. (*Remember:* You'll find post-processing videos on this on the book's webpage mentioned on page 185.)

The Moonscape Blend

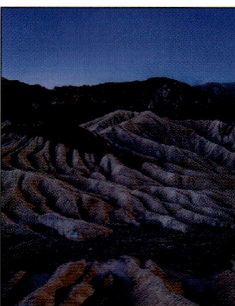
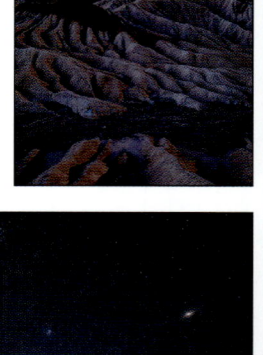
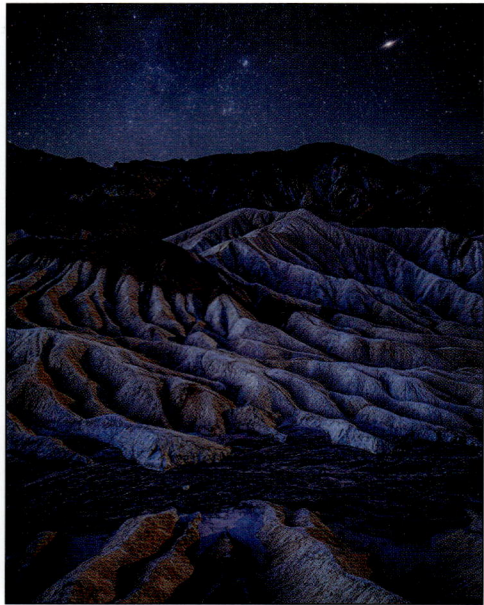

Most people don't realize this, but the moon isn't just a glowing rock in the sky—it's a built-in light source for night photography. Treat it like a dim, natural sun, and you can light up landscapes beautifully while still capturing the stars. The trick? Knowing how to balance moonlight with your night shot. (1) Choose the right moon phase (we looked at these on page 70). The best phases for moonscapes? First/last quarter moon: great balance of light and stars. Full moon: good for foregrounds but washes out the Milky Way. Crescent moon: adds moodier shadows with subtle lighting. (2) Shoot the moonlit foreground. Position yourself so the moonlight is hitting your subject from an angle, which adds depth and contrast—if it's overhead, shadows disappear, making everything look flat. You're aiming for a soft, natural glow over the scene. Settings for the foreground: ISO 800–1600 (low noise, good detail); aperture at f/4 to f/8 (for foreground detail); and shutter speed at 10–30 sec (long enough to soak in moonlight). (3) Capture the night sky. If the moon is bright, you may need a second exposure for the stars, otherwise, they'll be too faint or lost in the light pollution. Settings for the sky: ISO 3200–6400 (to pull in fainter stars), aperture at f/2.8 or wider; and shutter speed at 10–15 sec (to prevent star trails). (4) Blend in Photoshop. Open both images, placing the night sky shot on the top layer, and then use a layer mask to hide the overexposed sky from your foreground image, revealing the crisp night sky underneath, and then adjust the warmth, if needed—moonlight often looks too cool. And there you have it—using the moon as your personal night photography light source. No flashlights, no artificial lights, just good old lunar glow doing all the work for you.

The Astro-Tracking Blend

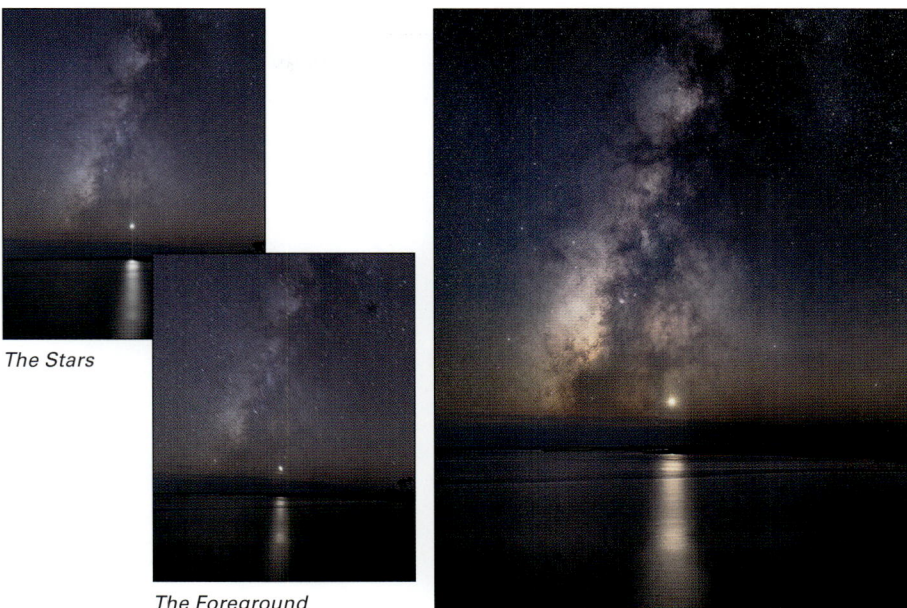

The Stars

The Foreground

If you've ever tried to shoot deep-space objects or the Milky Way with long exposures, you know the struggle—stars turn into streaks while your foreground stays sharp. Astro-tracking lets the stars stay perfectly still while your camera moves with them. The result? Insanely detailed, NASA-catalog-worthy stars. (1) Get the right gear. You'll need a star tracker, which moves your camera at the same speed as Earth's rotation (like Sky-Watcher's Star Adventurer, iOptron's SkyGuider Pro, or my favorite, Move-Shoot-Move's NOMAD). You'll also need a sturdy tripod and a ball head, or preferably what we call a "wedge" to align your tracker. (2) Track and shoot the stars. Set up your tracker, align it with Polaris (in the Northern Hemisphere) or Sigma Octantis (if you're down south), and mount your camera. If your alignment is off, the stars will drift, and your hard work goes out the window. You'll need Bulb mode here, since you're going beyond 30-second exposures since star trailing won't be an issue. Settings for star tracking: ISO 400–1600 (lower than usual since you're tracking); aperture open, but sharp (f/2.8 to f/8); and shutter speed at 1–7 minutes (depending on focal length—the wider your focal length, the longer you can go). (3) Shoot the foreground. Because your camera is moving with the stars, your foreground will blur. So, turn off the tracker and take a second shot with the same framing, focusing on the landscape. Settings for the foreground: ISO 400–1600 (depends on ambient light); aperture at f/4 to f/8 (for sharpness); and shutter speed at 30 seconds to a few minutes. (4) Blend in Photoshop. Open both shots as layers, then mask the blurred foreground from the star-tracked image to reveal the sharp, stationary foreground beneath, and then match the colors and contrast for a seamless blend. That's it—razor-sharp stars, crisp landscapes, and no weird motion blur. It takes a bit of set up, but once you get it right, your shots will look out of this world (literally).

Star Stacking

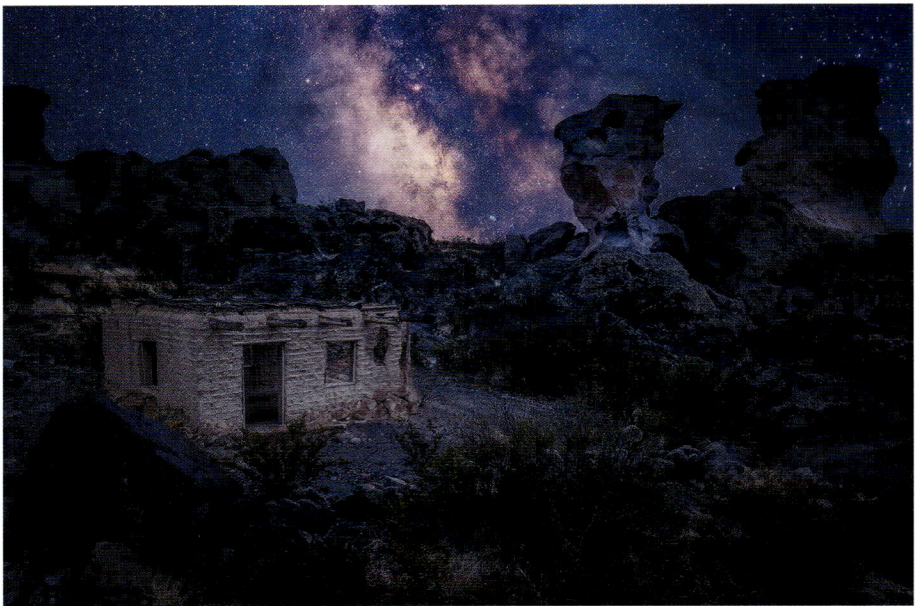

If you want ultra-detailed stars but don't feel like hauling around a star tracker and aligning it, star stacking is your new best friend. Instead of taking one long exposure and risking noise, you shoot multiple short exposures and stack them in post to get a cleaner, sharper result. Think of it as noise reduction on steroids. Couple stacking with added AI noise reduction, and even adding tracking to your stacking, and you have some of the cleanest images possible. (1) Set up your shot. Since you're shooting multiple frames, you need a sturdy tripod and an intervalometer (or your camera's built-in timer). Frame your composition with the stars you want, lock down your focus, and don't touch the camera until you're done. Settings for star stacking: ISO 6400–12800 (to capture faint stars); aperture wide open (f/2.8 or faster); shutter speed at 10–20 seconds (to avoid star trails); number of shots at 10–42 (more shots equals a cleaner image); and interval set at the shortest possible (like 1 second). (2) Shoot a foreground exposure (optional). If you want a perfectly sharp foreground, you might need a separate shot. Keep your camera in the same position but adjust your settings to properly expose the landscape. Settings for the foreground: ISO 800–3200 (lower for less noise); aperture at f/4 to f/8 (for detail); shutter speed at 30 seconds to a few minutes (in Bulb mode). (3) Stack in post. Load your star shots into Starry Landscape Stacker (for Mac) or Sequator (for Windows). These programs align the stars in every frame and blend them to reduce noise while keeping details razor sharp. (4) Blend with the foreground. If you shot a separate foreground image, bring both images into Photoshop, and using a layer mask, reveal the sharp foreground while keeping the stacked sky. A slight color balance adjustment will help everything look seamless. That's it! You just turned a noisy, single-frame star shot into a crystal-clear masterpiece—all without needing a fancy star tracker.

The Day-to-Night Conversion

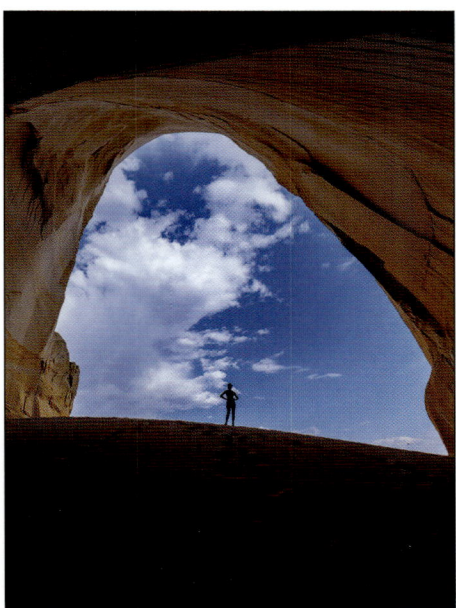
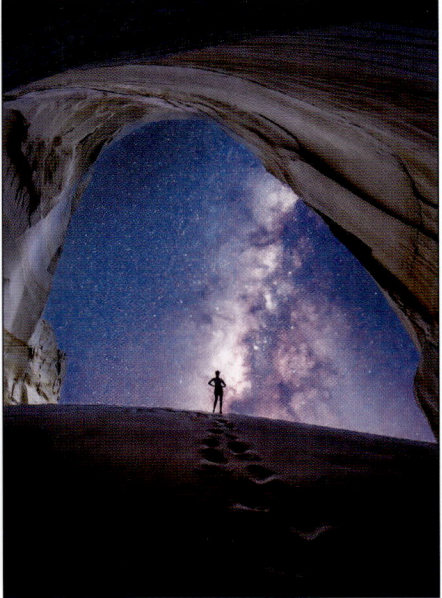

Another secret weapon for night photography: shoot during the day. Okay, not in broad, contrasty daylight—that would be cheating—but in soft, diffused light that blends seamlessly with a night sky. This trick is perfect for when you want a detailed, well-lit foreground without dealing with harsh lighting or noisy shadows. (1) Pick the right time to shoot. Day-to-night conversions work best when the light is soft—meaning no harsh shadows or glaring highlights. The goal is to capture a foreground that naturally blends with a night sky later in post. Ideal conditions include: overcast days (clouds diffuse light beautifully, giving even illumination) and golden hour (just before sunset—warm tones and soft light create a natural transition). Avoid shooting under direct sunlight—those hard shadows will scream "daytime" no matter how much editing you do. However, if you have to shoot in direct sunlight, shoot HDR and clamp down the highlights and fill the shadows to create less contrast. (2) Expose for the foreground. Since you're faking night, you want a darker, moody exposure—not a bright midday look. Underexpose slightly, at least by a stop to make the transition to night more convincing. Settings for the foreground: ISO 100–400 (cleanest image possible); aperture at f/8 to f/11 (sharp details); and adjust the shutter speed for a proper exposure. (3) Capture a real night sky. Once the actual night sky looks good, take your second exposure. If needed, shoot from the same location later that night (or you can use a stock Milky Way image that matches your scene's angle and direction). Settings for the night sky: ISO 6400 (to pull in stars); aperture at f/2.8 or wider; and shutter speed at 10–15 seconds (sharp stars, no trails). (4) Blend in Photoshop. Open both images as layers, then mask your day shot sky, replacing it with the night sky. Use curves and color grading to cool down highlights to make everything feel naturally nocturnal. That's it!

Light Painting While Moving the Light

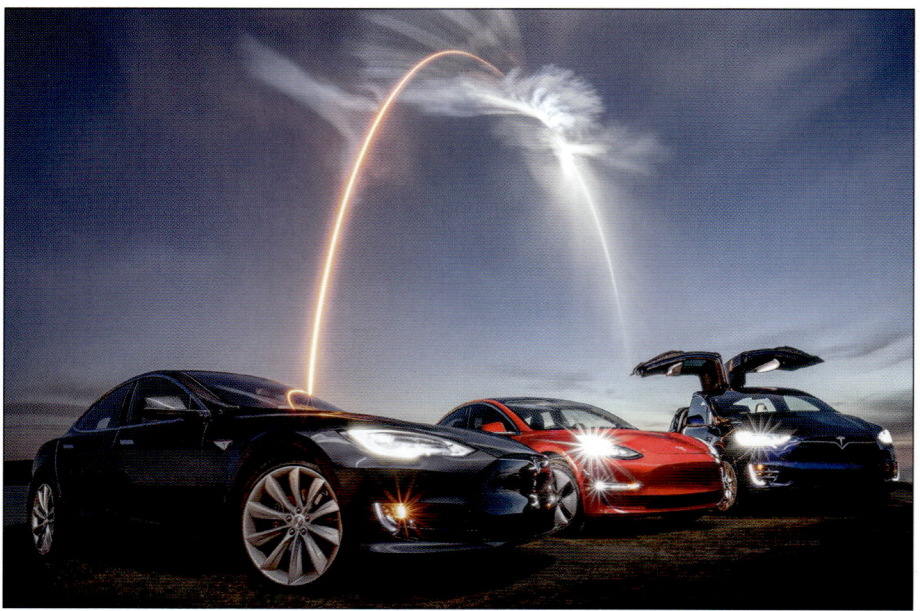

Light painting is like wielding a lightsaber for photography—you control exactly how your subject is lit. But instead of flashing a burst of light, continuous lights let you sculpt your scene, giving you precise control over exposure, direction, and mood. (1) Pick the right light source. You need a steady light source, not a flash. LED panels, handheld LED wands, RGB light sticks, and even basic flashlights (with the right color temperature) work great. The key is color temperature—match it to your scene to avoid weird tints in post. Warm LEDs (3200K) create a great warm glow to match the night's sky, cool LEDs (5600K) mimic sunlight and moonlight, and RGB LEDs let you get creative with color effects. (2) Set up your camera for a long exposure. Because you're "painting" with light, you need a long exposure to capture the light over time and lower your ISO. Mount your camera on a tripod and set a self-timer or remote trigger to avoid shake. Settings: ISO 400–800 (keep noise low); aperture f/5.6 to f/8 (sharp details), and shutter speed at 10–30 seconds (maybe even longer). (3) Light paint the scene. Once the shutter opens, move your light source to paint in the foreground—slow, steady sweeps work best. (*Pro Tips:* Move constantly to avoid harsh hot spots. Angle the light at 30, 45, or 90 degrees from the camera to create depth and avoid flat, unnatural lighting. Consider back lighting. Use side lighting for more dramatic textures.) (4) Shoot multiple passes. Light the foreground in one shot, the mid-ground in another, and then blend them for ultimate control. (5) Blend in Photoshop. Open and stack your best exposures as layers, use layer masks to blend only the best-lit parts, and then fine-tune with curves and color balance. Done right, continuous light painting looks like you set up an entire movie set for your night shot. And the best part? You're in full control of how the scene is lit—no unpredictable moonlight, no waiting for perfect conditions, just pure creativity.

Light Painting with the Lights on Stands

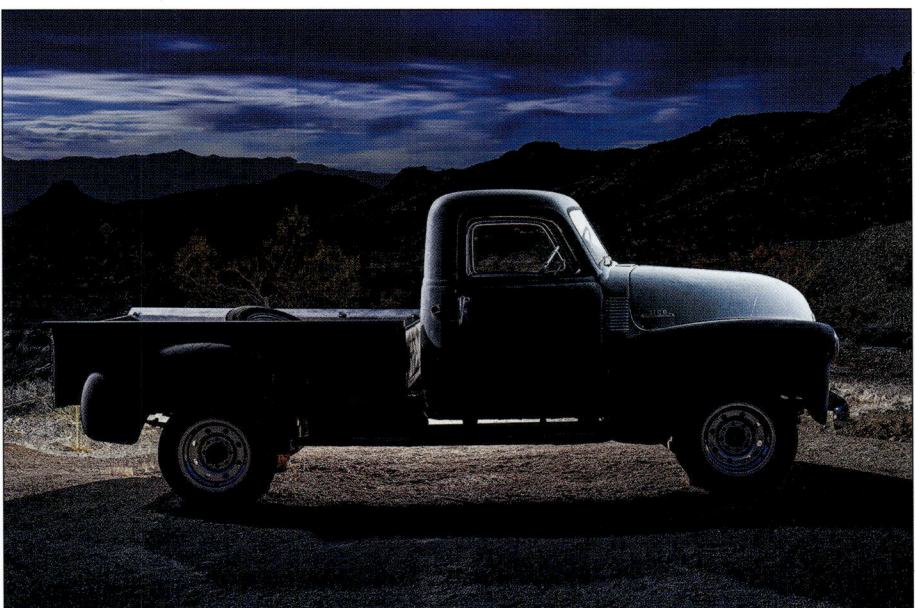

Light painting doesn't always mean running around waving a light. Sometimes, the best approach is to set up your lights like in a studio shoot. Using RGB LED panels or tubes on light stands allows for controlled, cinematic lighting while still keeping that surreal, night photography vibe. (1) Choose your RGB lights. Unlike hand-held light painting, where you move the light, this setup uses static lights to create a balanced, dramatic composition. The advantage? More control, cleaner exposures, repeatable lighting, and easier blending in post. (2) Set up your scene. Think of it like lighting a model in a studio, except your subject is a landscape, car, or architecture. Place the lights strategically to highlight essential elements. Basic setups: The key light (main source) is your brightest light, placed at an angle to create depth. The fill light is softer, opposite the key light to lift shadows. Accent lights are used for edge lighting, background glow, or adding colors. (*Pro Tip:* Use color gels or RGB settings to mix warm and cool tones for cinematic contrast.) (3) Dial in your settings. Since your lights are static, you can easily dial in exposure times better than traditional light painting, so you can balance ambient light and your RGBs for the perfect shot. Plus, the same scene can be shot with repeatable results. Settings: ISO 100–800 (keep noise minimal); aperture at f/5.6 to f/11 (sharp details); and shutter speed at 5–30 seconds (adjust based on LED brightness). (4) Capture multiple shots. Shoot different lighting setups that you can blend later or just use one frame. Try one frame with cool blue ambient light, another with warmer highlights, and one with a backlight for depth, or try all three together. (5) Edit in Photoshop. What's great about this technique is that what you see is what you get, so you can create it all in one exposure, or you can blend multiple exposures—it's up to you. Done right, this setup gives you full creative control—think of it as a Hollywood set, but under the stars.

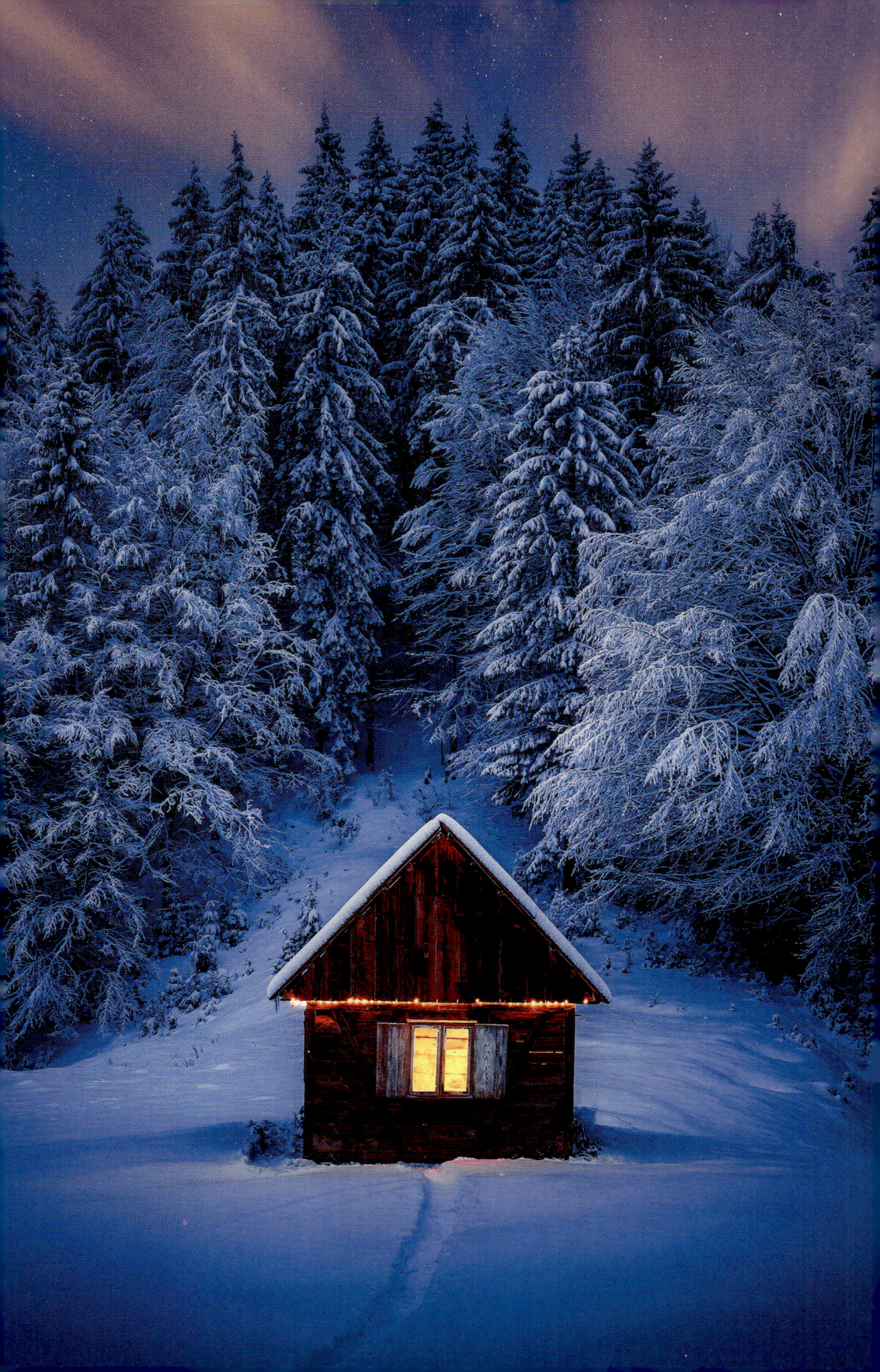

12

Post-Processing

Bringing Your Night Shots to Life

In the last chapter, we established that no one's best night photos come straight out of the camera. If you've ever taken what looked like an amazing shot in the field, only to get home and realize that the stars are too dim, the shadows are too noisy, or the colors are completely off, welcome to the club. This is where post-processing saves the day (or night). Editing night photos isn't about fixing mistakes; it's about unlocking the full potential of what you captured. That faint Milky Way core? It's in there. The shadow details you thought were lost? They're just waiting to be revealed. The trick is knowing how to bring everything out without overcooking it into an unrealistic mess. This chapter is all about fine-tuning your night shots for maximum impact. We'll cover how to balance exposure, recover highlights, bring out the Milky Way, and reduce noise without turning everything into a mushy blur. You'll learn how to use selective contrast adjustments to make your stars pop, why color grading matters more than you think, and how to blend multiple exposures for that perfect mix of sharp foreground and detailed sky. And of course, we have to talk about AI-powered noise reduction. Just a few years ago, shooting at ISO 6400 felt like a risky move. But now, with AI denoising tools, high-ISO images look cleaner than ever. We'll break down how to use them effectively, when to stack exposures instead, and how to get a crisp final image without losing the natural feel of the night. Post-processing isn't about making a bad shot good— it's about making a good shot great. And with the right techniques, your night photos will go from "pretty cool" to absolutely stunning. Let's edit.

Editing a RAW Image

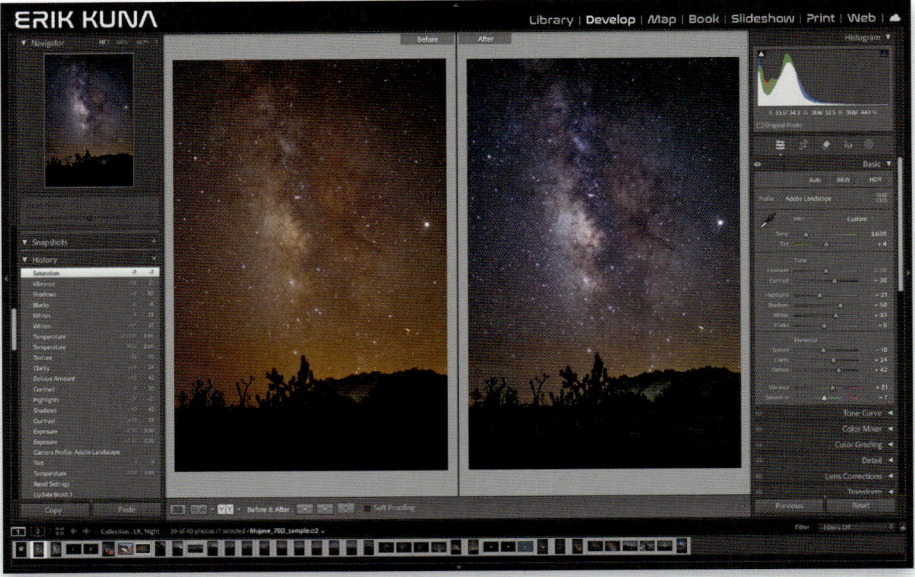

Shooting in RAW isn't optional for night photography—it's mandatory. RAW files hold all the light, detail, and color data your camera captured, letting you recover shadows, reduce noise, and fine-tune colors without destroying image quality. Here's how to process your night shots: (1) Fix the white balance. Cameras often misinterpret colors at night, so manually adjust the white balance (I'm doing this in Lightroom Classic here). A setting of 3200K–4200K works best for deep blue night skies. If the sky looks too green, shift the Tint slider slightly toward magenta, and vice versa. Be sure that the foreground and sky match—there's nothing that's more of a dead giveaway than a warm foreground under a cool sky. (2) Recover the shadows and highlights. Night photography is about balancing brightness and shadows without making it look fake. Adjusting the Shadows (+50 to +75) brings back foreground details without overexposing, and adjusting the Highlights (–20 to –40) pulls back blown-out stars. Adjust the Whites (+10 to +30) to make stars pop, and the Blacks (–10 to –30) to add depth and contrast. (Continued on the next page.)

Editing a RAW Image (continued)

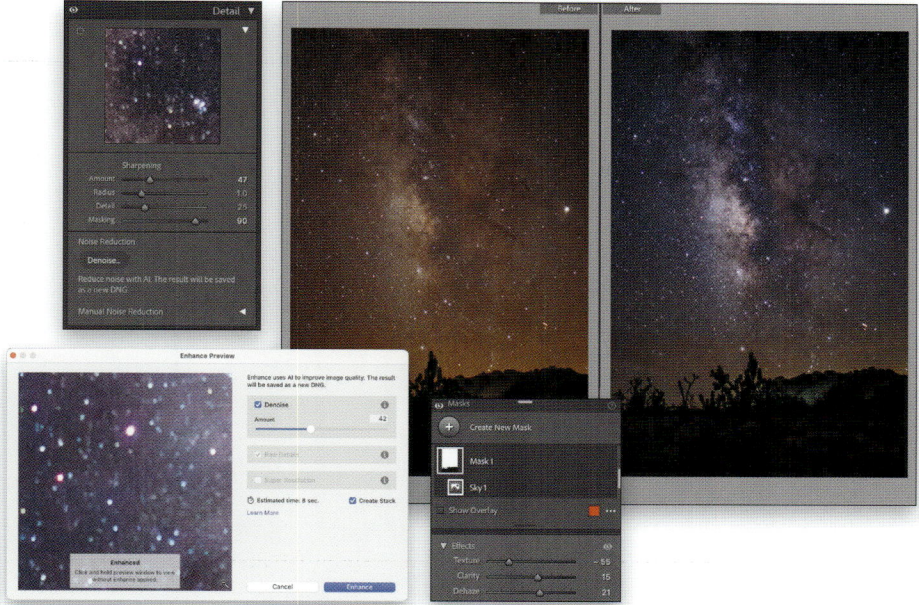

(3) Reduce noise without killing detail. High ISOs mean noise, but don't overdo noise reduction—it kills sharpness. However, Lightroom's (and Camera Raw's) AI Denoise does wonders now! In the Detail panel, run Denoise at around 20 to 50 with Raw Details turned on (it should be by default). Next, add Sharpening (40 to 70) and adjust the Masking (50 to 90)—press-and-hold the Option (PC: Alt) key while dragging this slider to avoid sharpening noise. (4) Boost (and remove) the stars without overprocessing. Create a Select Sky mask, then add Dehaze (10 to 25), which enhances the Milky Way. Add Clarity (15 to 40) to add detail while avoiding halos, and then add negative Texture (–20 to –55) to reduce the number of stars, which enhances the Milky Way. Trust me, it works. (5) Color grade for mood. In the Color Grading panel, add cool tones (blue/cyan) to the shadows for a realistic night feel. If your foreground looks too warm, reduce orange/yellow saturation in the HSL area of the Color Mixer panel (see page 157 for more on HSL). Final tip: Edit in low light. Bright screens can trick your eyes, so edit in a dimly lit environment for accuracy. (*Note:* Like I mentioned in the previous chapter, I created some post-processing videos showing you how to do these edits. You'll find them on the book's companion webpage mentioned on page 185.)

Editing a Single Exposure

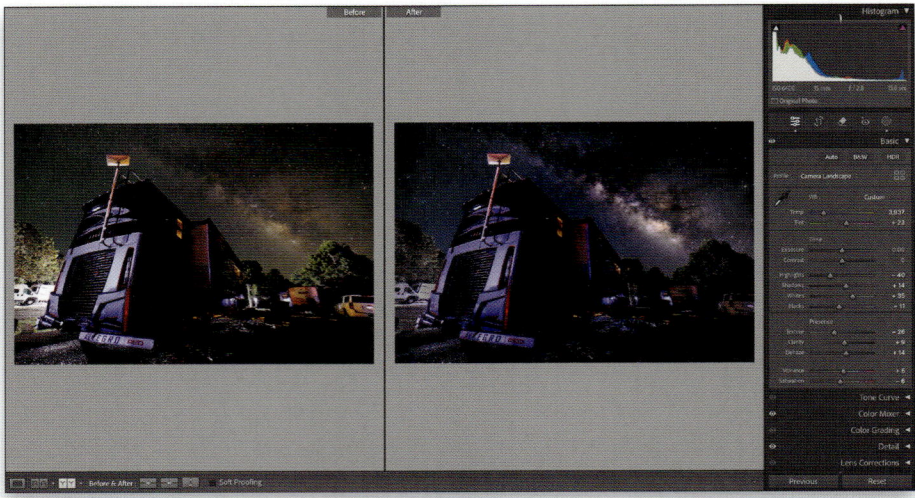

Not every night shot needs complex blending or stacking. Sometimes, a single exposure is all you need. The key is knowing how to bring out the best in that one frame without introducing noise, halos, or overcooked edits. Here's how to maximize detail, minimize noise, and create a stunning image: (1) Get the white balance right. Auto white balance struggles in the dark, so adjust it manually. Aim for a cooler temperature to keep the night sky looking natural, and make sure the foreground tones blend with the scene—no unnatural color shifts. (2) Balance the exposure without overdoing it. Night images need contrast and depth, but pushing shadows too far can ruin the mood. Recover highlights where needed, deepen blacks for a richer look, and make sure stars pop without overbrightening the scene. (3) Tackle noise smartly. High-ISO noise is inevitable, but today's AI noise reduction tools clean it up while preserving fine details. Apply noise reduction strategically and use sharpening carefully to avoid adding artifacts. (4) Enhance the stars without overprocessing. A touch of Dehaze and Clarity helps bring out the Milky Way, but too much can make stars look unnatural. Selectively brightening key stars or using radial adjustments can give them more presence without making the edit look forced. (5) Refine color for a natural night look. Cool tones in the shadows help maintain a nighttime feel, while subtle color grading can unify the image. Avoid oversaturating the sky or foreground—night photography should feel atmospheric, not artificial. Final tip: Edit in the right conditions. Make sure your monitor isn't too bright and that colors and contrast are accurate. Bright screens can trick your eyes, leading to over-darkened or overprocessed edits. Another tip: Send your image to your phone or tablet to look at the color and brightness there too! Keep adjustments subtle and stay true to the night scene. (*Note:* See page 150 for more specific setting suggestions.)

AI Noise Removal (It's a Game Changer)

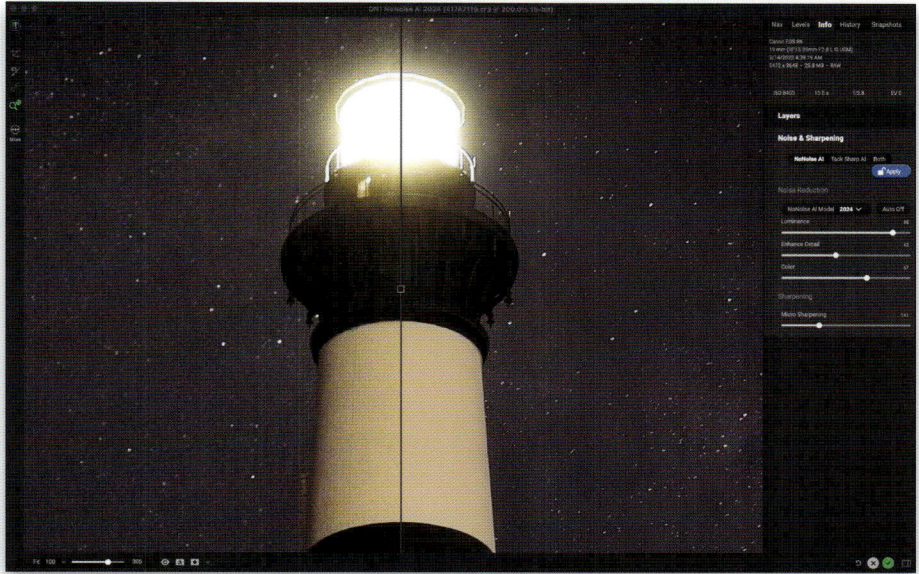

Just five years ago, noise reduction was a balancing act—reduce noise too much, and you lost sharpness; keep too much detail, and you were left with grainy, unusable images. The solution? Stacking multiple exposures to average out noise. But now, thanks to AI-driven noise removal, that's almost unnecessary because AI noise reduction replaces stacking. In the past, I relied on image stacking—combining multiple exposures to reduce noise naturally. While effective, it was time-consuming—aligning, blending, and masking layers in Photoshop wasn't exactly a quick fix. But now, AI-powered tools do in seconds what used to take hours. Programs like On1 NoNoise (seen here), Adobe Denoise, and Topaz DeNoise can remove noise while recovering fine details—without softening the image into mush. While old noise reduction tools blurred the image to hide noise, AI models analyze and rebuild lost details instead. Adobe AI Denoise (in Lightroom and Camera Raw) removes noise while preserving edges and fine details—perfect for high-ISO Milky Way shots. On1 NoNoise uses AI to intelligently smooth noise while keeping stars and textures crisp. Also, the impact on ISO choice means I'm no longer afraid to push my ISO to 6400 or even 12800. In the past, I'd hesitate because of noise, but now AI denoising makes high-ISO files cleaner than ISO 1600 shots from five years ago. Seriously. And it makes ISO 1600 shots look like ISO 400! So, if you're still stacking just to fix noise, feel free to stop. AI noise removal saves time, retains sharpness, and makes high-ISO night photography easier than ever. It's a game changer, and I wouldn't have believed it just five years ago. Or, heck, go nuts—stack and use AI noise reduction. It's only getting better and better. (*Note:* We'll look at stacking on page 161.)

Select Sky in Photoshop

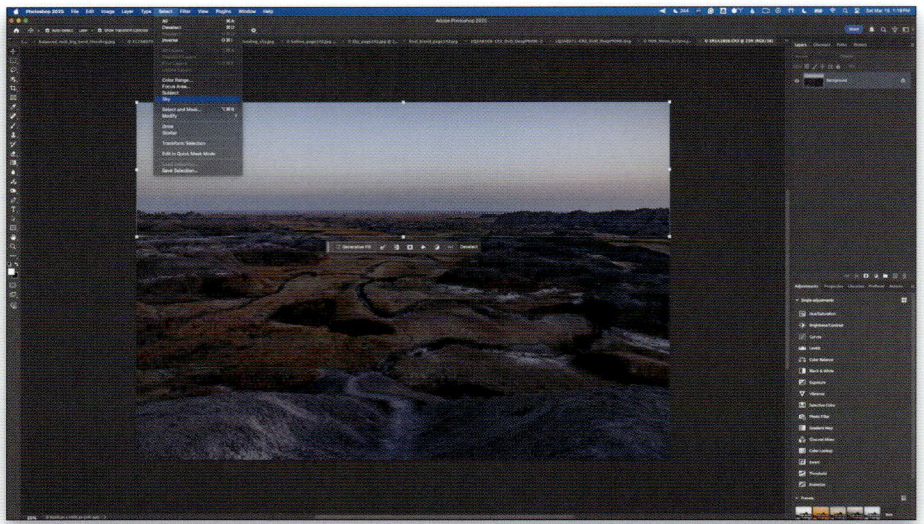

Sometimes, Sky Replacement (we'll look at this Photoshop feature more in a minute) just doesn't cooperate and you need to take control. Whether you're working with a blue hour foreground, a day-to-night conversion, or just need a cleaner Milky Way, Photoshop's Select Sky feature makes sky replacements fast and accurate while giving you control with a mask. Here's how to use it: (1) Open your foreground image. Be sure your foreground shot is well-exposed and ready for blending. If it was shot at blue hour or earlier in the evening, you'll want to darken it slightly in Camera Raw to match a night scene (just go under the Filter menu and choose Camera Raw filter). (2) Use Select Sky for a quick, clean mask. Go under the Select menu, choose Sky, and Photoshop's AI will detect and select the sky automatically. If the selection isn't perfect, choose any one of the Selection tools in the Toolbox on the left, and then click on Select and Mask up in the Options Bar. To refine the selection, in the Properties panel, increase the Feather slider (2.0–5.0 px) for a smoother transition and use the Refine Edge Brush tool (the second tool down in the toolbar on the left) to clean up tree lines, buildings, or tricky areas. At the bottom of the panel, click Invert, then choose Layer Mask from the Output To pop-up menu and click OK. (Continued on the next page.)

Select Sky in Photoshop (continued)

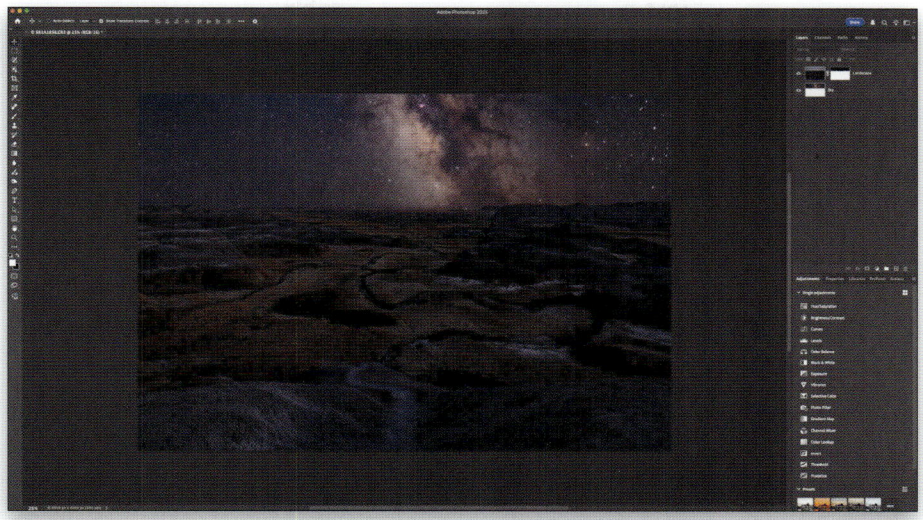

(3) Replace the sky. Open your night sky image, press Command-A (PC: Ctrl-A) to select it, and then Command-C (PC: Ctrl-C) to Copy it. Switch back to your foreground image, press Command-V (PC: Ctrl-V) to Paste your new sky into it, and then, in the Layers panel, click-and-drag its layer down below your foreground layer. Use the Move tool (V) and Free-Transform (Command-T [PC: Ctrl-T]) to resize and position the sky so it matches the perspective of your scene. If the horizon looks unnatural, lower the opacity of the night sky layer (at the top of the Layers panel) temporarily to align it properly. (4) Blend the foreground and sky seamlessly. Use Curves or Levels (under the Image menu, choose Adjustments) on the foreground to darken it so it looks like it was actually shot at night, and adjust the Color Balance to make the foreground and sky match (cool down warm tones if needed). If the edges look harsh, use a soft brush on the layer mask to gently blend transitions. Final tip: Add a glow for realism. Night skies aren't just a cutout swap—there's always some ambient light spill. So, you can add a new solid color (white) layer, then add a layer mask set to white, and then using a soft, black brush with a low opacity (around 3%), paint on the mask to reveal the glow where the sky meets the horizon. This helps create a more natural transition between the two elements. And that's it! With Select Sky, replacing a daytime sky with a starry night takes just minutes, and if it's done right, no one will ever know it was an edit.

Sky Replacement in Photoshop

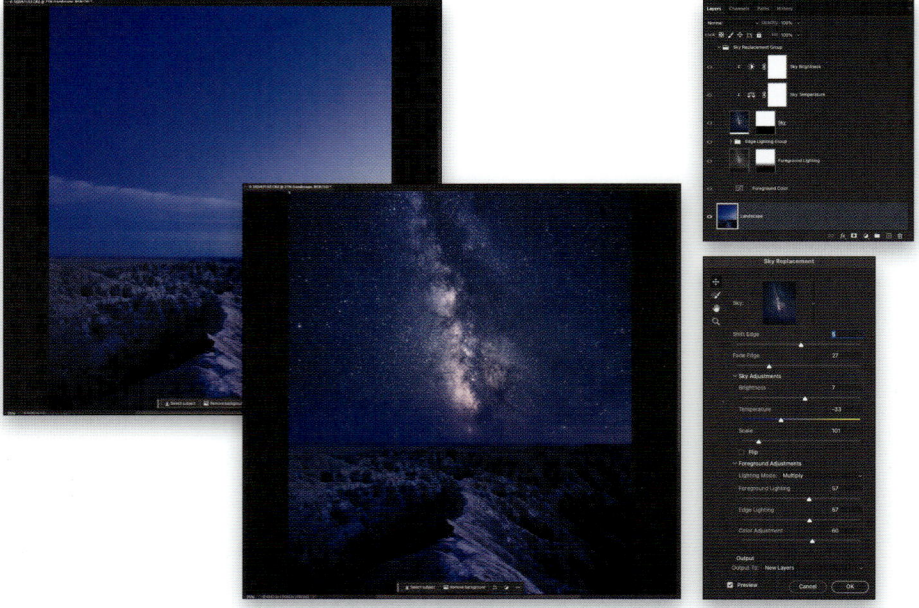

Photoshop's Sky Replacement feature makes swapping skies fast and automatic—perfect for turning a daytime or blue hour shot into a stunning night scene. The best part? It does all the masking and blending for you and you don't have to worry about all that glow and blending. Here's how to use it: (1) Open your foreground image. If your foreground was shot in daylight or blue hour, you might need to darken it slightly in Camera Raw to help the transition look natural (just go under the Filter menu and choose Camera Raw filter). (2) Open Sky Replacement. Go under the Edit menu, choose Sky Replacement, and Photoshop will automatically detect and mask the sky. The Sky Replacement dialog will appear and if you click on the Sky thumbnail, you'll see the different sky options. To import your own night sky to replace the current one, click on the Import Sky Images icon (the plus sign) at the bottom of the Sky menu. (3) Choose and position your night sky. Once you've selected your new sky, use the Scale slider to resize and/or reposition it for a proper perspective. (4) Blend the sky and foreground for a natural look. Use the Brightness and Temperature sliders to adjust the sky's mood to match the foreground, and use the Fade Edge slider to soften the transition between them. Under Foreground Adjustments, from the Lighting Mode pop-up menu, experiment with Multiply or Screen to blend the shadows realistically. (5) Fine-tune with layer masks (this is *big*). Click OK and Photoshop creates editable layers and masks, which you can refine using a soft brush, if needed. Finally, use Curves or Levels (under the Image menu, choose Adjustments) on the foreground (Background) layer to darken it to match the night scene and adjust the Color Balance to remove warm tones and keep it looking natural. And that's it! With Sky Replacement, you can swap in a perfect night sky in seconds—with none of the tedious masking work.

Complementary Tones & Presence

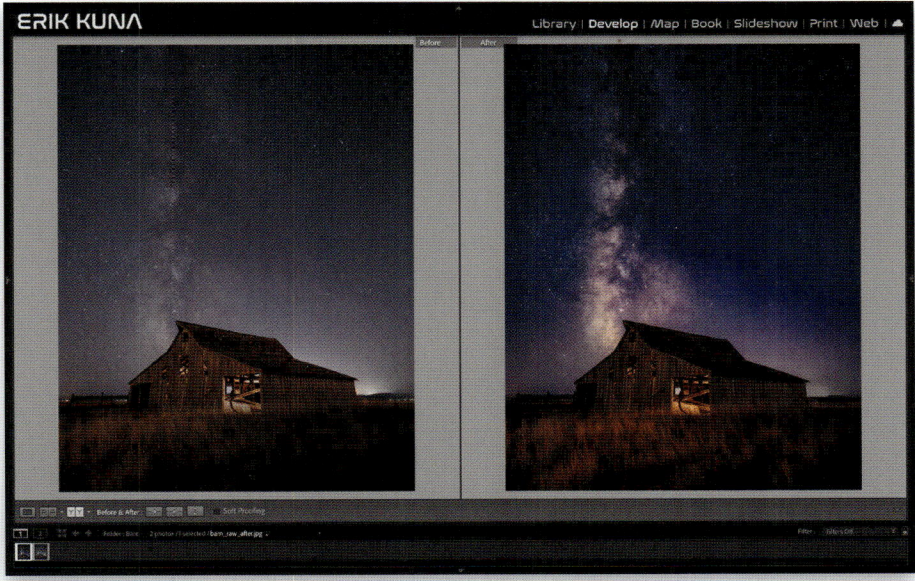

Night photography isn't just about capturing stars—it's about creating a mood. The right tones, colors, and contrast can make a night shot feel cinematic, ethereal, or even otherworldly. Get it wrong, and your image might feel flat, overly warm, or just "off." Here's how to master tones and presence in your shots: (1) Use the best color harmonies. Night scenes naturally lean toward cool tones, but the best images use a mix of warm and cool to create contrast and depth. Cool blue and cyan (monochromatic harmony) work best for Milky Way shots and deep-space scenes. Shift shadows toward deep blues and highlights toward cool cyans for a consistent night feel. Blue and orange (complementary contrast) are great for cityscapes or light-painted scenes where warm lights contrast against a cool night. Keep shadows cool (blue/cyan) and warm up highlights (yellow/orange) for cinematic contrast. Teal and purple (split-complementary mood) are ideal for surreal or moody astrophotography. Adding a subtle magenta cast to midtones makes nebulae and the galactic core pop. (2) Experiment with HSL (Hue, Saturation, Luminance). HSL adjustments fine-tune tones without making the image look overprocessed. Reduce yellow and green saturation because night photos often have an unwanted yellow-green tint (from light pollution or air glow). Desaturate greens and shift yellows toward orange for a cleaner look. Boost blue and teal luminance, which brightens the sky without overexposing stars. Reduce red and magenta saturation because too much can make the Milky Way look artificial. Keep these in check unless the scene has real magenta tones. Darken the blues slightly, which adds richness without flattening the image. Final tip: Use local adjustments for presence. Radial filters help emphasize the Milky Way or main subject. Dehaze (+10 to +20) enhances contrast in the sky, but use it sparingly, and a subtle vignette can keep focus on the subject while adding depth.

Lens Corrections & Optical Issues

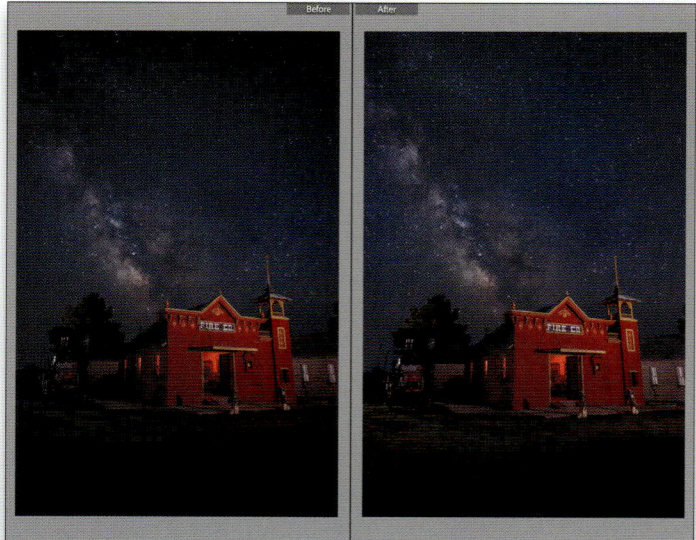
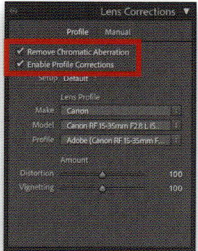
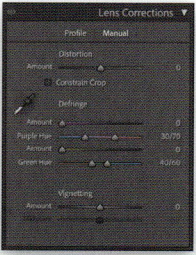

Night photography pushes lenses to their limits—wide apertures, high contrast, and bright stars against dark skies expose every optical flaw. Thankfully, Lightroom and Photoshop offer powerful correction tools to clean up distortion, color fringing, and aberrations. Here's how to fix common issues: (1) Turn on lens corrections first. Before making any other edits, go to the Lens Corrections panel in Lightroom (or the Optics panel in Camera Raw) and turn on Remove Chromatic Aberration, which fixes color fringing (more on this in a minute). Also turn on Enable (Use) Profile Corrections, which automatically corrects distortion and vignetting based on your lens. This instantly removes most barrel distortion, dark edges from vignetting, and warping—especially useful for wide-angle night shots. (2) Fix chromatic aberrations and color fringing. Night photos often show color fringes around bright stars and this happens when lenses struggle to focus on all colors at the same point. Once you turn on Remove Chromatic Aberration, if fringing is still visible, click on the Manual tab and then under Defringe, manually adjust the Purple Hue slider for magenta/purple fringing and the Green Hue slider for greenish halos. Use the Fringe Color Selector (Sample Fringe; the eyedropper) tool at the top left of the Defringe section to sample and remove stubborn color shifts. (Continued on the next page.)

Lens Corrections & Optical Issues (continued)

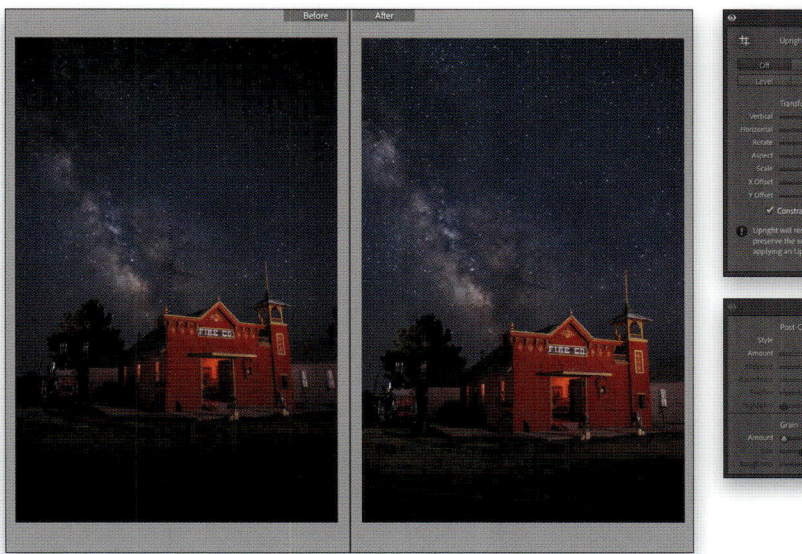
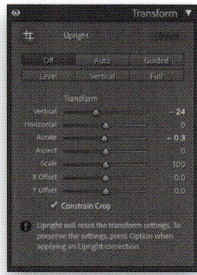
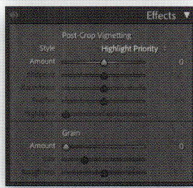

(3) Correct wide-angle distortion. Wide-angle lenses exaggerate foreground elements and stretch stars at the edges of the frame. So, use the Transform tools (in Lightroom's Transform panel; or in Camera Raw's Geometry panel, found nested with the Crop tool) to fix extreme distortion. If stars appear warped near the edges, go back to the Lens Corrections panel and in the Manual tab, try the Distortion correction, adjusting the Amount slider carefully. To subtly realign any unnatural stretching, in Photoshop, you can use Free Transform (Command-T [PC: Ctrl-T]) or Liquify (found beneath the Filter menu). (4) Remove unwanted vignetting. Most lenses darken the edges of an image at wide apertures (f/2.8 or faster). This is usually fixable, but sometimes you want to keep a little vignette for a natural look. Use the Lens Corrections panel's Vignetting Amount (or the Optics panel's Correction Amount Vignette) slider to brighten edges slightly—but don't overdo it. If you prefer a controlled vignette, use the Post-Crop Vignetting Amount slider (or the Vignette slider in Camera Raw) in the Effects panel instead for more artistic control. Final tip: Fix first, edit later. Lens corrections should be your first step in post-processing. By cleaning up distortions, fringing, and vignetting first, this ensures that every edit afterward looks natural and polished.

Blending Two Exposures

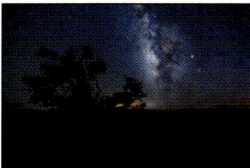

The Stars

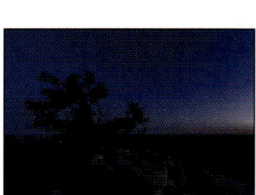

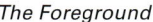

The Foreground

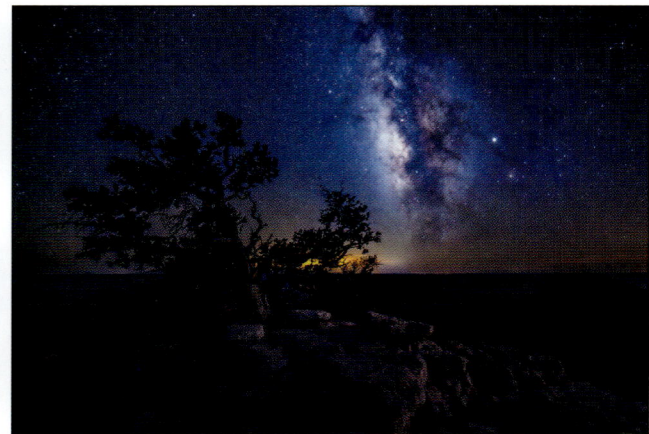

Blending two exposures is the secret to sharp, detailed foregrounds with a perfectly exposed night sky—but only when done right. A bad blend stands out immediately, so here's how to make it seamless. (1) Align your images in Photoshop (even with a tripod, slight shifts happen). Open both exposures in Photoshop, placing them as layers in the same document with the night sky layer on top (we looked at this in Chapter 12). Then, go under the Edit menu and choose Auto-Align Layers to ensure perfect positioning, and if needed, use Free Transform (Command-T [PC: Ctrl-T]) to fine-tune. (2) Create a smooth layer mask. Click on the Add Layer Mask icon at the bottom of the Layers panel to add a layer mask to the night sky layer on top. Then, get the Brush tool (B) and using a soft, black brush (30%–50% opacity), paint over the horizon to reveal the foreground on the layer below. For smooth transitions, use the Gradient tool (G) to create a black-to-white gradient mask—especially helpful for flat horizons. (3) Match exposure and contrast. One of the biggest giveaways of a bad blend is a foreground that's too bright, so use Curves or Levels (under the Image menu, choose Adjustments) to slightly darken the foreground layer. If the blend looks unnatural, adjust the Brightness/Contrast of each layer separately. (4) Refine edges. If the transition looks harsh, apply a slight Gaussian Blur (under the Filter menu, under Blur; 2–5 px) on the mask to soften the edges. Pay attention to objects breaking the horizon (trees, mountains), and if they look off, refine the mask with a smaller brush. (5) Add a natural glow. Night transitions are never harshly cut off—there's always a soft atmospheric glow. Use a low-opacity brush on a new layer (set to Soft Light mode) to paint a faint blue/cyan glow near the horizon. Final tip: Flip the image upside down. This helps you spot unnatural transitions because your brain focuses on tones and contrast instead of the subject.

Stacking Multiple Exposures

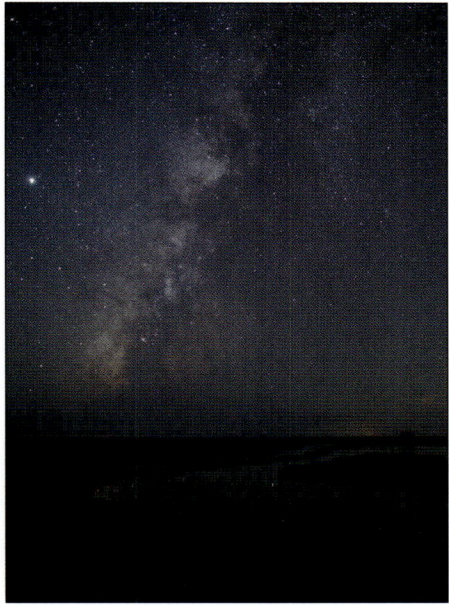 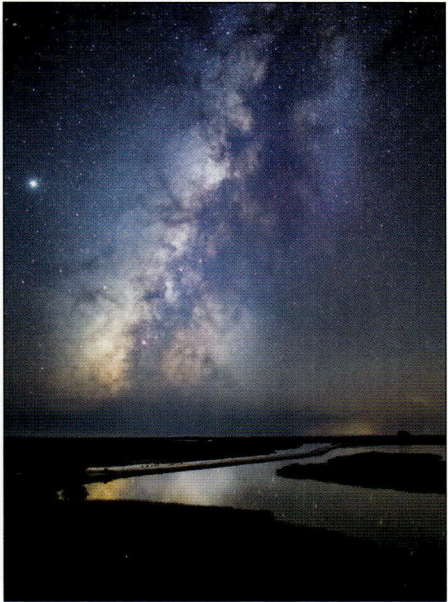

Stacking multiple exposures is one of the best ways to reduce noise and enhance details in night photography. Whether you're stacking for a cleaner Milky Way or for star trails, editing the images properly ensures the final result is sharp, smooth, and natural-looking. (1) Prepare your RAW files. Before stacking, process all your images consistently to avoid mismatches in color and exposure. Apply lens corrections and chromatic aberration removal to prevent edge distortions and adjust white balance, so all frames have the same color temperature. But, keep sharpening and noise reduction off for now—stacking will handle noise naturally. (2) Align and stack the images. For noise reduction stacking (deep sky, Milky Way, or landscapes), use Starry Landscape Stacker (for Mac) or Sequator (for Windows) to align and blend exposures. These tools keep stars sharp while averaging out noise. For star trails stacking, open your images as layers in one document in Photoshop, and then set the blending mode to Lighten to reveal trails. (3) Post-stack editing for a clean final image. Once stacked, the image will be cleaner, but it needs fine-tuning. Adjust Contrast and Clarity (using the Camera Raw filter) to bring out textures in the sky and use Curves or Levels to deepen shadows and brighten stars without overexposing. If trails or stars look soft, apply gentle sharpening using the High Pass filter (under the Filter menu) or the Texture slider (in the Camera Raw filter). (4) Final noise cleanup and refinements. Even after stacking, some noise may persist, so use AI noise reduction tools (Adobe Denoise, Topaz DeNoise, On1 NoNoise) sparingly to keep fine details. For star trail stacks, add a slight Gaussian Blur (1–2px) to trails for a more fluid motion effect. Final tip: Blend in a foreground for extra depth. If you shot a separate foreground, blend it in using a soft layer mask for a balanced looking image. (Remember: You'll find a video on this on the book's companion webpage.)

Tracking & Blending Images

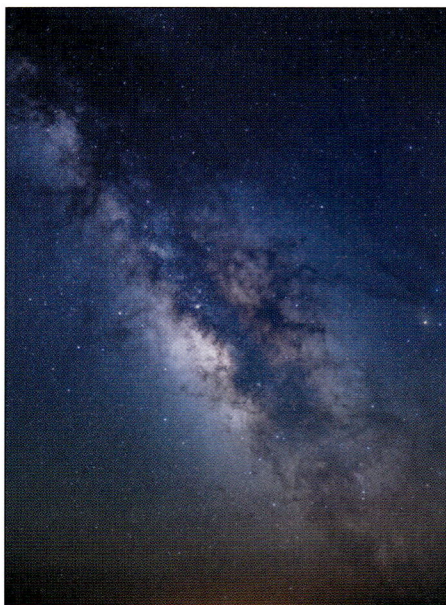 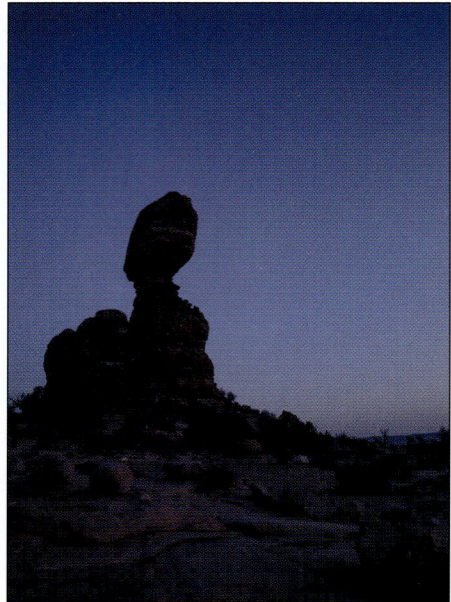

Using a star tracker lets you capture incredibly sharp, detailed stars without push-ing ISO to noisy extremes (see page 16 for more on this), but tracking introduces its own challenges in post. Since the tracker moves the camera with the sky, your foreground blurs, meaning blending in a separate, non-tracked foreground is key. Here's how to process and combine tracked exposures for the cleanest results: (1) Process your tracked sky exposure. Since tracking keeps stars sharp but intro-duces motion in the landscape, your main focus is enhancing celestial detail while keeping noise low. In Lightroom (or Camera Raw), apply lens corrections and defringe to clean up chromatic aberration on stars (see page 158), use Curves or Levels to stretch contrast, bringing out faint nebulae and dust lanes, and add a touch of Dehaze (+10 to +20) to emphasize structure in the Milky Way. Sharpen lightly—too much sharpening introduces weird artifacts in deep-space details. (2) Process your foreground exposure. Your non-tracked foreground shot will be sharper but likely darker, so the key is making sure it blends naturally. Keep white balance consistent with the sky shot—no warm foregrounds under a cool sky and use noise reduc-tion (if needed) to clean up shadow noise, but don't over-soften details. Darken your foreground slightly to match the night mood so it doesn't look artificially bright. (Continued on the next page.)

Tracking & Blending Images (continued)

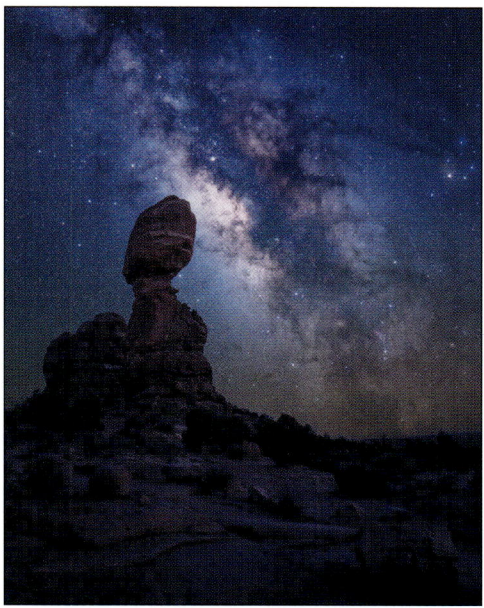

(3) Blend your sky and foreground in Photoshop. Since the tracker moves the camera, you can't just stack the images—you have to manually blend them. So, open both images as layers in the same document, placing the sharp foreground on top. Click on the Add Layer Mask icon at the bottom of the Layers panel to add a mask (you can also use Select Sky here; see page 154), then use a soft, black brush (30%–50% opacity) to mask in the sky exposure. If the horizon transition looks unnatural, apply a small Gaussian Blur (under the Filter menu, under Blur; 2–5 px) on the mask to soften the blend. (4) Match exposure and color for a seamless blend. Use Curves or Levels (under the Edit menu, choose Adjustments) to balance brightness between the sky and foreground. If the colors feel off, tweak the Color Balance to unify the tones, adding a faint blue glow at the horizon to simulate atmospheric light spill for realism. Final tip: Add local contrast for depth. Use the Dodge tool (O) on the brightest Milky Way areas to subtly enhance glow, and the Burn tool (Shift-O) on deep shadows to add richness. With a properly processed tracked image, you'll get razor-sharp stars, clean foregrounds, and an ultra-detailed Milky Way—without ISO noise ruining the shot.

Compositing

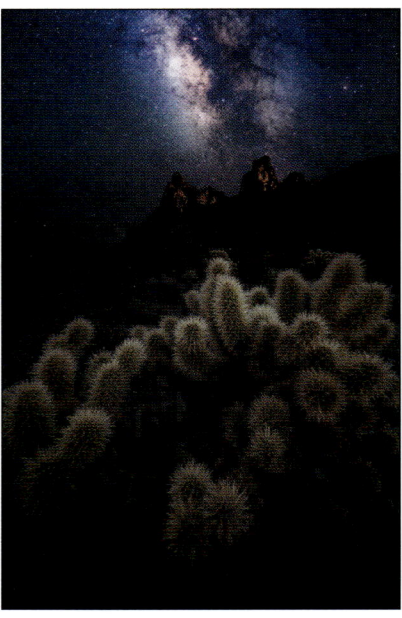

Compositing in night photography isn't just about blending exposures—it's about making sure every element feels realistic and cohesive. The dark tones, atmospheric glow, and natural light sources all play a role in selling the illusion. Here are a couple of examples and some advanced compositing tricks to ensure your final image looks seamless (remember, you can find a more detailed video on this on the book's companion webpage—see page 185): (1) Keep star alignments realistic. If you're replacing a sky or stitching multiple images, be mindful of star placement. The Milky Way moves predictably, and shifting its position too much can make your image look fake—especially if someone familiar with astronomy sees it. Use the Stellarium or PhotoPills app to check the Milky Way's real-world positioning for accuracy. If compositing multiple tracked images, align constellations properly so there are no mismatches (see page 71 for more on tracking). (2) Maintain light direction and shadows. Night photography still has directional light, whether from the moon, city glow, or artificial sources. If your foreground is lit from the left, but the sky suggests the moon was on the right, your brain will notice something's wrong—even if it can't explain why. Identify the primary light source in your scene (moon, ambient glow, light painting). If you're blending different exposures, adjust the shadows and highlights so the lighting matches. When adding foreground elements, use Curves to adjust the brightness and contrast to match the existing light. (Continued on the next page.)

Compositing (continued)

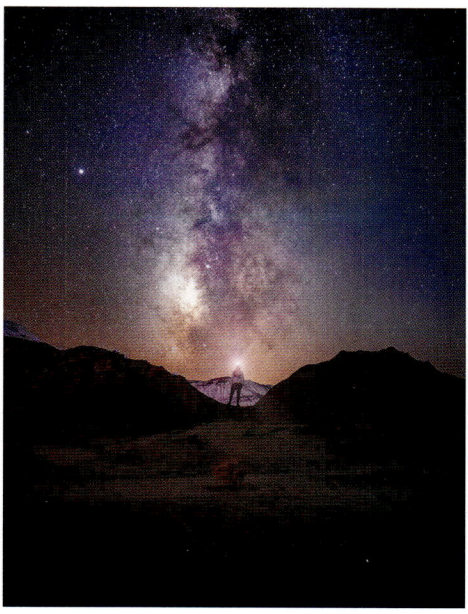

(3) Add atmospheric depth for realism. Night images aren't flat—there's natural depth created by air glow, haze, and light pollution. Without this, composites can feel too crisp and artificial, so add a subtle haze layer between the foreground and background for depth. Use Gradient Maps to introduce realistic color falloff (cooler at the top, warmer near the horizon). If adding distant elements (like mountains), reduce the contrast slightly to simulate atmospheric perspective. (4) Avoid "floating foregrounds." One of the biggest giveaways of a bad composite is when the foreground looks like it's floating and disconnected from the environment. Use a soft ground shadow or light spill at the base of the foreground to anchor it, and apply a slight blur or noise match to integrate sharp foregrounds with softer night skies. (5) Use subtle color contamination for believability. At night, colors from light pollution, moonlight, and star glow subtly mix into the scene. If an element looks too clean or untouched, it won't feel like part of the environment, so add a low-opacity color layer with the same hue as the scene's ambient light. Use Selective Color adjustments to slightly tint highlights and shadows toward the existing tones. If light sources are visible, introduce a faint color cast where they would naturally affect objects. Final tip: Step away and reevaluate. Night composites trick the eye—what looks perfect after an hour of editing might scream "Photoshopped" the next day. So, take breaks, zoom out, and view your image in different lighting conditions to catch inconsistencies. If something feels off, flip the image upside down, which helps your brain spot unnatural edits instantly. When done right, a night composite should feel like a single, perfect shot. By focusing on realistic alignment, depth, light interaction, and subtle color shifts, your composites will look natural, cinematic, and completely seamless.

Accurate Composite Blending

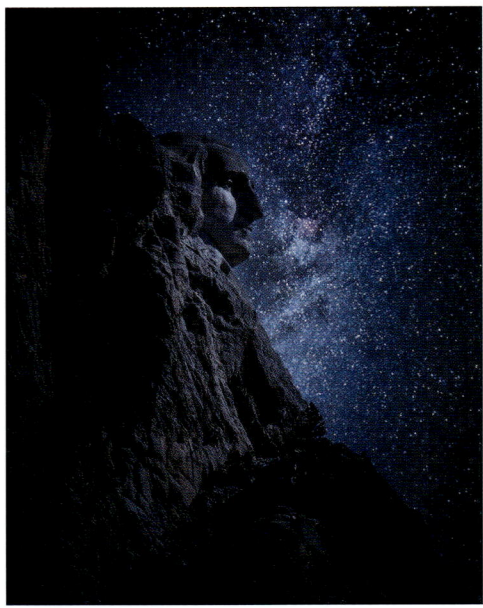

If you want to make a composite look real, blending isn't just about slapping two exposures together and hoping for the best. You have to match light, color, and exposure, so the final image looks like a seamless night shot—not a Frankenstein of mismatched parts. Here are a couple of examples along with how to do this: (1) Match the white balance first. Ever see a blend where the sky is a cool, deep blue, but the foreground looks like it was shot on Mars? That's because the white balance doesn't match. Fix this in Lightroom or Camera Raw before blending the images by making sure both have a similar color temperature. Your sky should be around 3200K–4200K (cooler tones work best for stars), and your foreground should match—if it's too warm (5000K+), it'll look fake. (2) Keep the foreground dark enough. A common mistake is making the foreground too bright. If it looks like it was shot at noon, your night composite is dead on arrival. Darken your foreground exposure using Curves, so it matches the mood of the night sky. But, avoid shadows that are too deep—they should have just enough detail to look natural. (3) Use feathered layer masks for seamless blending. A hard transition between exposures is a dead giveaway of a bad blend, so use a soft, feathered brush (30%–50% opacity) to blend your exposures in Photoshop. Also, try a black-to-white gradient mask for smoother sky replacements. If the edges look unnatural, blur the mask slightly using a 2–5 px Gaussian Blur. (Continued on the next page.)

Accurate Composite Blending (continued)

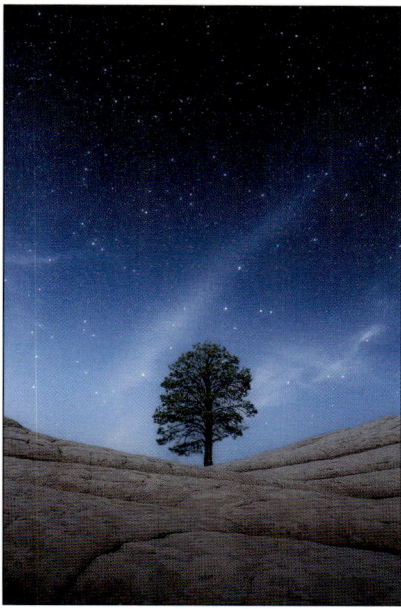

(4) Match exposure and contrast. Even if brightness levels are different in-camera, you can fix them in post. Use Levels or Curves (go under the Edit menu and choose Adjustments) to make the foreground exposure match the sky. Keep the contrast in check—if the sky is soft, don't make the foreground ultra-sharp. (5) Add a final color grade. Even if exposure and contrast match, the color can still feel "off." So, apply Color Balance or Selective Color to unify the tones. A subtle blue tint in the shadows helps the whole scene feel cohesive. Final tip: Like I've mentioned before, flip the image upside down. Your brain will focus on shapes and transitions instead of the subject. If anything feels "off," you'll spot it instantly when it's upside down! (*Note:* Once again, you can find detailed videos on all this on the book's companion webpage—see page 185.)

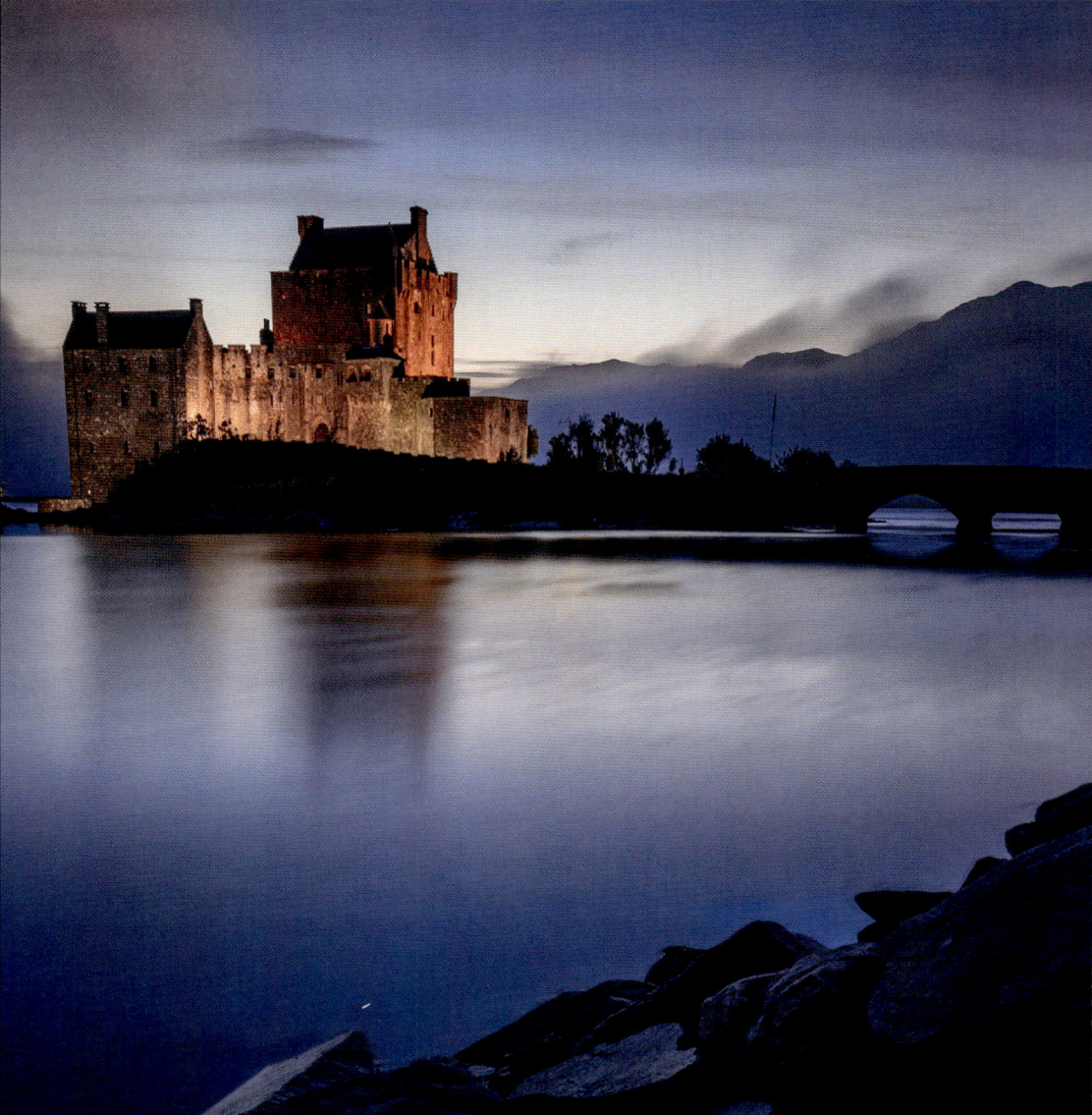

))))●● 13 ●●(((((

Printing & Sharing

Bringing Your Night Photography into the Real World

There's something special about seeing your night photography in print—holding it in your hands, seeing it on a wall, and knowing it's more than just pixels on a screen. A great print doesn't just display an image; it makes it tangible, permanent, and something people can truly experience. But getting from screen to print (without it looking like a dull, muddy mess) is where the real work begins. Printing night photography isn't as simple as hitting "Print" and hoping for the best. What looks amazing on your backlit screen can turn into a dark, lifeless print if you're not careful. This chapter is all about how to properly prepare your images for printing, choosing the right paper and medium, and making sure your work looks just as stunning in person as it does online. We'll break down the pros and cons of using a professional print lab vs. printing at home, why test prints are your best friend, and how to tweak brightness, contrast, and sharpness so your final print actually matches what you envisioned. We'll also dive into how to sell your prints, whether online, in galleries, or at local art shows, and how to price your work in a way that makes sense for both you and your audience. And of course, we can't ignore the digital side of sharing. Social media is a game-changer for photographers, but if you've ever uploaded an image to Instagram only to have it compressed into a blurry mess, you know that sizing and formatting matter. We'll cover the best settings for different platforms, how to make your photos stand out in an endless scroll of content, and why engagement is just as important as the photo itself when it comes to growing your audience. Your photography deserves to be seen. Whether it's hanging on a wall, sitting in a collector's gallery, or blowing up on social media. This chapter will help you get your work out there and make sure it looks incredible when you do.

Using a Professional Lab vs. Printing at Home

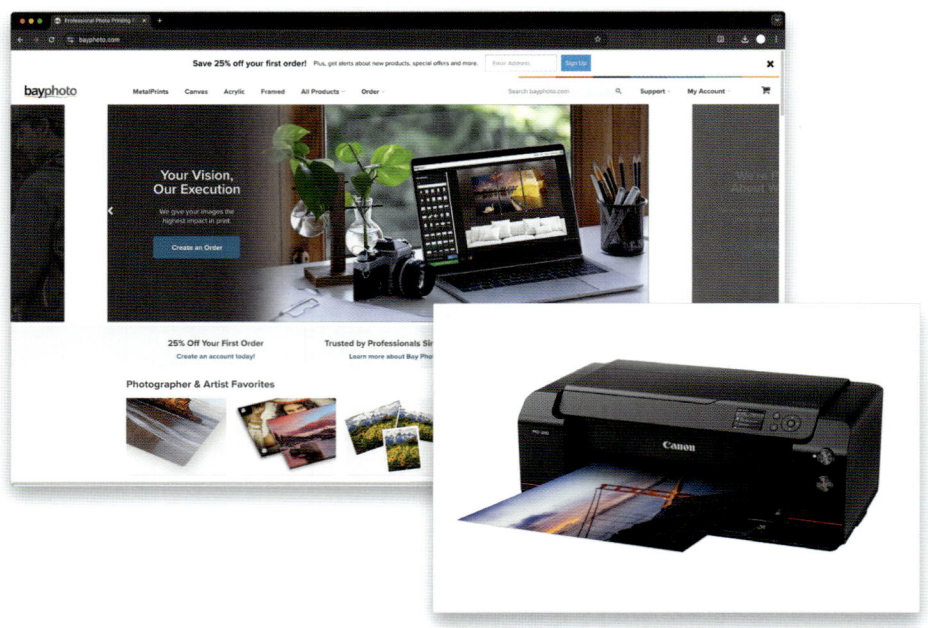

Choosing a lab like Bay Photo Lab or MPIX to print your photos offers significant advantages over home printing. Labs use high-quality materials and advanced printing technologies that ensure your photos display vibrant colors, deep blacks, and sharp details that do justice to the night sky. Additionally, they offer a wide range of sizes and finishes, allowing for customization. However, printing at home offers immediate control over the printing process, allowing you to experiment with different papers and settings to achieve your desired results. It's also convenient for quick prints or small batches, saving time and shipping costs. Using a lab for photo printing offers other advantages, like color calibration and quality control, and they ensure that images are printed with accurate colors that closely match what you see on your screen without wasting ink or paper. They also have quality control processes to address issues, provide customer support, and ensure a high-quality product every time. Labs offer the unique advantage of printing photos on various mediums, like metal, canvas, and acrylic, which can enhance the visual impact of your images. Again, on the other side, printing at home offers customization in paper type, color management, and calibration, allowing for a personal touch to each print. However, maintaining your printer is crucial. Another pro of using a lab is their capability to handle large format prints, which might be challenging or impossible to achieve with typical home printers. But, relying on labs can mean longer wait times from order to delivery compared to the instant gratification of home printing. Another consideration is the ongoing cost and impact of shipping, especially for frequent orders or single prints. Balancing all these factors will depend on your specific needs, priorities, and values as a photographer.

Running Test Prints

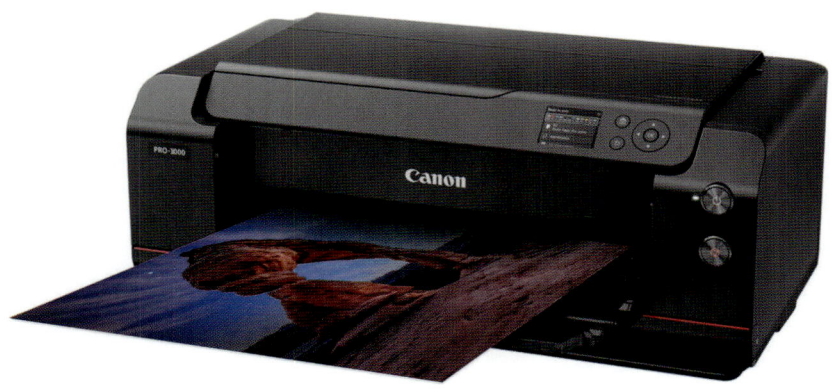

For any photographer, running test prints, whether at home or with a professional lab, is a critical step in achieving the perfect final product. Doing this allows you to evaluate the print's color accuracy, ensuring that what you see on your monitor gets translated onto the print. This happens since our screens are backlit and have difficulty accurately translating to print. For example, most photos will need brightness and exposure increases before printing to compensate (see the next page for more on this), and a test print is the best way to ensure accuracy. Test prints are also essential for assessing the impact of different papers or finishes on the final image and they can reveal issues with contrast, brightness, and detail that might not be visible onscreen. Adjusting these elements based on test prints can significantly enhance the quality of your final print. Moreover, test prints can save time and resources in the long run and they prevent the disappointment and cost of large or multiple final prints that don't meet expectations. If you're printing at home, this helps fine-tune your printer settings and helps you understand the nuances of your printer's output. If you're using a lab, they ensure your instructions are understood and executed correctly before proceeding with large-scale or more expensive prints. Ultimately, the goal of test printing is to bridge the gap between digital visualization and physical manifestation, making it an indispensable part of your workflow.

Increasing Brightness, Sharpness & Saturation

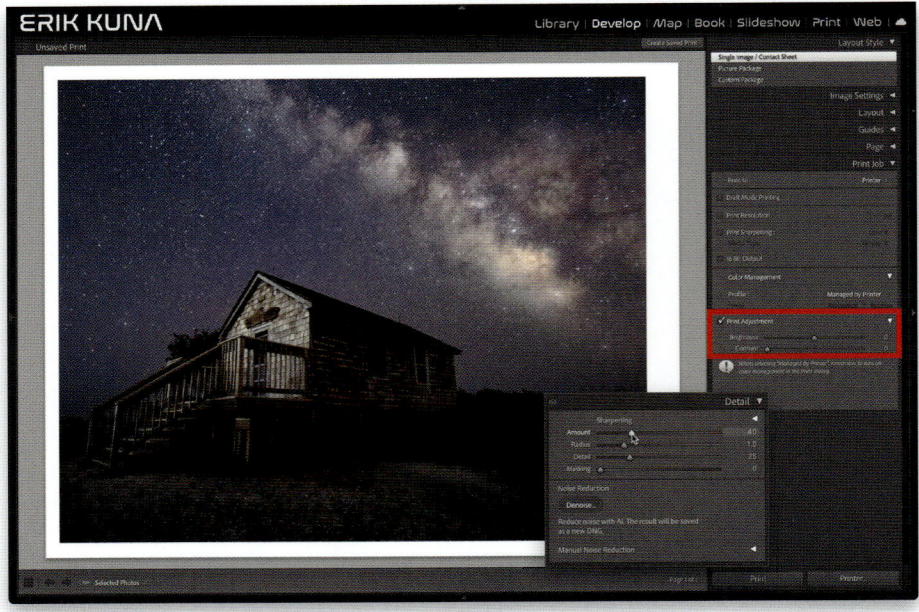

Adjusting the brightness and sharpness of a photo before printing is essential due to two main differences between screen displays and printed images. Firstly, computer monitors are backlit, making images appear brighter than they will on paper. To ensure the printed photo reflects your original vision, increasing the brightness compensates for the lack of back lighting in physical prints. This adjustment helps maintain the vibrancy and depth you see onscreen. Secondly, the physical nature of printing means that ink or pigment can bleed slightly on the paper, leading to a loss of sharpness and detail. To counteract this effect, applying additional sharpness to your digital file before printing is crucial. This ensures that the final printed image maintains the clarity and crispness you intended, counterbalancing the inherent spreading of ink on paper. These adjustments are vital to produce high-quality prints that faithfully represent your digital work. You might also adjust the color profile and saturation before printing. Matching the color profile to the printer's specifications ensures accurate reproduction of colors. This is less important when using a lab since they are equipped to match color profiles. Increasing saturation is also necessary to compensate for colors that appear more muted on paper than the vibrant display on backlit screens.

Selling Your Prints

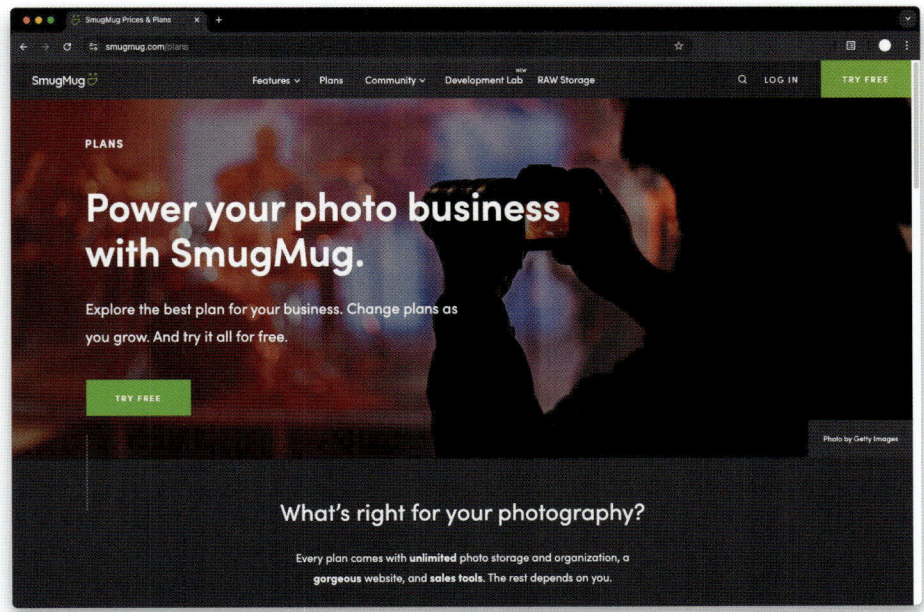

If you're looking to sell your work, the internet has broadened the horizon with numerous avenues, making it easy to get into print sales. Platforms like SmugMug and Art Storefronts offer robust online stores, which enable you to display and sell your work globally. These services handle the tasks of online transactions, print fulfillment, and even shipping, simplifying selling digital and physical copies of your work. Plus, these services tie right into print labs, making it easy to print, ship, and fulfill orders. They even handle customer support if there are any issues. However, if you're looking for a more hands-on approach, direct sales, though requiring more legwork in terms of marketing and customer interaction, provide a more personal touch and higher control over pricing. This method is ideal for photographers with an established client base or those who excel in personal selling. Local art shows and exhibitions are another valuable channel. They not only allow you to sell your work, but also to connect with the community, receive direct feedback, and increase your local visibility. These events can lead to networking opportunities with galleries and collectors, potentially opening more doors. Commissioned work represents a tailored approach to photography sales. By working directly with clients to create specific images or projects, you can leverage your skills in a more personalized setting, often leading to higher satisfaction and repeat business. Each method has its unique set of benefits and challenges, so the choice depends on your specific goals, resources, and the type of photography you specialize in. Ultimately, selling prints often involves a combination of these approaches, maximizing exposure and reach while building a diverse and sustainable photography business.

Sharing Your Work on Social Media

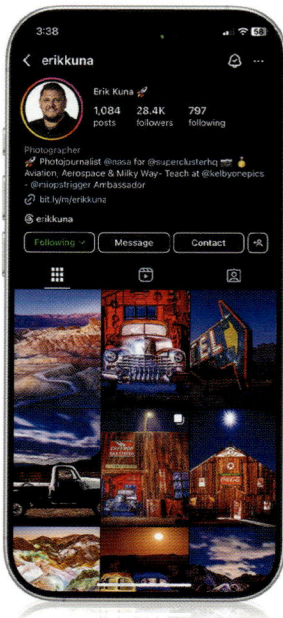

Sharing your photography on social media involves strategic engagement and authentic interaction. Focus on consistent posting with high-quality images that reflect your unique style and engage with your audience. Remember, social media is a tool for connection, so you'll want to prioritize genuine engagement over mere follower count. When sharing my photography on social media, I always focus on quality over quantity. Always prioritize the quality of your posts over the frequency. Each image should reflect your interaction, which isn't just about posting your work; it's about building a community. Respond to comments, participate in discussions, and show appreciation for your followers' support. Hashtags extend your reach, so use relevant and specific hashtags to get your work in front of the right audience. However, avoid over-stuffing your posts with hashtags, as it may seem like spam. Social media thrives on connections. Collaborate with other photographers and influencers to cross-promote each other's work. Building a network with other photographers and industry professionals can open up collaboration opportunities, and potential client leads. Participate in photography challenges to showcase your work to a broader audience. Join online groups and forums related to photography to share tips and experiences and get feedback. Your social media profiles should reflect your brand as a photographer. Use a consistent naming scheme, profile picture, and bio across platforms to make it easy for followers to recognize you. Social media trends evolve rapidly, so stay informed about new features, algorithms, and content types. Experiment with these changes to see what resonates best with your audience. Also, consider platforms that better reflect the audience you want to connect with as a photographer.

Sizing Your Images for Social Media

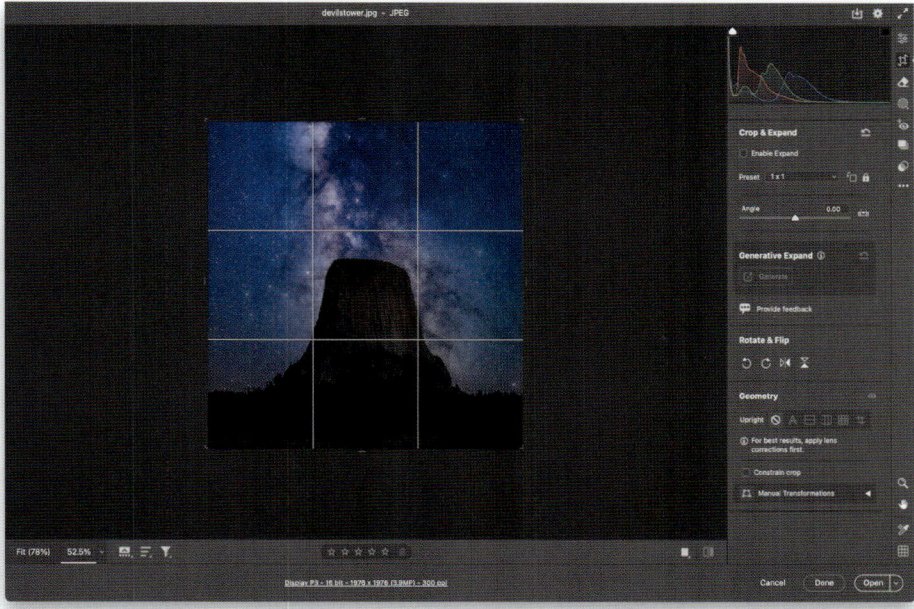

Understanding the importance of sizing images for social media is crucial for photographers who want their work to stand out in the digital crowd. Each social media platform has its own set of image size guidelines optimized for both desktop and mobile viewing. For instance, Instagram favors square 1:1 and vertical 5:4 aspect ratio images, while X's (formerly Twitter) layout is more accommodating to horizontal shots in the traditional 3:2 aspect of most cameras. This means that you must edit or creatively crop your images to ensure they fit within these confines without losing the impact of the visual story you're telling. Adapting to these requirements can be both a challenge and an opportunity for creativity—cropping an image to fit a specific aspect ratio could lead to discovering a more compelling composition that was not initially apparent. Alternatively, you might create custom layouts or use borders to maintain the original aspect ratio while adhering to platform specifications. Another advantage of cropping to the preferred aspect ratios of a social media platform can be the impact since it usually maximizes the size of the images. Moreover, properly sized images ensure faster loading times and better quality on viewers' feeds, enhancing engagement and the overall perception of your brand. To navigate this, you can use Photoshop and Lightroom or apps designed to resize and format images specifically for social media, saving time and maintaining consistency across posts. There's an art of sizing images for social media, allowing you to present your work in the best possible light across social media accounts. This careful consideration not only respects the experience you want the viewer to hold but also upholds the integrity and intention behind each photograph by ensuring it's what you want.

Increasing Your Audience on Social Media

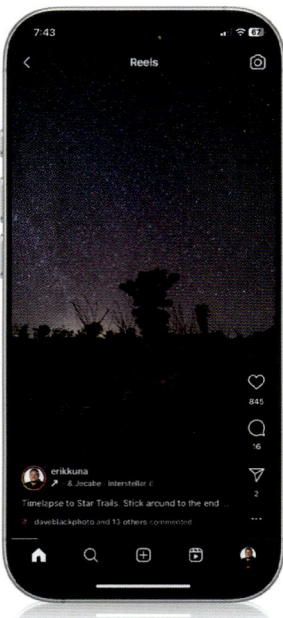

As a photographer, engagement, content quality, and strategic posting are key to effectively growing your audience on social media. Regularly sharing images highlighting your unique photographic style can attract followers who share your style. On certain platforms like Instagram, including well-researched hashtags helps broaden your visibility, making your work discoverable to a global audience. Like I've mentioned, actively engaging with your community by responding to comments, participating in discussions, and sharing behind-the-scenes content can foster a loyal following. At the same time, collaborating with other creatives can introduce your work to new audiences. Utilizing analytics tools to monitor engagement and audience growth allows you to adapt your strategy, focusing on the content that resonates most. Building a significant online presence is a gradual process that requires patience, creativity, and consistency in sharing your photographic journey. Another way you can really increase your audience nowadays is by increasing the number of videos (reels) you share—behind-the-scenes videos and personal stories are especially helpful. This allows your audience to connect with your work on another level. But, here's the biggest tip I can give you to online growth: consistency. You need to post as much high-quality content as you can. That's the number one way to ensure your growth online.

Finding Your Style

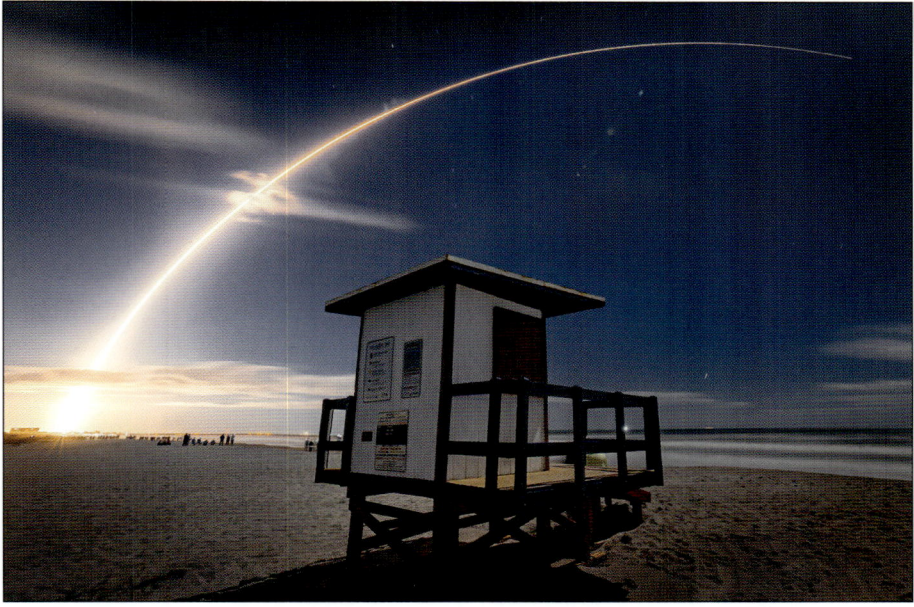

Finding your style as a photographer is akin to embarking on a personal journey where exploration, experimentation, and self-reflection are your companions. Initially, this path involves trying various subjects, techniques, lighting conditions, and compositions to gauge what truly captivates you. As you go deeper, analyzing your work for recurring themes or techniques that evoke a strong response helps you know your style. Engagement with diverse photographic genres, from street to landscape or portrait photography, can offer insights into what resonates with your creative side. This exploration period is crucial, as it allows you to discover a unique voice amidst the vast sea of other photographers and artists. Simultaneously, understanding the influences that drive your photography—be it the raw emotion of human connections, the serene beauty of nature, the dynamic tension of urban landscapes, or as in my case, the terrestrial mixed with the extraterrestrial—helps hone your style. The key lies in continuous shooting and refinement, allowing your style to evolve organically. Moreover, immersion in a community of photographers and creatives can spark new ideas, offering fresh perspectives that might influence your stylistic development. Constructive feedback from such communities is invaluable, providing an external viewpoint that can help fine-tune your vision. Definitely solicit critiques and feedback from photographers you respect. Remember, finding your style is not a destination but a continuous journey of growth and evolution. As your experiences and skills expand, so too will the uniqueness of your photographic voice. Stay curious, remain patient, and embrace the journey with an open heart and mind.

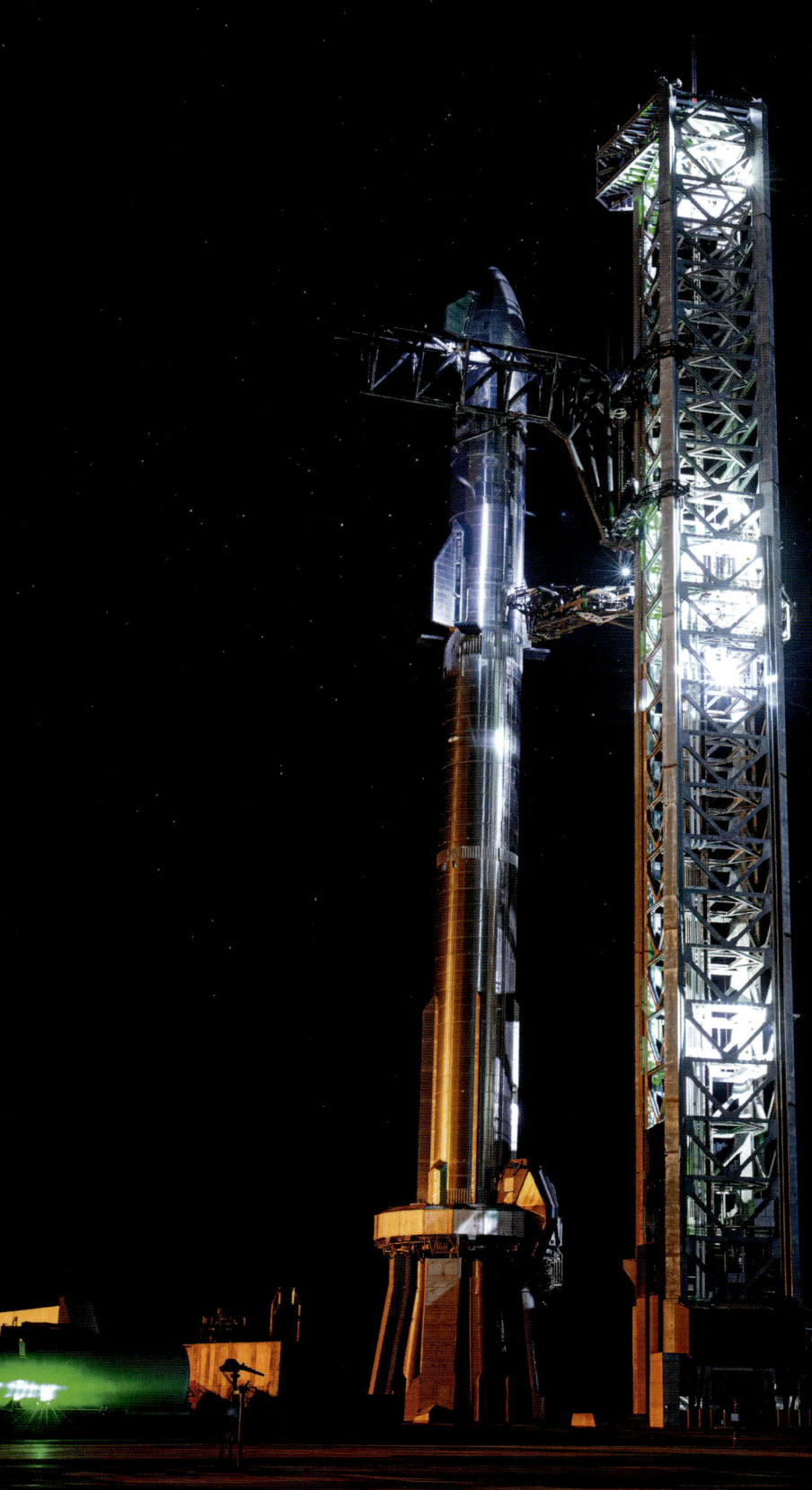

14

Wrapping It All Up

The Night Is Yours—Now Capture It

If you've made it this far, you're not just interested in night photography—you're committed. You've spent time dialing in your settings, learning how to compose in the dark, battling noise, and maybe even mastering the fine art of not blinding your friends with your headlamp. Now comes the most important part: what you do next. Night photography isn't about perfection; it's about adapting, experimenting, and embracing the unpredictability of shooting after dark. The conditions will never be perfect—clouds will roll in, the Milky Way will be just slightly out of frame, and your best shot of the night might come just as your battery dies. That's part of the game. The best night photographers aren't the ones who get lucky with perfect conditions; they're the ones who know how to work with what they've got and still create something stunning. So what now? Keep shooting. Keep learning. Keep pushing yourself. The more time you spend under the stars, the more everything becomes second nature. Whether you're stacking star trails, nailing that perfect single exposure, or finally getting comfortable with editing, every step builds on the last. And if a shot doesn't work out? That's actually good. That means you're pushing your limits. Beyond the camera, share your work, print your favorites, and don't let your best shots sit unseen on a hard drive. Whether you're posting online, selling prints, or just hanging one on your wall as a reminder of that perfect night, photography is meant to be experienced, not just stored. Most importantly, don't stop exploring. The night sky isn't going anywhere, but every time you step outside with your camera, you'll see it in a new way. The more you chase the night sky, the more it gives back. So, let's go seize the night.

Night Photography Dos

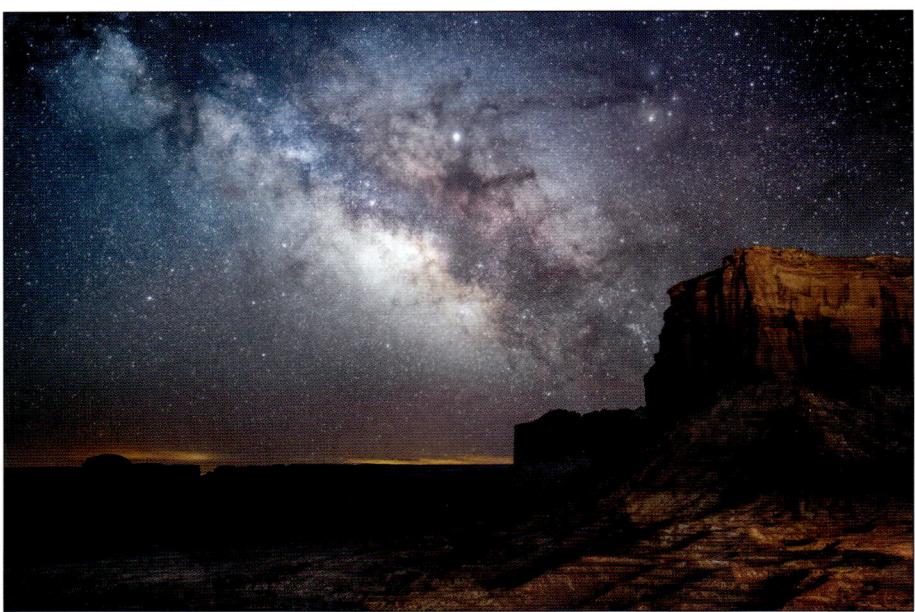

Night photography is part science, part art, and part patience. Nail the technique, and you'll get stunning, detailed images. Mess up, and you'll be fighting blurry stars, noisy shadows, or bad blends. Here's your quick hit list of what to do when shooting and editing your night photos:

- ✅ Use enough ISO to pick up the stars and Milky Way. Don't be afraid of ISO 3200, 6400, or even higher—modern noise reduction (especially AI) can clean it up in post.

- ✅ Shoot in RAW. JPEGs throw away details you'll need when editing night shots.

- ✅ Use a sturdy tripod. The sharper your starting image, the better your final edit will be.

- ✅ Manually focus on a bright star. Autofocus won't cut it at night—zoom in and use manual focus for perfect stars.

- ✅ Keep your foreground dark enough for a realistic night feel. Blue hour shots are great for blending, but don't overbrighten in post.

(*Note:* We looked at gear and settings in Chapters 1 and 3.)

Night Photography Dos (continued)

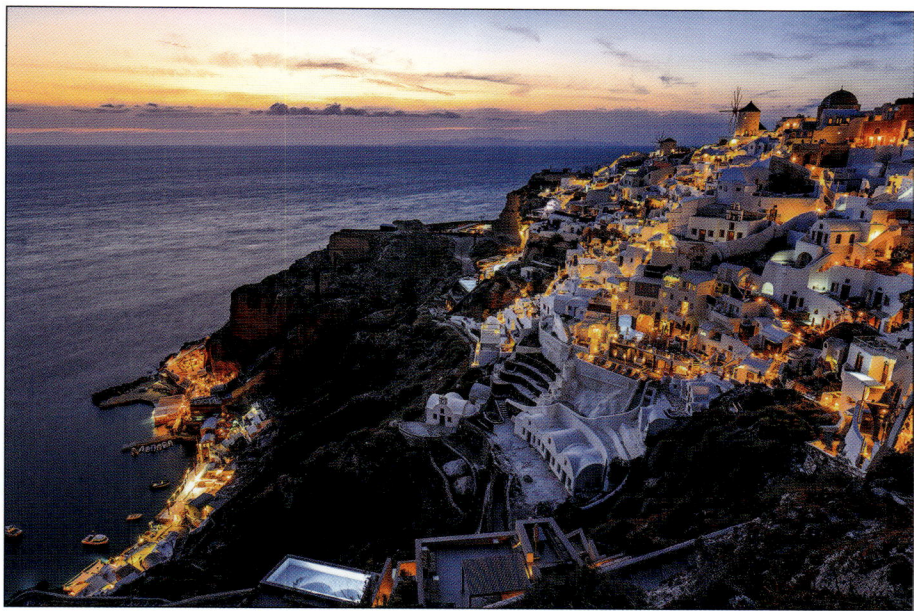

☑ Match white balance between your sky and foreground. Cool skies and warm landscapes scream "bad composite." Keep tones consistent.

☑ Use AI noise reduction sparingly. It's a game-changer, but too much can make your image look like plastic.

☑ Experiment with color grading. Night shots thrive on cool blues, teals, and subtle warm highlights—adjust for mood, not just accuracy.

☑ Blend exposures smoothly. Use soft, feathered layer masks and avoid hard edges when merging foregrounds and skies.

☑ Use radial filters to enhance the Milky Way. A subtle pop around the galactic core helps guide the viewer's eye.

☑ Keep shadows detailed but not too bright. Night shots should feel dark and atmospheric, not like they were taken at sunset.

☑ Check your final edit in different lighting. What looks great in a dark editing room might look off on a bright screen.

(*Note:* We looked at all of these post-processing techniques in Chapter 12.)

Night Photography Don'ts

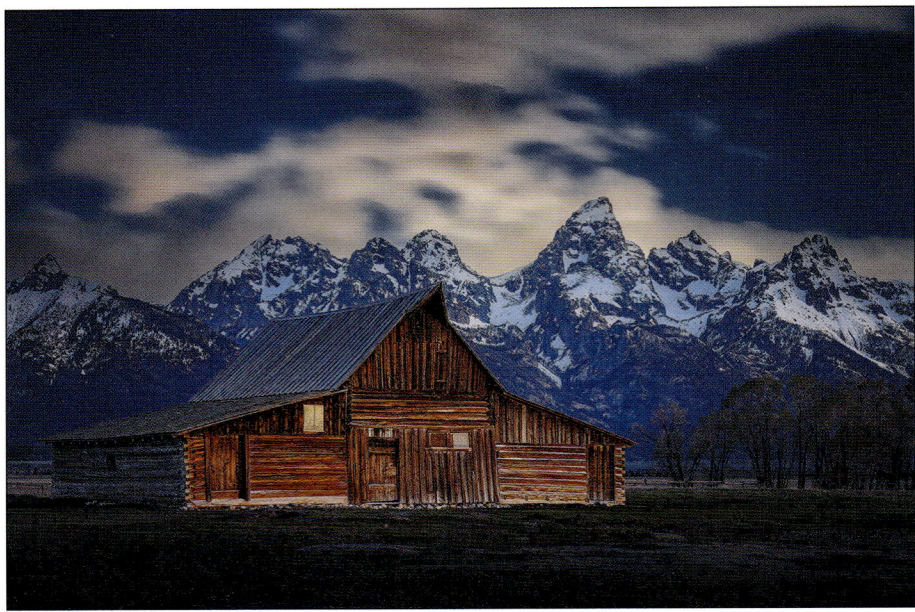

Great night photos aren't just about what you do right, they're about avoiding common mistakes that can ruin an otherwise epic shot. Here's what *not* to do when shooting and editing your night photos:

❌ Don't use too low an ISO. If you underexpose to avoid noise, you'll end up with dark, muddy shadows and weak stars. Noise is fixable—bad exposure isn't.

❌ Don't trust auto white balance. Night scenes confuse your camera, often making the sky too warm or purple. Set it manually!

❌ Don't overbrighten shadows. Night photos should feel dark and moody, not like they were taken in broad daylight.

❌ Don't use long exposures for pinpoint stars without tracking. Anything over 15–20 seconds (on a wide-angle lens) will turn stars into streaks.

(*Note:* We looked at gear and settings and in Chapters 1 and 3.)

Night Photography Don'ts (continued)

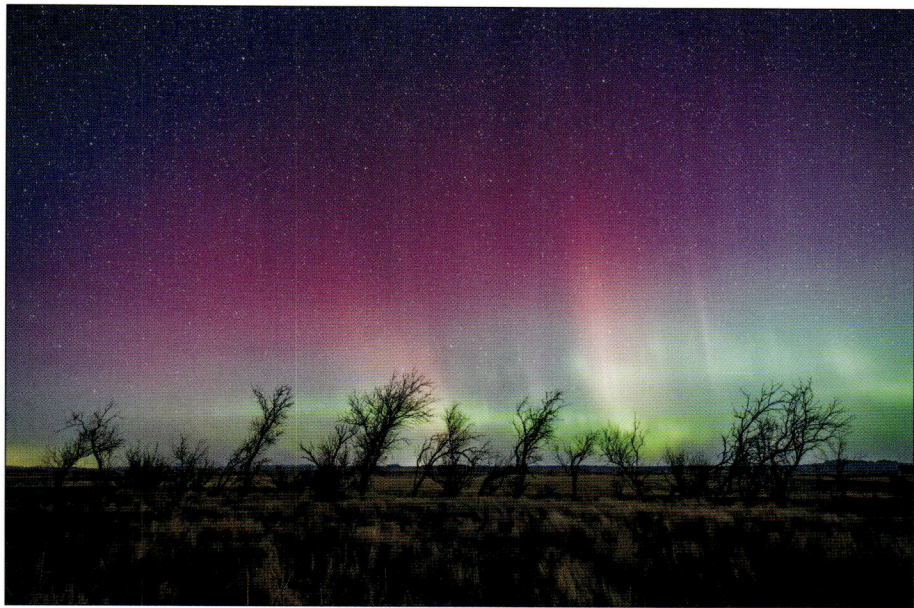

❌ Don't leave lens corrections off. Vignetting, distortion, and chromatic aberration are all worse at night—fix them first in post.

❌ Don't go overboard on Clarity or Dehaze. These are great tools, but too much makes the Milky Way look harsh and unnatural.

❌ Don't mix mismatched exposures in a composite. If your foreground is bright and golden but your sky is cool and dark, your edit will look fake.

❌ Don't ignore noise reduction. High-ISO noise is unavoidable, but AI noise removal tools can clean it up while keeping stars sharp—use them!

❌ Don't forget to align your layers when blending. Even small misalignments between sky and foreground make blends look off. Use Auto-Align in Photoshop if needed.

❌ Don't push saturation too far. Night skies should look vivid but natural—over-cooked blues, purples, and oranges scream "bad edit."

❌ Don't rush the edit. Take breaks, flip the image, and check it in different lighting conditions to catch mistakes before posting and sharing.

(*Note:* We looked at all of these post-processing techniques in Chapter 12.)

Just remember: The best night photos aren't overdone—they're balanced, natural, and immersive.

More Resources

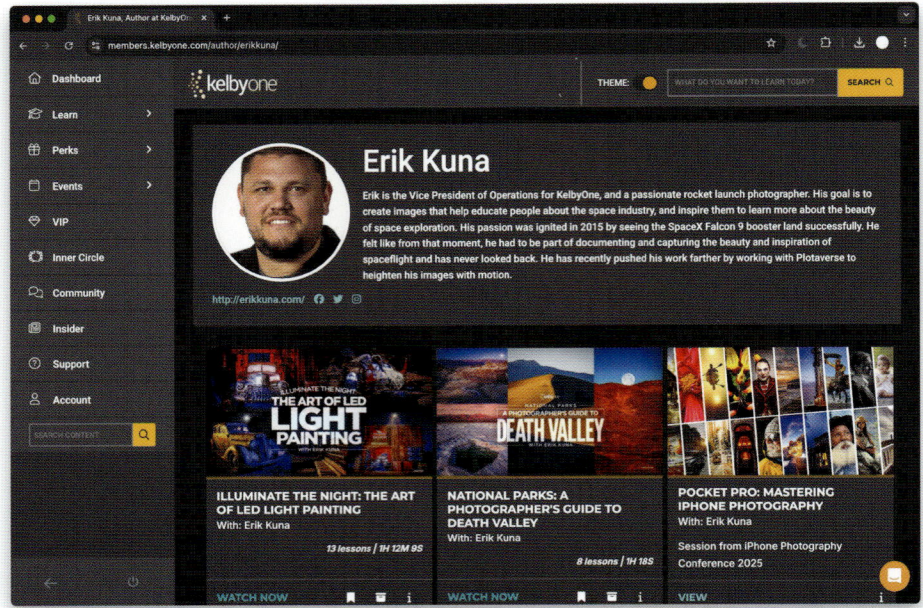

If you've made it this far, you're serious about mastering night photography—and trust me, there's always more to learn. The best way to level up your skills is through hands-on training, expert insights via video, and real-world workshops that go beyond what a single book can cover. That's why I've created a ton of night photography resources to help you continue improving:

Online Training & Classes

I teach in-depth night photography courses at KelbyOne.com, where I break down everything from camera settings to advanced post-processing techniques. Whether you're just getting started or looking to refine your edits, these courses will take you step by step through the process (search "Night Photography" to find my latest classes!). Some of my most popular classes include:

Astrophotography for Beginners—Mastering camera settings, Milky Way shots, and night sky compositions.

Advanced Night Photography Post-Processing—How to blend exposures, reduce noise, and enhance your night shots in Photoshop.

Light Painting Techniques—Creative ways to add artificial lighting to night photography for stunning results.

More Resources (continued)

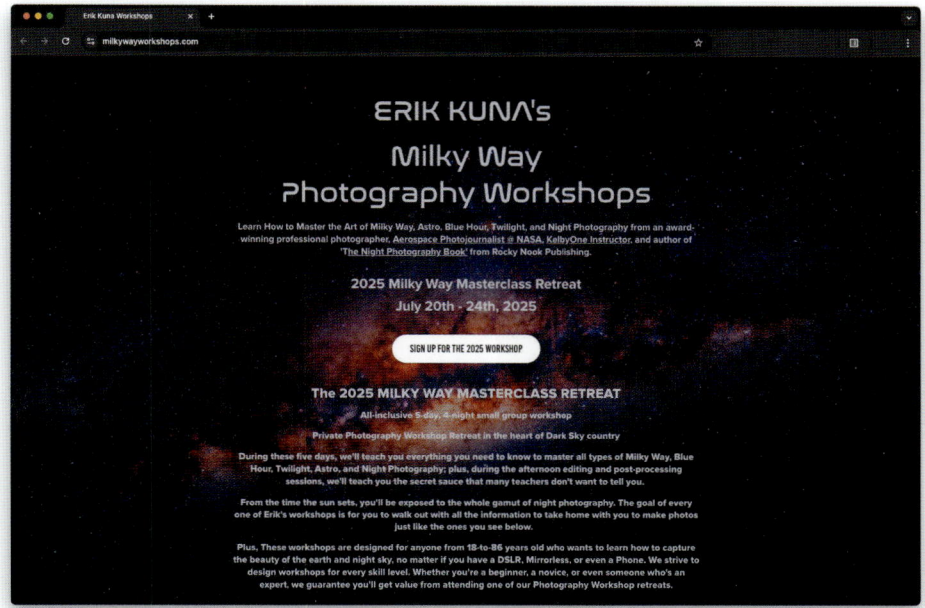

Companion Webpage

I created a webpage for this book where you'll find a bonus chapter with step-by-step photo recipes showing you exactly how to get those spectacular night photos. You'll also find some helpful videos there as well, where I walk you through some of the post-processing techniques we looked at in Chapters 11 and 12. You can find the webpage here: **kelbyone.com/books/nightphoto**.

Social Media

I regularly share tutorials, tips, and behind-the-scenes insights on my social media and on a weekly photography podcast I co-host with Scott Kelby called *The Grid*. Follow me for updates on the latest techniques, gear reviews, and night photography inspiration on Instagram, Facebook, and X (Twitter) at @ErikKuna.

Workshops

Want to learn in person? I also teach live workshops (you can check them out at MilkyWayWorkshops.com) and speak at photography conferences throughout the year, covering night photography techniques. Keep an eye out for upcoming events at KelbyOneLive.com and ErikKuna.com.

Night photography is a journey, and the best way to improve is by learning, experimenting, and pushing your creative limits. Check out these resources, keep shooting, and most importantly, have fun capturing the night sky!

A Final Thought...

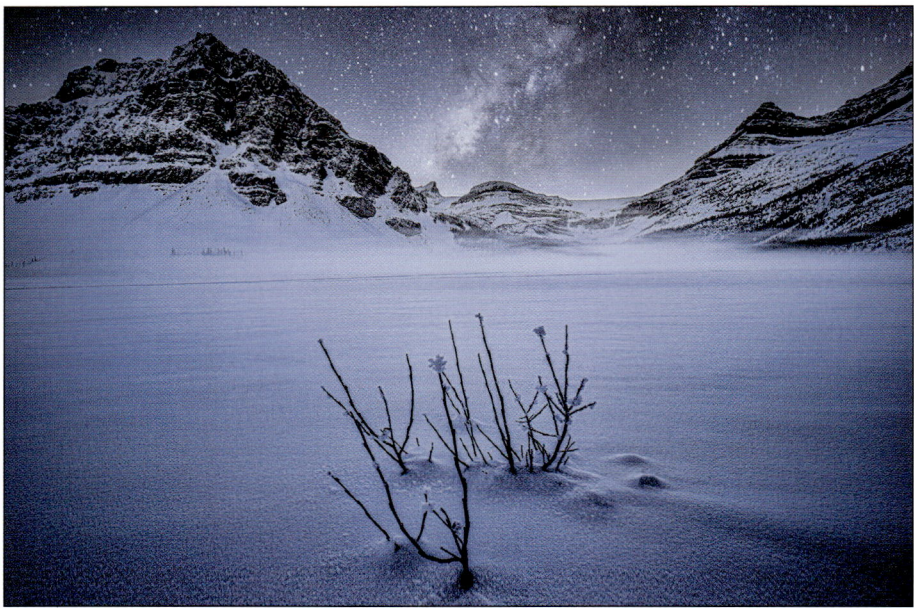

If there's one takeaway from everything we've covered here in this book, it's this: embrace the imperfections of the night. Night photography isn't about perfection; it's about problem-solving. The conditions will never be ideal. The stars will move, the wind will shake your tripod, light pollution will creep into your shot, and your camera will struggle to capture what your eyes can see. But that's the challenge—and the beauty—of it. Mastering night photography isn't about memorizing settings or using the "perfect" blend of ISO, aperture, and shutter speed. It's about knowing how to adapt when the conditions change. It's about understanding that every shot—whether a single exposure, a stacked Milky Way, or a carefully blended composite—is a balance between science and creativity.

...and the Most Important Lesson

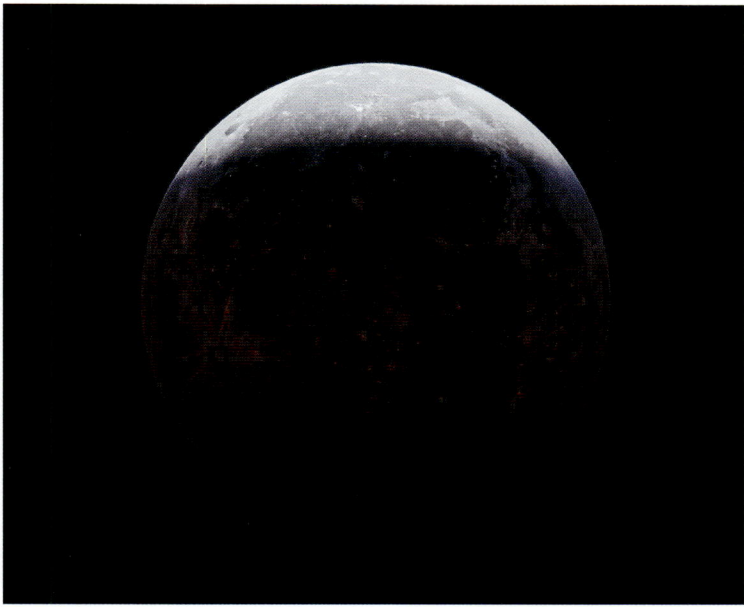

The truth about "perfect" night photos? The best night photographers aren't the ones who take flawless images straight out of the camera. They're the ones who know how to make the most out of what they've got, whether that means fixing a noisy sky in post, blending exposures to create the perfect balance of light, or using AI noise reduction instead of time-consuming stacking. Great night shots don't just happen. They're built—layer by layer, edit by edit, mistake by mistake—because it's more about the story the frame tells than the technical perfection. So, here are the real secrets:

- ☒ Don't obsess over perfection—obsess over progress.

- ☒ Don't fear high ISO—fear missing the shot.

- ☒ Don't force edits—let the image guide you.

And above all, don't stop experimenting because every night under the stars is a chance to learn something new. That's what separates a good night photographer from a great one—not just technical skill, but the ability to embrace the unknown and make the night your own. Now, the night is yours. Capture it!

INDEX

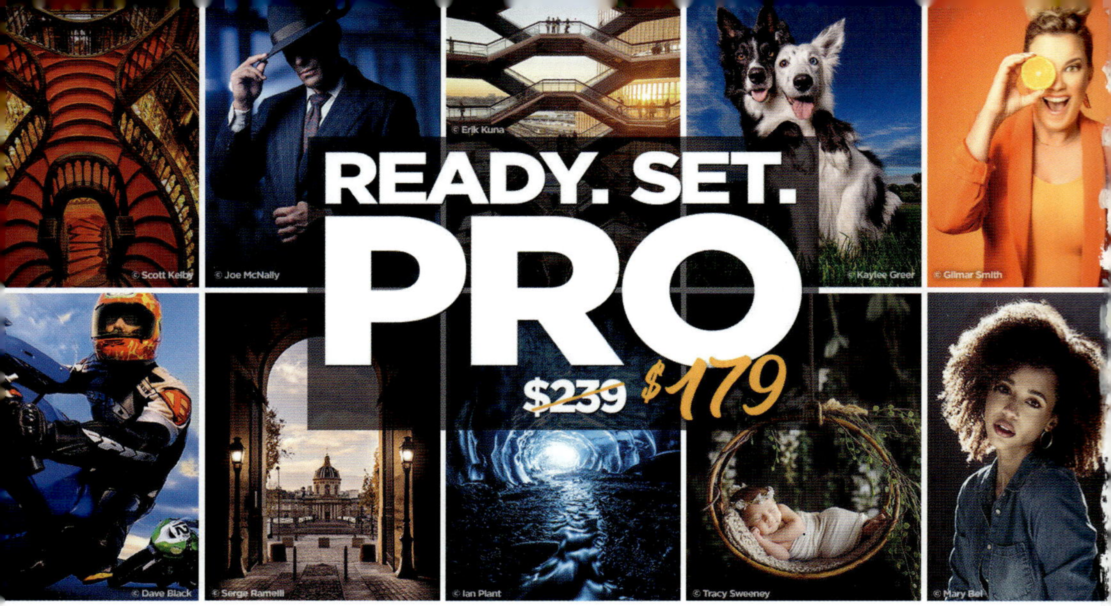

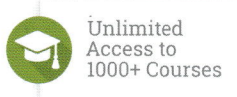
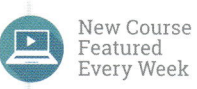
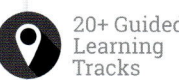
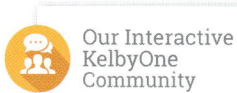
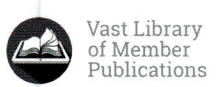
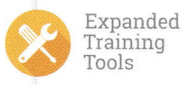
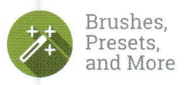
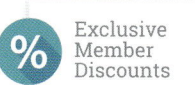
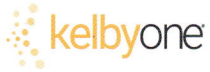